# The Vietnam War and American Culture

THE SOCIAL FOUNDATIONS OF AESTHETIC FORMS

The Social Foundations of Aesthetic Forms
A SERIES OF COLUMBIA UNIVERSITY PRESS
Jonathan Arac, Editor

# The Vietnam War and American Culture

EDITED BY
John Carlos Rowe and
Rick Berg

New York · Columbia University Press

COLUMBIA UNIVERSITY PRESS
NEW YORK   OXFORD

Library of Congress Cataloging-in-Publication Data

The Vietnam War and American culture / edited by John Carlos Rowe and
Rick Berg.
p.   cm.—(Social foundations of aesthetic forms series)
Includes bibliographical references and index.
ISBN 0-231-06732-1
ISBN 0-231-06733-X (pbk.)
1. United States Civilization—1970–   [1. Vietnamese Conflict,
1961–1975 United States.]   I. Rowe, John Carlos.   II. Berg,
Rick.   III. Series.
DS558.V56   1991                                                          90-22418
959.704'3—dc20                                                              CIP

Casebound editions of Columbia University Press
books are Smyth-Sewn and printed on permanent and
durable acid-free paper.

⊗

Printed in the United States of America
c 10 9 8 7 6 5 4 3 2 1
p 10 9 8 7 6 5 4 3 2

To all the veterans—men, women, children—of the war in Vietnam.

# Contents

## Contents

# PREFACE

Although most of the essays in this collection refer to literary works, their primary concerns are not literary. All the contributors to this volume understand that literary responses to the war constitute only a small part of American culture's massive effort over the past quarter century to "cover the war." We think that the Vietnam War and its reception have decisively changed familiar notions of literature's role as social criticism. Of course, it was not just the "war" in some narrowly understood sense that brought about such changes in literature's critical function, but the cultural, political, and economic forces that led us into war. And it was not due simply to the fact that the Vietnam War was a "television" war that literature seems to have lost some of its authority to criticize our social history.

What the cultural reception of the Vietnam War has made manifestly clear is that American ideology is itself an extraordinarily canny artist, capable of accommodating the most vigorous criticism and for that very reason powerfully resistant to significant social and political changes. Attentive as all the contributors are to the subtleties of power in our society, each suggests ways that informed social criticism can bring about necessary changes in the ways we understand other peoples and ourselves. Insofar as literature may contribute both to such criticism and social change, we must begin to understand it as merely one of the many powerful media that influence us and in some degree can be used by us. Just how "available" the media of television, film, and politics are to us is certainly one of the problems posed in this collection. Access to the mass media must be considered part of all campaigns for greater civil rights. Even with our presently limited access to such media, however, we think it is still possible to speak of *popular media*, which are capable of questioning, resisting, and sometimes overcoming the misinformation often so subtly communicated by mass media.

It is, of course, no longer possible to speak of some clear distinction between "mass" and "popular" media, just as it is impossible to imagine any specific boundary separating mass culture from popular culture. But this confusion of realms need not mean merely that popular resistance to mass domination is impossible; it can also mean that the genuinely popular and critical media might find a larger and more sophisticated audience than expected. In this volume, literature is often viewed as performing ideological work contrary to its vaunted critical and educational functions. Yet, in other contexts, literature is interpreted as sharing its potential for ideological criticism, reform, and transformation with the media of popular music, television, and film. The important literary texts about the Vietnam War are often treated critically in this volume, because we no longer have full confidence in literature's traditionally humane purposes. We are as skeptical of novels and poems as we are of television news and mass-market films.

Thus we have worked carefully to avoid the common impression that the study of how America has represented the Vietnam War is primarily the work of *literary criticism*. The cultural criticism we offer in this volume is in many respects at odds with literary criticism, even when literary criticism is genuinely comparative, culturally diverse, and multidisciplinary. Cultural criticism can be effective only when it focuses on the relations among those cultural media that have political significance in both their production and their reception. Finally, cultural criticism cannot contribute significantly to *cultural politics* until it investigates carefully the ways in which apparently discrete media work in more profoundly coordinated ways—both for purposes of social control and potentially in the interests of a more just society.

*Acknowledgments*

This collection of essays on the ways the Vietnam War has been interpreted in American culture grew out of a special issue we edited for *Cultural Critique* (Spring 1986), entitled "American Representations of Vietnam." In this book, we have added new essays on revisionist histories of the war, popular music, and feminism. The essays that first appeared in *Cultural Critique* have been substantially revised, and we think that the present collection offers a more balanced treatment of the American representations of the Vietnam War in history, the mass media, and popular media.

We thank Donna Przybylowicz and Abdul JanMohamed, editors of *Cultural Critique*, both for permission to reprint revised versions of essays that first appeared in that journal and for their generous support of this project. We also wish to thank the editors of *Social Text* for permission to reprint David James' "The Vietnam War and American Music" as chapter 9 and Rutgers University Press for permission to include Rick Berg's "Losing Vietnam: Covering the War in an Age of Technology" as chapter 5. Among the many people who provided support and encouragement for this collection, Edward Said and David Lloyd deserve special mention.

# The Vietnam War and
# American Culture

# The Vietnam War and American Memory

## RICK BERG AND
## JOHN CARLOS ROWE

Fifteen years ago, Americans didn't want to talk about Vietnam. Most of us never knew very much about the peoples, history, cultures, and languages of Vietnam; the word referred to the war. The singular form which we used in talking about *the* Vietnam War helped us forget that it was merely one among the countless colonial wars waged in Southeast Asia over the last thousand years. As soon as we could talk about Vietnam—the cultures, peoples, their history—as *our war*, then even the issue of political responsibility for that war was simplified and historically contained. Nothing else about Vietnam seemed to matter very much to Americans in the mid-1970s except the undeniable fact that we had *lost* that war. Refusing to talk about "Vietnam" was thus a collective defense against what those who had protested the war had tried to tell us. Our part in the wars fought to subjugate the Vietnamese people to various colonial rulers was merely the latest chapter in a long history. Our responsibility for "that war" connected us to the ugly history of Western colonialism. Had we looked closely at that responsibility, we would also have understood the essential relation between our foreign and domestic policies. Even as we revolted against European colonial domination, we were consolidating our domination of native Americans and building an economy with the stolen labor and lives of Africans. Little was said of Vietnam in 1976, that bicentennial year, when we so nostalgically celebrated the "revolutionary spirit." Few of us wanted to recall, especially then, that it was of the great revolutions that Ho Chi Minh had studied. In that year, amid the tall ships, the consumer collectibles, the television docudramas, and those celebrity sound-bytes ("Bicentennial Minutes"), Vietnam might have reminded us not only of our recent and bitter conflicts at home, of our human losses in the war, but also of a longer, uncanny history that flatly contradicted

1

our fondest myths of the revolutionary American as politically committed, practical, self-reliant, democratic, and honest.

The silence with which we greeted the veterans of that war was symptomatic of this collective repression of what we had made of ourselves. How, then, are we to account for the ways that "Vietnam" has become today an *unavoidable* word in American culture, a term in everyone's vocabulary, however various its meanings, and this in spite of the fact that the United States still has not resumed diplomatic relations with the Republic of Vietnam and maintains an economic embargo against it that has hobbled its postwar social and economic reconstruction? Vietnam has certainly become a *commodity* sold on television and in popular films, a marketable image in children's video games and toys and comic books, a "subject" for art exhibitions and publishers' catalogues. Seldom does this "Vietnam" refer to the Vietnamese and other Southeast Asians (Laotians, Kampucheans, Thais, Burmese) still suffering the consequences of western colonialism. Despite documentaries on "Boat People," news coverage of refugee camps on the Thai border and in Hong Kong, and public discussions of the Southeast Asian immigrants in the United States, "Vietnam" now refers primarily to *our* wounds of war. It is almost as if following a "respectful silence," we have committed ourselves to the bittersweet work of mourning our loss: of the war, our national innocence, the lives of our sons and daughters. The popular term for this public and often theatrical mourning suggests that we have not really come to terms with what we lost in Vietnam. American idealism didn't die; we are simply in the course of "healing" the wounds those ideals suffered in *our* war.

We may speak casually of the "body politic," the "collective unconscious," the "communal spirit," but we ought to know that cultures aren't "bodies" or "psyches." Myths and ideals can't really be "wounded." We are obsessed with the trauma and injury we have suffered, as if the United States, not Vietnam and Kampuchea, were the country to suffer the bombings, the napalm air strikes, the search-and-destroy missions, the systematic deforestation, the "hamlet resettlement" programs. The cultural and economic means by which we have commodified Vietnam have been our means of keeping silent about the political and historical realities of our involvement in western imperialism. And yet these same means of imagining Vietnam as the mirror we hold up to ourselves, as the searching, critical "self-image" of our collective failure as a democratic people, are themselves the essence of the new brand of imperialism that we continue to sell in the furthest reaches of the world.

We did not go to Vietnam in search of raw materials, cheap labor, new commercial markets. Unlike the French, we didn't want Vietnamese rubber. Unlike the Japanese, we didn't want their hardwood. Unlike the Chinese, we didn't want the fertile lands of the Mekong Delta. We wanted something abstract, utterly immaterial, and (finally) fantastic: a "sphere of influence," a counterweight in the imaginary game of "balance of power" politics. It is not incidental that we used a metaphor from a game of the European aristocracy to describe Vietnam: a *domino*. The pieces in the game represent the player's power; they are thus named for the "master," *dominus*, whom they ultimately announce. It was this sort of representation of the United States that we wanted in Vietnam: a mirror-image of ourselves that, however distorted, would confirm our existence. In Peter Davis' antiwar documentary, *Winning Hearts and Minds*, the perversity of this self-image is captured in the figure of a Saigon businessman, lovingly describing the economic "opportunities" of the war, and in the dining room of a South Vietnamese country club, where the war's famine and death are as remote as in Los Angeles or Columbus.

When we failed to sell America to the Vietnamese, we tried to sell Vietnam to America. *That* Vietnam is the war-surplus of our new imperialism, and it should hardly surprise us that it has virtually nothing to tell us of Vietnamese history, culture, and politics. Just what this "Vietnam" signifies today in American culture is what this collection of essays attempts to address, and one of its most important and troubling connotations involves the very concept of social and political "community." The very effort to address just how the Vietnam War challenged traditional notions of American community is crucial to any useful historical understanding of that war. Yet even as this issue played a central role in the turn from "silence" to endless discussion of Vietnam, it was already being ꜀urned from proper memory to the purposes of forgetting.

In the 1980s, the political issues of the Vietnam War were increasingly related to the crisis of the American middle-class family. During the war, David Rabe argued in plays like *Sticks and Bones* (1969) that the typical American family ought to be considered one of the contributing factors in the war and, perhaps, western militarism in general. Rabe focused specifically on the plight of the

3

returning veteran, and the inability of the family to deal with his physical and psychic trauma. Beyond that important contemporary question, Rabe asked his viewers to consider the ways in which the middle-class family reproduced domestically the values and attitudes of the public sphere. However it has been normalized as part of the western rite of passage to adulthood, Oedipal conflict and its gendered hierarchies of father, son, and mother involve modes of domestic aggression that may play formative roles in forms of more public violence. In less complicated terms, C.D.B. Bryan pursued a similar thesis in *Friendly Fire* (1976) by arguing that the war required a reconsideration of the family's dependence on the moral leadership of the state. In their effort to discover how their son, Michael, was killed by U.S. army artillery in the war, Peg and Gene Mullen discover the extent of the governmental cover-up of its essentially immoral conduct in the war. Such disillusionment provokes a reconsideration of the family's confidence in state authority that awakens Peg Mullen to a political activism utterly contrary to the conventional role of an Iowa farm-wife.

No community in the United States was unaffected by the Vietnam War. The Pentagon and Congress invaded not only Southeast Asia but the American family, forcing ordinary citizens to reconsider conventional responsibilities to their families and local communities. Honest and civic-minded citizens served on local draft boards and their review panels, forced to decide which neighbors' children would go to war. In order to do so, they were compelled often to repeat the patriotic clichés and cold war jargon of the government in order to justify decisions they knew would have very material consequences for their communities. In short, the conduct of foreign policy depended upon its reproduction in the behavior of responsible citizens and its legitimation by the domestic authority of the nuclear family. For those refusing to serve in Vietnam, these were by no means abstract issues. With the terms for "conscientious objection" rewritten so narrowly as to exclude virtually any ethical objection to military service other than those justified by certified religious affiliations, "draft dodgers" had only the choices of prison or emigration. In both cases, the moral decision to refuse military service meant exile from the family. For young men between the ages of eighteen and twenty-three—the average age of those drafted to fight in Vietnam was *nineteen*—the enormity of such a decision to abandon the security of the nuclear family can hardly be exaggerated. Nevertheless, such issues were oddly transformed in the popular representation of Vietnam in America in the 1980s. Rather than exploring just how our myths of the individual and the nuclear family had contributed to the war, the mass media focused instead on how our failure in Vietnam was reflected in the *breakdown* of the nuclear family and our loss of confidence in "American individualism."

The Vietnam War, together with dramatic changes in the domestic economy of the United States in the 1960s and 1970s, fundamentally challenged the complacent ideal of the apolitical, hard-working, patriotic American family marketed so relentlessly in the popular films and on network television of the 1950s. Any one of the millions of working women in the 1950s, many of whom continued to work in jobs created by the defense economy of World War II, could have exposed the myth of the bourgeois family shaped by such media stereotypes as Donna Reed, Lucille Ball, Gracie Allen, and June Cleaver. Well before that myth entered its period of "fantastic" solutions in the late 1960s, such as *Bewitched* and *I Dream of Jeannie* and *The Odd Couple*, the realities of two-income families, the new teenaged "working class," dramatic increases in divorces, and the transience of middle-class professionals made the "ideal" of the white, middle-class family appear a quaint anachronism.

The Vietnam War revealed explicitly the fiction of the middle-class, nuclear family as fundamental to American ideals and values. In fact, the working classes, the unemployed, and oppressed minorities were drafted in much greater proportion and saw more combat than the sons of the middle-class. Those citizens likely to benefit least from our vaunted "economic opportunities" made the greatest sacrifices in that war. As some veterans have complained, they were sent to fight a war against peoples suffering a colonial and racial domination that they themselves had experienced in the United States. Conservative critics of the antiwar movement in the United States often insisted that the protest on college campuses had more to do with bourgeois "guilt," if not the personal fears of white, middle-class students, than it had to do with real political commitment. Such criticism ignores, of course, the efforts made by many antiwar groups to develop coalitions with minority activists and the women's rights movement in the late 1960s. Even so, the failure of such coalitions to achieve genuine political power in the United States of the 1970s may have resulted in part from the inability of middle-class liberals to question adequately how the myths of the nuclear family and the self-reliant individual had contributed to our social problems. The Vietnam War exposed the illusion of a "classless" America committed to cultural diversity and equal opportunity.

"Healing" the wounds of the Vietnam War in the 1980s came to involve some fantastic "therapy" for the nuclear family. The very family that had so often contributed consciously or inadvertently to the war effort began to look like a *solution* to the very political problems it had helped produce. Perhaps the most perverse version of this work of cultural revision was the projection of this anxiety concerning the American family to the Vietnamese and to veterans of the war. The previously "invisible" Vietnamese were represented in the mass media of the late 1970s and throughout the 1980s as peasant families caught between the equally alien antagonists of American troops and the Vietcong.

The "stock shot" of this period is a family of Vietnamese villagers "mistakenly" killed by U.S. troops or "murdered" by the Vietcong. The conventional moral conclusions were complementary: we ended up killing those we had come to protect; the politics of Communism revealed its immorality in the war it waged against the family. The typical scene in the humble village hootch was too often "composed" to remind us that families, however superficially different, are all alike. Gruesomely dead, graphically wounded, or alone surviving, the Vietnamese child came to represent, often in sustained close-up, what Americans had done to their own children. Even gestures made by the media to represent the extended Vietnamese peasant family generally went no further than images of a grandmother or grandfather amid the corpses. Little serious attention was paid to the complex ancestral authorities and religious traditions governing village life, to the central role many South Vietnamese peasants played in the military victory of the Vietcong and North Vietnamese Army, or to the problems of urbanization facing the many Vietnamese fleeing the country for the cities. Rural "family life" in Vietnam remained center-stage for those interested in representing the Vietnamese, and all too often it looked more like life in Iowa than in Vietnam. Our imaginary construction of "the Vietnamese peasant" was built on our own nostalgia for rural American and its solid family values. Had we taken the time to read the letters and diaries written by young men and women who made up the Vietcong and North Vietnamese Army, we would have understood that their principal concerns, even above their own personal sufferings, were for their immediate and extended families. But we had successfully transformed the "invisibility" of our enemy, which was its most brilliant military strategy in this guerilla war, into a cultural and human "invisibility."

By the same token, the veteran returning to the "world" from the war was transformed from the psychotic killer of popular films and television in the 1970s into a misunderstood neurotic struggling to rediscover the virtues of domestic happiness and gainful employment. Such films as *In Country* and *Distant Thunder* translated the trauma of the war into a family trauma, especially appropriate to the moral rhetoric of the Reagan administration. The nuclear family may not have kept its sons and daughters from going to Vietnam, but that same family structure was offered as therapy for veterans of the war. Often enough, the only fond memory the veteran brought home from the war was of the strong personal ties developed with others in combat or field hospitals. The labor shared under fire was generally described in domestic metaphors, using such conventional terms as "family" feeling or "brotherhood" and "sisterhood" in arms. Ignoring the artificiality of such relations, as well as the general alienation of combat troops and support personnel during the war (subject as they were to frequent duty-rotations and brief tours of duty), the media tried to refunction such psychic bonds in the interests of redeeming the embattled American family.

Thus, liberal documentaries—such as HBO's *Soldiers in Hiding* —stressed the "costs" to the family of the veteran's failure to "adjust" to normal life in the United States. The more radical proposal that perhaps "normal life" was in part to blame for the War and deserved more searching critical examination was ignored. Only rarely—in such films as *Cease Fire* or *Who'll Stop the Rain?*—were we reminded that the economic and social motives for U.S. foreign policies in Vietnam were at the very heart of "normal life" in capitalist America. The idea that those veterans who refused to "adapt" to America might be deliberately repudiating a socioeconomic order that had supported our violence in Vietnam was unthinkable for a society intent upon "healing" its wounded psyche.

In similar fashion, the "assimilation" of Vietnamese and Kampuchean immigrants into the culture of the United States focused primarily on the apparently universal yearning for the freedoms

7

and comforts of middle-class life in the West. What the Pentagon and Congress had ignored, it would appear from the media in the 1980s, was the "personal" factor in war. *The Killing Fields*, for example, although nominally about the Khmer Rouge's genocide in Kampuchea, focused on personal relations and family ties as the most "natural" resistances to war and political domination. Yet without some political organization to protest the remilitarization of America that occurred during the Reagan administration and resulted in such follies as the Iran-Contra affair, the invasion of Grenada, and our Middle-Eastern and Central American foreign policies, the "resistance" of good citizens and the "virtues" of their respect for individuals could hardly be effective. George Roy Hill's film *Southern Comfort* (1983) brought the war "home" in a different way by arguing that the racism and ethnocentrism that both took us to Vietnam and prevented us from understanding Vietnamese culture are part of the psychological "equipment" of the decent American citizen. More explicitly, Michael Cimino's *Year of the Dragon* and Louis Malle's *Alamo Bay* (1985) argued that our conduct in Vietnam was only one manifestation of our long history of racism toward Asian peoples. For Cimino and Malle, such "Orientalism" had traditionally performed its most perversely efficient work in personal and working relations. They challenged the thesis that the war was exclusively the responsibility of remote governments and abstract politics. Xenophobia, economically motivated "nationalism" and racism were for them fundamental facts of everyday life in America.

Yet political discussions of the Vietnam War that related issues of race, class, gender, and family to myths of the "American individual" and the "essential goodness" of the American people were efficiently controlled in the 1980s by stereotypes of the political activist. The accepted forms of political activism echoed ironically the complaints of "Hawks" during the war that antiwar activists must "learn to work within the system." The answer at the time was obvious enough: the "system" is corrupt and cannot be reformed from within. By the 1980s, however, the "activism" of veterans of the war was distributed neatly among three general categories: an "obsession" with the war that combined symptoms of Post-Traumatic Stress Syndrome with the residual adolescence of the New Left; efforts to "heal" the wounds of the war by rebuilding the family and the economy; work within existing legal and political institutions to redress specific wrongs. In the first category, even Sylvester Stallone's fighting machine, Rambo, would first appear to viewers in *First Blood* as a refunctioned "hippy," wearing his tattered fatigue jacket, long hair, and "drifting" the highways of America. By the same token, the fire-breathing Rambo of *Rambo: First Blood, Part II* and his avatars in a host of films devoted nominally to "rescuing" POWs from Vietnam had as their primary aim the "restoration" of shattered American families. Armed to the teeth, Rambo himself could declare to his coworker, the Vietnamese woman Co, that his fondest hope was to find a peaceful domestic life.

In the 1980s, the popular enthusiasm for Rambo seemed an entirely predictable consequence of the mass media's inclination to offer wish-fulfilling fantasies (rather than critical investigations) of the Vietnam War. Rambo fought the war again, now against such "enemies" as the U.S., Soviet, Vietnamese, and Chinese governments, in order to "win" the Vietnam War for an imaginary "American people." But much more was at stake than simply a kind of collective reaction formation to the terrible knowledge of our immoral actions in Vietnam, not only as a government but as a *people*. From *Coming Home* to the Rambo films, the mass media had encouraged us to believe that we, the people, had not wanted the Vietnam War, which was merely a "mistake" of a government that had exceeded the *controls* of its people. By scapegoating the government, fiction films, novels, personal records, documentaries, and docudramas stressed again and again the inherent goodness of the American people and their collective ability to achieve a moral *consensus* when presented the bare "facts." Thus the disabled veteran at the end of *Coming Home* may find political purpose in addressing high school students about the evils of war on the self-evidence of his experience in Vietnam: his crippled body is represented as an irrefutable icon for his antiwar message. More recently, Chris (in Oliver Stone's *Platoon*) can encourage his audience to "teach" their children about the war in the confidence that its self-evident immorality will be revealed. Thus the third and most acceptable category for political activism growing out of our outrage regarding the Vietnam War has become the image of the veteran as politician. Long before Oliver Stone and Ron Kovic turned Kovic's *Born on the Fourth of July* into a box-office success, well before Ron Kovic considered running for Congress for the 38th

District in California, veterans of the war on both sides of the
political spectrum claimed special abilities for governmental leadership on the basis of their experiences in Vietnam.

Of course, many veterans of the Vietnam War have held political
offices and pursued political causes in distinguished ways. But the
popular image of the "political veteran" often served the larger
purpose of reaffirming the very political institutions and practices
that had taken us to Vietnam in the first place. Too often in the
1980s, "healing the wounds" meant patching up our conventional
myths and values, rather than subjecting them to necessary criticism and revision. No longer irreverent or mad, the Vietnam veteran in the 1980s was celebrated by the mass media and offered a
certain compensatory heroism. There had been few parades for
returning veterans during and at the end of the war; there were no
monuments. In a speech delivered to a convention of the Veterans
of Foreign Wars (a veterans' group notorious for excluding Vietnam
veterans) in the 1980 presidential campaign, Ronald Reagan announced the end of the Vietnam "syndrome": "It is time we recognized that ours was, in truth, a noble cause." Four years later, at
the burial of the unknown Vietnam serviceman, President Reagan
declared: "An American hero has returned home. . . . He accepted
his mission and did his duty. And his honest patriotism over-
whelms us." In 1985, there was a belated "national" celebration, a
"Welcome Home" that merely announced a new *use* for the veteran. In police and crime melodramas on television, the veteran
became a source of wisdom and experience, especially where violence and weaponry required such special knowledge. Fictional
veterans like Crockett on *Miami Vice* or Magnum on *Magnum, P.I.*
typified the new image of the veteran who had learned in Vietnam
how to address the social problems of urban America. Their "Vietnam Experience" was often enough a private matter, revealed only
in the urgency of the moment and then with becoming modesty
and humility. Like Rambo, these urban warriors were reluctant to
fight, but when conflict was unavoidable their military training
assured us that they were "prepared."

Such heroism neglected, of course, the generally uncelebrated
activism of real veterans who worked within the legal and political
system to improve medical and educational benefits for veterans,
to publicize the still-growing unemployment and suicide rates of
veterans, to bring a class action suit against Dow Chemical and the
federal government for the effects of Agent Orange on veterans and

their children. In fact, their courageous efforts have never been adequately rewarded. The "success" of the class action suit for the production and use of Agent Orange in Vietnam was purely symbolic: the average award was $20,000. The figures for suicides by veterans continue to climb—ranging today between 60,000 and 100,000—outnumbering U.S. troops and personnel killed during the war. These activist veterans worked to remind us that the "casualties of war" include the suicides, the physically and psychically disabled, the unemployed, the homeless, and the countless veterans in U.S. prisons. Yet, the heroism of these activists was largely forgotten amid the construction of the "heroic" veteran celebrated in the mass media. In the 1980s, monuments and memorials to those who died in Vietnam were funded and built across the country, but the "survivors" found little satisfaction in such pyramids. Our compassion for the veteran remained abstract, a mere gesture to assuage our collective guilt.

Maya Lin's eloquent Vietnam Veterans' Memorial was unveiled in Washington, D.C. in 1982. As Michael Clark argues in his essay in this collection, the visitor reads not only the names of our dead carved in the stone, but also the melancholy reflections of those other, more ideal monuments to American nationalism that its polished black granite strategically reflects: the Washington Monument, the Capitol, the Jefferson Memorial. The criticism of both war and nationalism achieved so simply in this memorial certainly prompted its "revision" with the more conventional sculpture of those "soldiers in arms" added later to the Memorial's site. Powerfully moving as Lin's unrevised memorial is, however, it is dedicated exclusively to *our* veterans of the war. There is still no "memorial" for the "Vietnam War" that acknowledges the sufferings of the Vietnamese, the Kampucheans, and Americans at home.

As important and still urgent as the real circumstances of our Vietnam veterans are for our critical understanding of the Vietnam War's significance for America's future, we must acknowledge that the veteran's *experience* of the war both in Vietnam and in the United States by no means encompasses the significance of Vietnam for American culture. As this collection of essays suggests, understanding the significance of the Vietnam War in the history of the United States and the larger global politics of which that history is such a crucial part involves far more than simply "experience" of the war or antiwar sentiments, however earnestly offered. The experiences of the veterans of Vietnam are by no means inconsequential; they can contribute significantly to our historical understanding. But it is important for us to remember how long the "history" of the Vietnam War is, and how it must be considered only one part of the even longer and more complex histories of the Vietnamese people and western imperialism. These histories are no longer divisible, but we must be careful not to "forget" the Vietnamese as we attempt to explore the historical motives that led the United States to Vietnam.

Those motives are profoundly related to the ways in which Americans have conceived of and represented themselves. Long before most Americans even knew that Vietnam existed, we had imagined "Vietnams" of many different sorts. Just how we "misunderstood" the peoples and cultures of Vietnam has to be studied in relation to other cultural misunderstandings whose residual elements have shaped our collective myth of Vietnam. Noam Chomsky argues convincingly that our conduct in Vietnam may be traced to our annexation of the Philippines, together with the Far Eastern policy that we developed during the Spanish-American War. Certainly the overtly "benign" imperialism developed by Secretary of State John Hay under Presidents McKinley and Theodore Roosevelt has much to teach us about our eventual conduct in Korea and Vietnam, as well as our current foreign policies in Asia. The "dominos" we hoped to keep from falling in Southeast Asia were first "set up" by us in the years between the Spanish-American and Russo-Japanese wars, when we were intent upon "balancing" the growing threats of Russia and Japan in Asia and assuming global authority from the waning European empires of Great Britain and Spain.

Yet, the historical path from our annexation of the Philippines and the Portsmouth Treaty concluding the Russo-Japanese War to the Paris Peace Talks and the final chaos of our dishonorable evacuation of Americans from Saigon is hardly a straight one. Our misguided efforts in the 1980s to "heal" the wounds of Vietnam were accompanied by a host of "revisionary" histories, the most influential of which are discussed in the essay by Stephen Vlastos in this collection. Speculations by Guenter Lewy in *America in Vietnam* (1978) on how we might have "won" the war had we not made such fundamental errors in military strategy and political administration of the South Vietnamese government are complemented by Stanley Karnow's conclusion in *Vietnam: A History* (1983) that the Vietnam War was a war that "nobody won." Such revisionary histories were unable to address the fundamental problem that complicates any strictly historical treatment of the United States' role in Vietnam and Asia. The "living-room war" has its roots in the far more extensive historical question of how American political power in the twentieth century—the period of its global dominance as a "superpower"—has depended upon the ability of the United States to *represent* itself both to its own citizens and other peoples of the world. Of course, these revisionary histories of the Vietnam War are themselves part of that representation of American ideology and thus disinclined to reflect upon their own complicity in foreign policies based on mythic and idealized conceptions of the American self, family, and moral righteousness.

From John Hay (the first Secretary of State to understand the importance of the press conference) to Henry Kissinger, America's imperial ambitions have focused on the exportation of "lifestyles," "attitudes," and "values." It was not *territory* that we hoped to conquer in Vietnam, but "hearts and minds." The generation of Americans that fought the Vietnam War had been raised largely in the anticommunist ethos of the cold war, which had used the threat of Communist "mind-control" and "propaganda" to encourage us to believe ourselves "better dead than Red." Such slogans, however, were rarely applied to our own efforts to manipulate the lives and behaviors of other peoples. Our "educational" missions to Vietnam in the late 1950s and early 1960s, the quixotic "Hamlet Resettlement Program" during the war, and the economic and military "assistance" we showered on puppet governments in South Vietnam are only some examples of the "propaganda" we used in Southeast Asia.

The ugly term "American propaganda" still haunts our thinking about how we may best *teach* the many subjects related to the Vietnam War and Vietnamese culture. As Claudia Springer's and Carol Lynn Mithers' essays suggest, the boundary distinguishing literature or film from "propaganda" must be reconsidered in the wake of Vietnam. Perhaps the reason that the Vietnam War remains a relatively neglected subject in high school and college curricula is that any history of the war raises fundamental and often unanswerable questions about how American history has been written and taught. By the same token, no course concerned with the "literature" of the Vietnam War can ignore the ways in which fiction and history are implicated, as well as how "serious" literature and the mass media still contribute to our cultural efforts to "colonize" Vietnam as a part of the "American Experience." Of course, there is now a long list of courses and a substantial bibliography of traditional scholarship that have ignored just such issues, focusing instead upon the presumed "facts" of the historical record or the "special qualities" of the "Vietnam novel" or "Vietnam film."

To speak of Vietnam either in terms of an artistic "genre" or a specific "period" in *our* history is simply another means of ignoring the challenge the Vietnam War poses to our abiding cultural myths of America and Americans. By this we do not mean to argue that "Vietnam" is an unanswerable mystery, some terrible anomaly in the American experience—yet another version of the "mystery" of that "Orient" invented by the Western imagination. Quite the contrary, the Vietnam War simply exposes the irrationality of an American ideology that has shaped far more than our foreign policies and military actions over the last hundred years. It is an ideology that has informed our very conception of academic and educational disciplines in ways that should make us suspicious of even the best-intentioned efforts to develop programs in "Vietnam Studies" and courses on "The Vietnam War." We must not forget that research programs in political science, linguistics, Oriental languages and cultures, funded by the Department of Defense at Michigan State, Cornell, the School for Advanced International Studies at Johns Hopkins, and a host of other American colleges and universities provided much of the *misinformation* about Vietnam and Southeast Asia that directed our diplomacy and military action during the war.

When antiwar students occupied university buildings, shut down classes, and burned R.O.T.C. facilities on campuses across the country, public outrage focused on the "irrationality" of these demonstrators attacking institutions of higher learning. When these same students insisted upon curricular reforms, new faculty, student involvement in university administration, many Americans concluded that protest against the war was merely a disguise for less compelling "campus unrest" and adolescent high-jinks. In fact, many student activists in the antiwar movement understood the political functions of higher education in the United States, despite the long traditions of "disinterested inquiry" to which faculty and university administrators appealed. For many of those students, the most visible signs of the American university's complicity in the Vietnam War were reserve officer training programs, weapons' research funded by the Department of Defense, and military recruiters on campus. Still others understood the subtler and more pervasive roles higher education continues to play in the legitimation of American ideology. The emphasis which humanists placed on western cultural traditions and aesthetic values encouraged an ethnocentrism fundamental to racism at home and colonialism abroad. With considerable insight and intellectual maturity, many student demonstrators in the 1960s understood that the "military-industrial complex" promoting the war in Vietnam had a powerful and often willing ally in the American academy.

This complicity of our educational institutions with American ideology that revealed its contradictions in the Vietnam War remains one of the most important issues for us to address. Admittedly, it complicates profoundly the task of "teaching" the Vietnam War, even though the history of that war and of Southeast Asia remains an urgent educational topic for a generation of students born *after* the war was technically concluded. Too often the courses that deal with Vietnam as a topic in history, political science, sociology, literature, and media studies are concerned with "correcting" the misrepresentations of Vietnam in the mass media. Our scholarly habits encourage us to provide more deliberate, factually accurate, and rationally defensible accounts of the war, the Vietnamese, and their reception in America. From all that we have written about the transformation of American silence about Vietnam in the 1970s into the endless debate of Vietnam in the 1980s, it would seem perverse for us to criticize the scholarly and educational purposes of setting the historical record straight. Yet, there can be no "accurate" treatment of what Vietnam means for American culture until these very teachers reconsider the material practices that have shaped curricula, instruction, and research projects in our universities for decades before and after the Vietnam War. The disciplinary practices that student demonstrators understood to be part of our military involvement in Vietnam did not change significantly after 1975. The continuing urgency of the political issues raised by the Vietnam War argue for less academic specialization and more multidisciplinary treatment of such questions. Above all, the ethnocentrism and racism that helped motivate our war effort are only reinforced by curricula designed to celebrate the progressive destiny of Western societies. To teach "Vietnam" today means also to embrace the aims of multicultural diversity at all levels of American education. If we hope to address the political

15

issues raised by Vietnam, rather than merely "heal" the wounds our idealism has suffered, then we will have to discover the rich heritages of other peoples. Rather than working to "reclaim a legacy" as William Bennett has argued, or promoting a "cultural literacy" such as E. D. Hirsch, Jr. has advocated, we ought to use Vietnam as an occasion to teach our students that genuine cultural literacy begins with practical knowledge of cultures other than our own. Whatever "legacy" we hope to pass on to our students must include what our own teachers left out of the curriculum.

Could it be that the "market" for mass-media treatments of Vietnam in the 1980s has a more positive, albeit still unrealized, dimension to it? When accused of cynically exploiting the passive public, television and film producers appeal to the conventional excuse of advertisers: "We simply give the people what they want." It is possible, however, that the many different peoples that we complacently call "Americans" continue to consume the vast array of media products associated with the name of Vietnam because they are still dissatisfied with the answers they have been given. Perhaps there is still some capacity for self-criticism, and thus social reform, in the politically and culturally diverse United States to which scholars and teachers may appeal. Should such an optimistic possibility be salvageable from the continuing mystification of Vietnam's significance in American culture, then the critical, analytical, and historical work of scholars and teachers may find a larger audience whose interests in learning are motivated by their desires for genuinely progressive social and political change. To accomplish this work, we may well have to reopen the "wounds" of the Vietnam War before we can ever hope to address the real causes of such violence.

As we watch the collapse of Stalinist regimes in Eastern Europe, epochal reforms within the Soviet Union, student challenges to the repressive leadership in the Peoples' Republic of China, we are encouraged by our government and the news media in the United States to believe that we are confronting a certain "end" to "history" as we have known it and that the confrontational politics of the cold war have finally been overcome. We are less plausibly encouraged by these same sources to believe that we have won a great victory, that the "freedoms" of liberal capitalism and its democratic institutions have demonstrated their superiority. Such a vainglorious claim still belongs to the rhetoric of the cold war and has direct bearing on our understanding of the Vietnam War's significance. Too often "healing" the wounds of Vietnam has meant in the 1980s "winning" a war that we decisively and justifiably *lost*. The same ideological argument that sent us imaginatively *back* to Vietnam, either in the character of Rambo or the form of our continuing economic and diplomatic "blockade" of Vietnam, shapes our complacent belief that we are the "victors" of the cold war.

Amid the self-congratulation and banal patriotism with which our government and media generally greet these dramatic changes around the world, there is growing sentiment in the United States that we demonstrate materially and symbolically our support for these political movements. Certainly this includes the economic assistance which Czechoslovakian President Havel has suggested that the United States extend to the new societies and economies taking shape in Eastern Europe. It also ought to include a more forthright and candid assessment of our own social failings, in order to begin the work of reforming our domestic and international conduct. Perhaps even more efficiently than economic assistance, such self-criticism will allow us to share the emancipatory and democratic aims of these new societies. Rather than congratulate ourselves upon a great victory, we ought to take inspiration from these revolutionary movements to find the means of changing the social, political, economic, and even psychological factors that shaped our responsibility for the cold war. Some of these same historical conditions still cause us to keep many of our own citizens, as well as so many other peoples in the third world, out in the cold.

# PART ONE

# The Vietnam War and History

# ONE
# Visions of Righteousness
## NOAM CHOMSKY

In one of his sermons on human rights, President Carter explained that we owe Vietnam no debt and have no responsibility to render it any assistance because "the destruction was actual."[1] If words have meaning, this must stand among the most astonishing statements in diplomatic history. What is most interesting about this statement is the reaction to it among educated Americans: null. Furthermore, the occasional reference to it, and what it means, evokes no comment and no interest. It is considered neither appalling, nor even noteworthy, and it is felt to have no bearing on Carter's standing as patron saint of human rights, any more than do his actions: his dedicated support for Indonesian atrocities in Timor and the successful terrorist campaign undertaken in El Salvador to destroy the popular organizations that were defended by the assassinated Archbishop Romero; his huge increase in the flow of arms to Israel in parallel with its 1978 invasion of Lebanon, its subsequent large-scale bombing of civilians, and its rapid expansion into the occupied territories; etc. All of this is a tribute to the successes of a system of indoctrination that has few if any peers.

These successes permit the commissars to issue pronouncements of quite impressive audacity. Thus, Zbigniew Brzezinski thunders that the Soviet invasion of Afgahnistan is:

> A classical foreign invasion, waged with Nazi-like brutality. Scorched villages, executed hostages, massive bombings, even chemical warfare . . . [with] several hundred thousand killed and maimed by Soviet military operations that qualify as genocidal in their intent and effect. . . . It needs to be said directly, and over and over again, that Soviet policy in Afghanistan is the fourth greatest exercise in social holocaust of our contemporary age: it ranks only after Stalin's multimillion massacres; after Hitler's genocide of the European Jews and partially of the Slavs; and

21

after Pol Pot's decimation of is own people; it is, moreover, happening right now.[2]

While the descriptive words are fair enough, when issuing from this source they merit all the admiration accorded similar pronouncements by Brzezinski's Soviet models with regard to American crimes, which he somehow seems to have overlooked in his ranking of atrocities of the modern age. To mention a few: the U.S. wars in Indochina, to which his condemnation applies in full except that there were *many millions* "killed and maimed" and the level of destruction was far greater; the Indonesian massacres of 1965 backed enthusiastically by the United States with half a million murdered; the Timor massacres conducted under Brzezinski's aegis with hundreds of thousands "killed and maimed" and the remnants left in the state of Biafra and the Thai-Cambodian border, an operation that is "happening right now" thanks to U.S. silence and support; the murder, often with hideous torture and mutilation, of over 100,000 people in El Salvador and Guatemala since 1978, operations carried out thanks to the support of the United States and its proxies, and most definitely "happening right now." But the readers of the *National Interest* will find nothing amiss in Brzezinski's presentation, since in Vietnam "the destruction was mutual" and the other cases, if known at all, have been easily assimilated into the preferred model of American benevolence. An auspicious opening for a new "conservative" journal of international affairs.

"It is scandalous," Brzezinski writes, "that so much of the conventionally liberal community, always so ready to embrace victims of American or Israeli or any other unfashionable 'imperialism,' is so reticent on the subject" of Afghanistan. Surely one might expect liberals in Congress or the press to desist from their ceaseless efforts on behalf of the PLO and the guerrillas in El Salvador long enough to notice Soviet crimes; perhaps they might even follow Brzezinski to the Khyber Pass so that they can strike heroic poses there before a camera crew. One should not, incidentally, dismiss this characterization of the "liberal community" on grounds of its transparent absurdity. Rather, it should be understood as a typical example of a campaign carefully designed to eliminate even the limited critique of crimes by the United States and its clients that is sometimes voiced, a campaign that reflects the natural commitments of the totalitarian right, which regards anything less than full subservience as an intolerable deviation from political correctness.

Some feel that there was a debt but that it has been amply repaid. Under the headline "The Debt to the Indochinese Is Becoming a Fiscal Drain," Bernard Gwertzman of the *New York Times* quotes a State Department official who "said he believed the United States has now paid its moral debt for its involvement on the losing side in Indochina." The remark, which passed without comment, is illuminating: we owe no debt for mass slaughter and for leaving three countries in ruins, no debt to the millions of maimed and orphaned, to the peasants who still die today from unexploded ordnance. Rather, our moral debt results only from the fact that we did not win—or as the party line has it, that South Vietnam (i.e., the client regime that we established as a cover for our attack against South Vietnam, which had as much legitimacy as the Afghan regime established by the USSR) lost the war to North Vietnam—the official enemy, since the U.S. attack against the South cannot be conceded. By this logic, if the Russians win in Afghanistan, they will have no moral debt at all. Proceeding further, how have we paid our moral debt for failing to win? By resettling Vietnamese refugees fleeing the lands we ravaged, "one of the largest, most dramatic humanitarian efforts in history" according to Roger Winter, director of the U.S. Committee for Refugees. But "despite the pride," Gwertzman reports, "some voices in the Reagan Administration and in Congress are once again asking whether the war debt has now been paid. . . ."[3]

Invariably, the reader of the press who believes that the lowest depths have already been reached is proved wrong. In March 1968, as U.S. atrocities in South Vietnam were reaching their peak, the *Times* ran an item headed "Army Exhibit Bars Simulating Shooting at Vietnamese Hut," reporting an attempt by demonstrators to disrupt an exhibit in the Chicago Museum of Science and Industry: "Beginning today, visitors can no longer enter a helicopter for simulated firing of a machine gun at targets in a diorama of the Vietnam Central Highlands. The targets were a hut, two bridges and an ammunition dump, and a light flashed when a hit was scored." The *Times* is bitterly scornful of the peaceniks who demonstrated in protest at this amusing exhibit, which was such great fun for the kiddies, even objecting "to children being permitted to 'fire' at the hut, even though no people appear. . . ." Citing this item at the time, I asked whether "what is needed in the United States

23

is dissent—or denazification," a question that elicited much outrage; the question stands, however.[4]

To see how the moral level has improved since, we may turn to the *Times* sixteen years later, where we find a report on a new board game designed by a Princeton student called "Vietnam: 1965–1975." One player "takes the role of the United States and South Vietnam, and the other represents North Vietnam and the Vietcong." The inventor hopes the game will lead people to "experiment with new ideas, new approaches" to the war. We may ask another question: how would we react to a report in *Pravda* of a board game sold in Moscow, in which one player "takes the role of the USSR and Afghanistan, and the other represents Pakistan, the CIA, China, and the rebels," designed to lead people to "experiment with new ideas, new approaches" to the war—perhaps supplied with some accessory information concerning the "bandits terrorizing Afghanistan," who, according to Western sources, initiated their attacks from Pakistan with support from this United States-Chinese ally in 1973, six years before the USSR sent forces to "defend the legitimate government"?[5]

The American system of indoctrination is not satisfied with "mutual destruction" that effaces all responsibility for some of the major war crimes of the modern era. Rather, the perpetrator of the crimes must be seen as the injured party. We find headlines in the nation's press reading: "Vietnam, Trying to be Nicer, Still has Long Way to Go."[6] "It's about time the Vietnamese demonstrated some good will," said Charles Printz of Human Rights Advocates International, referring to negotiations about Amerasian children who constitute a tiny fraction of the victims of the savage U.S. aggression in Indochina. Crossette adds that the Vietnamese have also not been sufficiently forthcoming on the matter of remains of American soldiers, though their behavior is improving somewhat: "There has been progress, albeit slow, on the missing Americans." The unresolved problem of the war is what they did to us. This point of view may be understood by invoking the terminology contrived by Adlai Stevenson—the hero of Brzezenski's "liberal community"—at the United Nations in May 1964, when he explained that we were in South Vietnam to combat "internal aggression," that is, the aggression of South Vietnamese peasants against U.S. military forces and their clients in South Vietnam. Since we were simply defending ourselves from aggression, it makes sense to consider ourselves the victims of the Vietnamese.[7]

This picture of aggrieved innocence, carefully crafted by the propaganda system and lovingly nurtured by the educated classes, must surely count as one of the most remarkable phenomena of the modern age. Its roots lie deep in the national culture. "The conquerors of America glorified the devastation they wrought in visions of righteousness," Francis Jennings observes, "and their descendants have been reluctant to peer through the aura."[8] No one who surveys the story of the conquest of the national territory, or the reaction to it over three-and-a-half centuries, can doubt the accuracy of this indictment. In Memphis in 1831, Alexis de Tocqueville watched in "the middle of the winter" when the "cold was unusually severe" as "three or four thousand soldiers drive before them the wandering races of the aborigines," who "brought in their train the wounded and the sick, with children newly born and old men on the verge of death," a "solemn spectacle" that would never fade from his memory: "the triumphal march of civilization across the desert." They were the lucky ones, the ones who had escaped the ravages of Andrew Jackson who, years earlier, had urged his men to exterminate the "blood thirsty barbarians" and "cannibals" and to "distroy [sic] those deluded victims doomed to distruction [sic] by their own restless and savage conduct"—as they did, killing women and children, stripping the skin from the bodies of the dead for bridle reins and cutting the tip of each dead Indian's nose to count the number of "savage dogs" who had been removed from the path of civilization. De Tocqueville was particularly impressed by the way the pioneers could deprive Indians of their rights and exterminate them "with singular felicity, tranquilly, legally, philanthropically, without shedding blood, and without violating a single great principle of morality in the eyes of the world." It was impossible to destroy people with "more respect for the laws of humanity."[9]

The story continues with no essential change in later years. The American conquest of the Philippines, led by men who had learned their craft in the Indian wars, ranks among the most barbaric episodes of modern history. In the island of Luzon alone, some 600,000 natives perished from the war or diseases caused by it. General Jacob Smith, who gave orders to turn the island of Samar into a "howling wilderness," to "kill and burn" ("the more you kill and burn the better you will please me") was retired with no punishment by President Roosevelt, who made it clear that Smith's only sin was his "loose and violent talk." Roosevelt, who went on to receive the Nobel Peace Prize, explained that "I also heartily approve of the employment of the sternest measure necessary" against the cruel and treacherous savages who "disregard . . . the rules of civilized warfare," and who had furthermore "assailed our sovereignty" (President McKinley) in an earlier act of internal aggression. The director of all Presbyterian missions hailed the conquest as "a great step toward the civilization and evangelization of the world," while another missionary explained that the notorious "water cure" was not really "torture" because "the victim has it in his own power to stop the process" by divulging what he knows "before the operation has gone far enough to seriously hurt him," and a leading Episcopal Bishop lauded General Smith's tactics as necessary "to purge the natives," who were "treacherous and barbarous," of the "evil effects" of "a degenerate form of Christianity." The press chimed in with similar sentiments. "Whether we like it or not," the *New York Criterion* explained, "we must go on slaughtering the natives in English fashion, and taking what muddy glory lies in the wholesale killing until they have learned to respect our arms. The more difficult task of getting them to respect our intentions will follow." Similar thoughts were expressed as we were slaughtering the natives in South Vietnam, and we hear them again today, often in almost these words, with regard to our current exploits in Central America. The reference to the "English fashion" will be understood by any student of American history, by anyone who recalls how the settlers, including the saintly Puritans and George Washington, taught the natives that war in the English fashion is a system of extermination, directed specifically against women and children.

For Theodore Roosevelt, the murderers in the Philippines were fighting "for the triumph of civilization over the black chaos of savagery and barbarism," while President Taft observed that "there never was a war conducted, whether against inferior races or not, in which there were more compassion and more restraint and more generosity" than in this campaign of wholesale slaughter and mass torture and terror. Stuart Chreighton Miller, who records these horrors and the reaction to them in some detail and observes that they have largely disappeared from history, assures the reader that "the American interventions both in Vietnam and in the Philippines were motivated in part by good intentions to elevate or to aid the victims"; Soviet scholars say the same about Afghanistan, with comparable justice.[10]

General Smith's subordinate Littleton Waller was acquitted in court-martial proceedings, since he had only been following orders: namely, to kill every male Filipino over the age of ten. He went on to become a Major-General, and to take charge of Woodrow Wilson's atrocities as he celebrated his doctrine of self-determination by invading Haiti and the Dominican Republic, where his warriors murdered, raped, burned villages, established concentration camps that provided labor for the U.S. companies, reinstituted virtual slavery, demolished the political system and any vestige of intellectual freedom, and generally reduced the countries to misery while enriching U.S. sugar companies. According to the approved version, these exploits not only illustrate the Wilsonian doctrine of self-determination to which we are dedicated as a matter of definition, but also serve as a notable example of how "the overall effect of American power on other societies was to further liberty, pluralism, and democracy." So we are informed by Harvard scholar Samuel Huntington, who adds that "No Dominican could doubt but that his country was a far, far better place to live in 1922 than it was in 1916," including those tortured by the benefactors and those whose families they murdered or whose villages they burned for the benefit of U.S. sugar companies.[11]

The record of U.S. intervention in Central America and the Caribbean, to the present day, adds further shameful chapters to the story of terror, torture, slavery, starvation and repression, all conducted with the most touching innocence, and with endless benevolence—particularly with regard to the U.S. investors whose representatives design these admirable exercises. The worst period in this sordid history was initiated by the Kennedy administration, which established the basic structure of state terrorism that has massacred tens of thousands since as an integral part of the Alliance for Progress; this cynical program, devised in fear of "another Castro," fostered a form of "development" in which crop lands were converted to export for the benefit of U.S. corporations and their local associates while the population sank into misery and starvation, necessitating an efficient system of state terror to ensure "stability" and "order." We can witness its achievements today, for example, in El Salvador, where Presidents Carter and Reagan organized the slaughter of some 60,000 people to mounting applause in the United States as the terror appeared to be showing signs of success. During the post-World War II period, as U.S. power greatly expanded, similar projects were undertaken over a much wider range, with massacres in Greece, Korea (prior to what we call "the Korean War," some 100,000 had been killed in South Korea, primarily in U.S.-run counterinsurgency campaigns undertaken as a part of our successful effort to destroy the indigenous political system and install our chosen clients), Southeast Asia, and elsewhere, all with inspiring professions of noble intent and the enthusiastic acclaim of the educated classes, as long as violence appears to be successful.[12]

In brief, a major theme of our history from the earliest days has been a combination of hideous atrocities and protestations of awesome benevolence. It should come as no great surprise to students of American history that we are the injured party in Indochina.

Contrary to much illusion, there was little principled opposition to the Indochina war among the articulate intelligentsia. One detailed study undertaken in 1970, at the peak of antiwar protest, revealed that the "American intellectual elite" came to oppose the war for the same "pragmatic reasons" that had convinced business circles that this investment should be liquidated. Very few opposed the war on the grounds that led all to condemn the Soviet invasion of Czechoslavakia: not that it failed, or that it was too bloody, but that aggression is wrong. In striking contrast, as late as 1982— after years of unremitting propaganda with virtually no dissenting voice permitted expression to a large audience—over 70 percent of the general population (but far fewer "opinion leaders") still regarded the war as "fundamentally wrong and immoral," not merely "a mistake."[13]

The technical terms for this failure of the indoctrination system is the "Vietnam syndrome," a dread disease that spread over the population with such symptoms as distaste for aggression and massacre, what Norman Podhoretz calls the "sickly inhibitions against the use of military force," which he hopes were finally overcome with the grand triumph of American arms in Grenada.[14] The malady, however, persists, and continues to inhibit the state executive in Central America and elsewhere. The major U.S. defeat in Indochina was at home: much of the population rejected the approved stance of passivity, apathy and obedience. Great efforts were made through the 1970s to overcome this "crisis of democracy," as it was called, but with less success than reliance on articulate opinion would suggest.

There was, to be sure, debate over the wisdom of the war. The hawks, such as Joseph Alsop, argued that with sufficient violence the United States could succeed in its aims, while the doves doubted this conclusion, through emphasizing that "we all pray that Mr. Alsop will be right" and that "we may all be saluting the wisdom and statesmanship of the American government" if it succeeds in subjugating Vietnam (what we would call: "liberating Vietnam") while leaving it "a land of ruin and wreck" (Arthur Schlesinger). Few would deny that the war began with "blundering efforts to do good" (Anthony Lewis) in "an excess of righteousness and disinterested benevolence" (John King Fairbanks), that it was "a failed crusade" undertaken for motives that were "noble" though "illusory" and with the "loftiest intentions" (Stanley Karnow, in his best-selling history). These are the voices of the doves. As noted, much of the population rejected the hawk/dove consensus of elite circles, a fact of lasting significance. It was that part of the population that concerned the planners in Washington, for example, Defense Secretary Robert McNamara, who asked in a secret memo of May 19, 1967, whether expansion of the American war might "polarize opinion to the extent that 'doves' in the US will get out of hand—massive refusals to serve, or to fight, or to cooperate, or worse?"[15]

It is worth recalling a few facts. The United States was deeply committed to the French effort to reconquer their former colony, recognizing throughout that the enemy was the nationalist movement of Vietnam. The death toll was about a half-million. When France withdrew, the United States dedicated itself at once to subverting the 1954 Geneva settlement, installing in the south a terrorist regime that had killed perhaps 70,000 "Viet Cong" by 1961, evoking resistance which, from 1959, was supported from the northern half of the country temporarily divided by the 1954 settlement that the United States had undermined. In 1961–1962, President Kennedy launched a direct attack against rural South Vietnam with large-scale bombing and defoliation as part of a program designed to drive millions of people to camps where they would be "protected" by armed guards and barbed wire from the guerrillas whom, the United States conceded, they were willingly supporting. The United States maintained that it was invited in, but as the London *Economist* accurately observed, "an invader is an invader unless invited in by a government with a claim to legitimacy." The United States never regarded the clients it installed as having any such claim, and in fact it regularly replaced them when they failed to exhibit sufficient enthusiasm for the American attack or sought

29

to implement the neutralist settlement that was advocated on all sides and was considered the prime danger by the aggressors, since it would undermine the basis for their war against South Vietnam. In short, the United States invaded South Vietnam, where it proceeded to compound the crime of aggression with numerous and quite appalling crimes against humanity throughout Indochina.

The *Economist*, of course, was not referring to Vietnam but to a similar Soviet fraud concerning Afghanistan. With regard to official enemies, Western intellectuals are able to perceive that $2 + 2 = 4$. Their Soviet counterparts have the same clear vision with regard to the United States.

From 1961 to 1965, the United States expanded the war against South Vietnam while fending off the threat of neutralization and political settlement, which was severe at the time. This was regarded as an intolerable prospect, since our "minnow" could not compete politically with their "whale," as explained by Douglas Pike, the leading government specialist on the National Liberation Front (in essence, the former Viet Minh, the anti-French resistance, "Viet Cong" in U.S. propaganda). Pike further explained that the NLF "maintained that its contest with the GVN [the American-installed client regime] and the United States should be fought out at the political level and that the use of massed military might was in itself illegitimate" until forced by the United States "to use counter-force to survive." The aggressors succeeded in shifting the conflict from the political to the military arena, a major victory since it is in that arena alone that they reign supreme, while the propaganda system then exploited the use of "counter-force to survive" by the South Vietnamese enemy as proof that they were "terrorists" from whom we must defend South Vietnam by attacking and destroying it. Still more interestingly, this version of history is now close to received doctrine.

In 1965, the United States began the direct land invasion of South Vietnam, along with the bombing of the North, and (at three times the level) the systematic bombardment of the South, which bore the brunt of the U.S. aggression throughout. By then, some 170,000 South Vietnamese had been killed, many of them "under the crushing weight of American armor, napalm, jet bombers and, finally, vomiting gases," in the words of hawkish military historian Bernard Fall. The United States then escalated the war against the South, also extending it to Laos and Cambodia where perhaps another half-million to a million were killed, while the Vietnamese death toll may well have reached or passed three million, while the land was destroyed and the societies demolished in one of the major catastrophes of the modern era[16]—a respectable achievement in the days before we fell victim to the "sickly inhibitions against the use of military force."

Throughout 1964, as the United States planned the extension of its aggression to North Vietnam, planners were aware that heightened U.S. military actions might lead to North Vietnamese "ground action in South Vietnam or Laos" in retaliation (William Bundy, November 1964). The United States later claimed that North Vietnamese troops began leaving for the South in October 1964, two months after the U.S. bombing of North Vietnam during the fabricated Tonkin Gulf incident. As late as July 1965, the Pentagon was still concerned over the "probability" that there might be North Vietnamese units in or near the South—five months after the regular bombing of North Vietnam, three months after the direct U.S. land invasion of the South, over three years after the beginning of U.S. bombing of the South, ten years after the U.S. subversion of the political accords that were to unify the country, and with the death toll in the South probably approaching 200,000. Thankfully, North Vietnamese units finally arrived as anticipated, thus making it possible for the propaganda system to shift from defense of South Vietnam against internal aggression to defense against North Vietnamese aggression. As late as the Tet offensive in January 1968, North Vietnamese troops appear to have been at about the level of the mercenary forces (Korean, Thai) brought in by the United States from January 1965 as part of the effort to subjugate South Vietnam, and according to the Pentagon there still were only South Vietnamese fighting in the Mekong Delta, where the most savage fighting took place at the time. U.S. military forces, of course, vastly exceeded all others in numbers, firepower, and atrocities.

The party line holds that "North Vietnam, not the Vietcong, was always the enemy," as John Corry observes in reporting the basic message of an NBC "White Paper" on the war.[17] This stand is conventional in the mainstream. Corry is particularly indignant that anyone should question this higher truth propounded by the state propaganda system. As proof of the absurdity of such "liberal mythology," he cites the battle of Ia Drang valley in November 1965: "It was clear then that North Vietnam was in the war. Nonetheless, liberal mythology insisted that the war was being waged only by the Vietcong, mostly righteous peasants." Corry presents no example of anyone who denied that there were North Vietnamese troops in the South in November 1965, since there was none, even among the few opponents of the war, who at that time and for several years after included very few representatives of mainstream liberalism. As noted earlier, principled objection to the war was a highly marginal phenomenon among American intellectuals even at the height of opposition to it. Corry's argument for North Vietnamese aggression, however, is as impressive as any that has been presented.

The NBC "White Paper" was one of a rash of retrospectives on the tenth anniversary of the war's end, devoted to "The War that Went Wrong, The Lessons it Taught."[18] They present a sad picture of U.S. intellectual culture, a picture of dishonesty and moral cowardice. Their most striking feature is what is missing: the American wars in Indochina. It is a classic example of Hamlet without the Prince of Denmark. Apart from a few scattered sentences, the rare allusions to the war in these lengthy presentations are devoted to the suffering of the American invaders. The *Wall Street Journal,* for example, refers to "the $180 million in chemical companies' compensation to Agent Orange victims"—U.S. soldiers, not the South Vietnamese victims, whose suffering was and is vastly greater.[19] It is difficult to exaggerate the significance of these startling facts.

There is an occasional glimpse of reality. *Time* opens its inquiry by recalling the trauma of the American soldiers, facing an enemy that "dissolved by day into the villages, into the other Vietnamese. They maddened the Americans with the mystery of who they were —the unseen man who shot from the tree line, or laid a wire across the trail with a Claymore mine at the other end, the mama-san who did the wash, the child concealing a grenade." No doubt one could find similar complaints in the Nazi press about the Balkans.

The meaning of these facts is almost never perceived. *Time* goes so far as to claim that the "subversion" was "orchestrated" by Moscow, so that the United States had to send troops to "defend" South Vietnam, echoing the fantasies concocted in scholarship, for example, by Walt Rostow, who maintains that in his effort "to gain the balance of power in Eurasia," Stalin turned "to the East, to back Mao and to enflame the North Korean and Indochinese Communists."[20] Few can comprehend—surely not the editors of *Time* —the significance of the analysis by the military command and civilian officials of the aggressors:

> The success of this unique system of war depends upon almost complete unity of action of the entire populations. That such unity is a fact is too obvious to admit of discussion; how it is brought about and maintained is not so plain. Intimidation has undoubtedly accomplished much to this end, but fear as the only motive is hardly sufficient to account for the united and spontaneous action of several millions of people. . . . [The only collaborators are] intriguers, disreputable or ignorant, who we had rigged out with sometimes high ranks, which became tools in their hands for plundering the country without scruple. . . . Despised, they possessed neither the spiritual culture nor the moral fibre that would have allowed them to understand and carry out their task.

The words are those of General Arthur MacArthur describing the Philippine war of national liberation in 1900 and the French resident-minister in Vietnam in 1897,[21] but they apply with considerable accuracy to the U.S. war against Vietnam, as the *Time* quote illustrates, in its own way.

Throughout, the familiar convenient innocence served admirably, as in the days when we were "slaughtering the natives" in the Philippines, Latin America, and elsewhere, preparing the way to "getting them to respect our intentions." In February 1965, the United States initiated the regular bombardment of North Vietnam, and more significantly, as Bernard Fall observed, began "to wage unlimited aerial warfare inside [South Vietnam] at the price of literally pounding the place to bits," the decision that "changed the character of the Vietnam war" more than any other.[22] These moves inspired the distinguished liberal commentator of the *New York Times*, James Reston, "to clarify America's present and future policy in Vietnam":

> The guiding principle of American foreign policy since 1945 has been that no state shall use military force or the threat of military force to achieve its political objectives. And the companion of this principle has been that the United States would use its influence and its power, when necessary and where it could be effective, against any state that defied this principle.

This is the principle that was "at stake in Vietnam," where "the United States is now challenging the Communist effort to seek power by the more cunning technique of military subversion" (the United States having blocked all efforts at political settlement because it knew the indigenous opposition would easily win a political contest, after ten years of murderous repression and three years of U.S. Air Force bombing in the South).[23]

In November 1967, when Bernard Fall, long a committed advocate of U.S. support for the Saigon regime, pleaded for an end to the war because "Viet-Nam as a cultural and historic entity . . . is threatened with extinction . . . [as] . . . the countryside literally dies under the blows of the largest military machine ever unleashed on an area of this size," Reston explained that America

> is fighting a war now on the principle that military power shall not compel South Vietnam to do what it does not want to do, that man does not belong to the state. This is the deepest conviction of Western Civilization, and rests on the old doctrine that the individual belongs not to the state but to his Creator, and therefore has "inalienable rights" as a person, which no magistrate or political force may violate.[24]

The same touching faith in American innocence and benevolence in Indochina—as elsewhere throughout our history—persists until today in any commentary that can reach a substantial audience, untroubled by the plain facts. Much of the population understood and still remembers the truth, though this too will pass as the system of indoctrination erases historical memories and establishes the "truths" that are deemed more satisfactory.

By 1967, popular protest had reached a significant scale although elite groups remained loyal to the cause (apart from the bombing of North Vietnam, which was regarded as a potential threat to us since it might lead to a broader war drawing in China and the USSR, from which we might not be immune—the "toughest" question, according to the McNamara memo cited earlier, and the only serious question among "respectable" critics of the war). The massacre of innocents is a problem only among emotional or irresponsible types, or among the "aging adolescents on college faculties who found it rejuvenating to play 'revolution'," in Stuart Creighton Miller's words. Decent and respectable people remain silent and obedient, devoting themselves to personal gain, concerned only that we too might ultimately face unacceptable threat —a stance not without recent historical precedent elsewhere. In contrast to the war protesters, two commentators explain, "decent, patriotic Americans demanded—and in the person of Ronald Reagan have apparently achieved—a return to pride and patriotism, a reaffirmation of the values and virtues that had been trampled upon by the Vietnam-spawned counterculture,"[25] most crucially the virtues of marching in the parade chanting praises for their leaders as they conduct their necessary chores, as in Indochina and El Salvador.

The U.S. attack reached its peak of intensity and horror after the Tet offensive, with the post-Tet pacification campaigns—actually mass murder operations launched against defenseless civilians, as in Operation Speedy Express in the Mekong Delta—and mounting atrocities in Laos and Cambodia, called here "secret wars," a technical term referring to executive wars that the press does not expose, though it has ample evidence concerning them, and that are later denounced with much outrage, when the proper time has come, and attributed to evil men whom we have sternly excluded from the body politic, another sign of our profound decency and honor. By 1970, if not before, it was becoming clear that U.S. policy would "create a situation in which, indeed, North Vietnam will necessarily dominate Indochina, for no other viable society will remain."[26] This predictable consequence of U.S. savagery would later be used as a post hoc justification for it, in another propaganda achievement that Goebbels would have admired.

It is a most revealing fact that there is no such event in history as the American attack against South Vietnam launched by Kennedy and escalated by his successors. Rather, history records only "a defense of freedom,"[27] a "failed crusade" (Stanley Karnow) that was perhaps unwise, the doves maintain. At a comparable level of integrity, Soviet party hacks extol the "defense of Afghanistan" against "bandits" and "terrorists" organized by the CIA. They, at least, can plead fear of totalitarian violence, while their Western counterparts can offer no such excuse for their servility.

The extent of this servility is revealed throughout the tenth anniversary retrospectives, not only by the omission of the war itself, but also by the interpretation provided. The *New York Times* writes sardonically of the "ignorance" of the American people, only 60 percent of whom are aware that the United States "sided with South Vietnam"[28]—as Nazi Germany sided with France, as the USSR now sides with Afghanistan. Given that we were defending South Vietnam, it must be that the critics of this noble if flawed enterprise sided with Hanoi, and that is indeed what the party line maintains; that opposition to American aggression entails no such support, just as opposition to Soviet aggression entails no support for either the feudalist forces of the Afghan resistance or Pakistan or the United States, is an elementary point that would not surpass the capacity of an intelligent ten-year-old, though it inevitably escapes the mind of the commissar. The *Times* alleges that North Vietnam was "portrayed by some American intellectuals as the repository of moral rectitude." No examples are given, nor is evidence presented to support these charges, and the actual record is, as always, scrupulously ignored. Critics of the antiwar movement are quoted on its "moral failure of terrifying proportions," but those who opposed U.S. atrocities are given no opportunity to explain the basis for their opposition to U.S. aggression and massacre or to assign these critics and the *New York Times* their proper place in history, including those who regard themselves as "doves" because of their occasional twitters of protest when the cost to us became too great. We learn that the opponents of the war "brandished moral principles and brushed aside complexity," but hear nothing of what they had to say—exactly as was the case throughout the war. A current pretense is that the mainstream media were open to principled critics of the war during these years, indeed that they dominated the media. In fact, they were almost entirely excluded, as is easily demonstrated, and now we are permitted to hear accounts of their alleged crimes, but not, of course, their actual words, exactly as one would expect in a properly functioning system of indoctrination.

The *Times* informs us that Vietnam "now stands exposed as the Prussia of Southeast Asia" because since 1975 the Vietnamese have "unleashed a series of pitiless attacks against their neighbors," referring to the Vietnamese invasion that overthrew the Pol Pot regime (after two years of border attacks from Cambodia), the regime that we now support despite pretenses to the contrary, emphasizing the "continuity" of the current Khmer Rouge-based coalition with the Pol Pot regime (see below). The Khmer Rouge receive "massive support" from our ally China, Nayan Chanda reports, while the United States has more than doubled its support to the coalition. Deng Xiaoping, expressing the Chinese stand (which we tacitly and materially support), states: "I do not understand why some want to remove Pol Pot. It is true that he made some mistakes in the past but now he is leading the fight against the Vietnamese aggressors."[29] As explained by the government's leading specialist on Indochinese communism, now director of the Indochina archives at the University of California in Berkeley, Pol

Pot was the "charismatic" leader of a "bloody but successful peasant revolution with a substantial residue of popular support," under which "on a statistical basis, most [peasants] . . . did not experience much in the way of brutality."[30] Though the *Times* is outraged at the Prussian-style aggression that overthrew our current Khmer Rouge ally, and at the current Vietnamese insistence that a political settlement must exclude Pol Pot, the reader of its pages will find little factual material about any of these matters. There are, incidentally, countries that have "unleashed a series of pitiless attacks against their neighbors" in these years, for example, Israel, with its invasions of Lebanon in 1978 and 1982, but as an American client state, Israel inherits the right of aggression so that it does not merit the bitter criticism that Vietnam deserves for overthrowing Pol Pot; and in any event, its invasion of Lebanon was a "liberation," as the *Times* explained at the time, always carefully excluding Lebanese opinion on the matter, as obviously irrelevant.[31]

The *Times* recognizes that the United States did suffer "shame" during its Indochina wars: "the shame of defeat." Victory, we are to assume, would not have been shameful, and the record of aggression and atrocities supported by the *Times* obviously evokes no shame. Rather, the United States thought it was "resisting" Communists "when it intervened in Indochina"; how we "resist" the natives in their land, the *Times* does not explain.

That the United States lost the war in Indochina is "an inescapable fact" *(Wall Street Journal)*, repeated without question throughout the retrospectives and in American commentary generally. When some doctrine is universally proclaimed without qualification, a rational mind will at once inquire as to whether it is true. In this case, it is false, though to see why, it is necessary to escape the confines of the propaganda system and to investigate the rich documentary record that lays out the planning and motives for the American war against the Indochinese, which persisted for almost thirty years. Those who undertake this task will discover that a rather different conclusion is in order.

The United States did not achieve its maximal goals in Indochina, but it did gain a partial victory. Despite talk by Eisenhower and others about Vietnamese raw materials, the primary U.S. concern was not Indochina, but rather the "domino effect," the demonstration effect of successful independent development that might cause "the rot to spread" to Thailand and beyond, possibly ultimately drawing Japan into a "New Order" from which the United

States would be excluded. This threat was averted. The countries of Indochina will be lucky to survive; they will not endanger global order by social and economic success in a framework that denies the West the freedom to exploit, infecting regions beyond, as had been feared. It might parenthetically be noted that although this interpretation of the American aggression is supported by substantial evidence, there is no hint of its existence, and surely no reference to the extensive documentation substantiating it, in the standard histories, since such facts do not conform to the required image of aggrieved benevolence. Again, we see here the operation of the Orwellian principle that Ignorance is Strength.

Meanwhile, the United States moved forcefully to buttress the second line of defense. In 1965, the United States backed a military coup in Indonesia (the most important "domino," short of Japan) while American liberals lauded the "dramatic changes" that took place there—the most dramatic being the massacre of hundreds of thousands of landless peasants—as a proof that we were right to defend South Vietnam by demolishing it, thus encouraging the Indonesian generals to prevent any rot from spreading there. In 1972, the United States backed the overthrow of Philippine democracy behind the "shield" provided by its successes in Indochina, thus averting the threat of national capitalism there with a terror-and-torture state on the preferred Latin American model. A move toward democracy in Thailand in 1973 evoked some concern, and a reduction in economic aid and increase in military aid in preparation for the military coup that took place with U.S. support in 1976. Thailand had a particularly important role in the U.S. regional system since 1954, when the National Security Council laid out a plan of subversion and eventual aggression throughout Southeast Asia in response to the Geneva Accords, with Thailand "as the focal point of U.S. covert and psychological operations," including "covert operations on a large and effective scale" throughout Indochina, with the explicit intention of "making more difficult the control by the Viet Minh of North Vietnam." Subsequently Thailand served as a major base for the U.S. attacks on Vietnam and Laos.[32]

In short, the United States won a regional victory, and even a substantial local victory in Indochina, left in ruins. That the United States suffered a "defeat" in Indochina is a natural perception on the part of those of limitless ambition, who understand "defeat" to mean the achievement only of major goals, while certain minor ones remain beyond our grasp.

Postwar U.S. policy has been designed to ensure that the victory is maintained by maximizing suffering and oppression in Indochina, which then evokes further joy and gloating here. Since "the destruction is mutual," as is readily demonstrated by a stroll through New York, Boston, Vinh, Quang Ngai Province, and the Plain of Jars, we are entitled to deny reparations, aid, and trade, and to block development funds. The extent of U.S. sadism is noteworthy, as is the (null) reaction to it. In 1977, when India tried to send one-hundred buffalos to Vietnam to replenish the herds destroyed by U.S. violence, the United States threatened to cancel "food for peace" aid while the press featured photographs of peasants in Cambodia pulling plows as proof of Communist barbarity; the photographs in this case turned out to be fabrications of Thai intelligence, but authentic ones could no doubt have been obtained, throughout Indochina. The Carter administration even denied rice to Laos (despite a cynical pretense to the contrary), where the agricultural system was destroyed by U.S. terror-bombing. Oxfam America was not permitted to send solar pumps to Cambodia for irrigation in 1983; in 1981, the U.S. government sought to block a shipment of school supplies and educational kits to Cambodia by the Mennonite Church. Meanwhile, from the first days of the Khmer Rouge takeover in 1975, the West was consumed with horror over their atrocities, described as "genocide" at a time when deaths had reached the thousands in mid-1975. Current scholarship (in conformity to the estimates of U.S. intelligence) indicates that the Khmer Rouge may have been responsible for a half-million to a million deaths; these atrocities took place primarily in 1978, largely unknown to the West, in the context of the escalating war with Vietnam.[33]

The nature of the profound Western agony over Cambodia as a sociocultural phenomenon can be assessed by comparing it to the reaction to comparable and simultaneous atrocities in Timor. There, the United States bore primary responsibility and the atrocities could have been terminated at once, as distinct from Cambodia, where nothing could be done but the blame could be placed on the official enemy. The excuses now produced for this shameful behavior are instructive. Thus, William Shawcross rejects the obvious (and obviously correct) interpretation of the comparative response to Timor and Cambodia in favor of a "more structurally serious explanation": "a comparative lack of sources" and a lack of access to refugees.[34] Lisbon is a two hour's flight from London, and even Australia is not notably harder to reach than the Thai-Cambodia border, but the many Timorese refugees in Lisbon and Australia were ignored by the media, which preferred "facts" offered by State Department handouts and Indonesian generals. Similarly, the media ignored readily available refugee studies from sources at least as credible as those used as the basis for the impotent but ideologically serviceable outrage over the Khmer Rouge, and disregarded highly credible witnesses who reached New York and Washington along with additional evidence from church sources and others. The coverage of Timor actually declined sharply as massacres increased. The real reason for this difference in scope and character of coverage is not difficult to discern, though not very comfortable for Western opinion, and becomes still more obvious when a broader range of cases is considered.[35]

The latest phase of this tragicomedy is the current pretense, initiated by William Shawcross in an inspired agitprop achievement,[36] that there was relative silence in the West over the Khmer Rouge. This is a variant of the Brzezinski ploy concerning the "liberal community," noted earlier; in the real world, condemnations virtually unprecedented in their severity extended from mass circulation journals such as the *Readers Digest* and *TV Guide* to the *New York Review of Books*, including the press quite generally (1976– early 1977). Furthermore, Shawcross argues, this "silence" was the result of "left-wing skepticism" so powerful that it silenced governments and journals throughout the West; even had such "skepticism" existed on the part of people systematically excluded from the media and mainstream discussion, the idea that this consequence could ensue is a construction of such audacity that one must admire its creators, Shawcross in particular.[37]

I do not, incidentally, exempt myself from this critique with regard to Cambodia and Timor. I condemned the "barbarity" and "brutal practice" of the Khmer Rouge in 1977,[38] long before speaking or writing a word on the American-backed atrocities in Timor, which on moral grounds posed a far more serious issue for Westerners. It is difficult even for those who try to be alert to such matters to extricate themselves from a propaganda system of overwhelming efficiency and power.

Now, Western moralists remain silent as their governments provide the means for the Indonesian generals to consummate their massacres, while the United States backs the Democratic Kampuchea coalition, largely based on the Khmer Rouge, because of its "continuity" with the Pol Pot regime, so the State Department explains, adding that this Khmer Rouge-based coalition is "unquestionably" more representative of the Cambodian people than the resistance is of the Timorese.[39] The reason for this stance was explained by our ally Deng Xiaoping: "It is wise for China to force the Vietnamese to stay in Kampuchea because that way they will suffer more and more. . . ."[40] This makes good sense, since the prime motive is to "bleed Vietnam," to ensure that suffering and brutality reach the maximum possible level so that we can exult in our benevolence in undertaking our "noble crusade" in earlier years.

The elementary truths about these terrible years survive in the memories of those who opposed the U.S. war against South Vietnam, then all of Indochina, but there is no doubt that the approved version will sooner or later be established by the custodians of history, perhaps to be exposed by crusading intellectuals a century or two hence, if "Western civilization" endures that long.

As the earlier discussion indicated, the creation of convenient "visions of righteousness" is not an invention of the intellectuals of the Vietnam era; nor, of course, is the malady confined to the United States, though one might wonder how many others compare with us in its virulence. Each atrocity has been readily handled, either forgotten, or dismissed as an unfortunate error due to our naiveté, or revised to serve as a proof of the magnificence of our intentions. Furthermore, the record of historical fact is not permitted to disturb the basic principles of interpretation of U.S. foreign policy over quite a broad spectrum of mainstream opinion, even by those who recognize that something may be amiss. Thus, Norman Graebner, a historian of the "realist" school influenced by George Kennan, formulates as unquestioned fact the conventional doctrine that U.S. foreign policy has been guided by the "Wilsonian principles of peace and self-determination." But he notices—and this is unusual—that the United States "generally ignored the principles of self-determination in Asia and Africa [he excludes the most obvious case: Latin America] where it had some chance of success and promoted it behind the Iron and Bamboo curtains where it had no chance of success at all." That is, in regions where our influence and power might have led to the realization of our principles, we ignored them, while we proclaimed them with enthusiasm with regard to enemy terrain. His conclusion is that this is "ironic," but the facts do not shake the conviction that we are committed to the Wilsonian principle of self-determination.[41] That doctrine holds, even if refuted by the historical facts. If only natural scientists were permitted such convenient methods, how easy their tasks would be.

Commentators who keep to the party line have an easy task; they need not consider mere facts, always a great convenience for writers and political analysts. Thus, Charles Krauthammer asserts that "left isolationism" has become "the ideology of the Democratic Party": "There is no retreat from the grand Wilsonian commitment to the spread of American values," namely human rights and democracy, but these "isolationists" reject the use of force to achieve our noble objectives. In contrast, "right isolationism" (Irving Kristol, Caspar Weinberger and the Joint Chiefs, etc.) calls for "retreat from Wilsonian goals" in favor of defense of interests. He also speaks of "the selectivity of the fervor for reforming the world" among "left isolationists," who have an "obsessive" focus on the Philippines, El Salvador, Korea, and Taiwan but, he would like us to believe, would never be heard voicing a criticism of the Soviet Union, Cuba, or Libya. The latter assertion might be considered too exotic to merit discussion among sane people, but as noted earlier, that would miss the point, which is to eliminate even that margin of criticism that might constrain state violence, for example, the occasional peep of protest over U.S.-organized terror in El Salvador which, if truth be told, is comparable to that attributable to Pol Pot at the time when the chorus of condemnation was reaching an early peak of intensity in 1977. Crucially, it is unnecessary to establish that there is or ever was a "grand Wilsonian commitment," apart from rhetoric; that is a given, a premise for respectable discussion.

To take an example from the field of scholarship, consider the study of the "Vietnam trauma" by Paul Kattenburg, one of the few early dissenters on Vietnam within the U.S. government and now Jacobson Professor of Public Affairs at the University of South Carolina.[42] Kattenburg is concerned to identify the "salient features central to the American tradition and experience which have made the United States perform its superpower role in what we might term a particularistic way." He holds that "principles and ideals hold a cardinal place in the U.S. national ethos and crucially distinguish U.S. performance in the superpower role"—a standard view, commonly set forth in the United States, Britain, and elsewhere in scholarly work on modern history. These principles and ideals, he explains, were "laid down by the founding fathers, those pure geniuses of detached contemplation" and "refined by subsequent leading figures of thought and action" from John Adams to Theodore Roosevelt, Woodrow Wilson, and Franklin Roosevelt; such Kim Il Sung-ism with regard to the "pure geniuses," etc., is also far from rare. These principles, he continues, were "tested and retested in the process of settling the continent [as Indians, blacks, Mexicans, immigrant workers, and others can testify], healing the North-South breach, developing the economy from the wilderness in the spirit of free enterprise, and fighting World Wars I and II, not so much for interests as for the survival of the very principles by which most Americans were guiding their lives."

It is this unique legacy that explains the way Americans act "in the superpower role." The Americans approached this role, "devoid of artifice or deception," with "the mind set of an emancipator":

> In such a mind set, one need not feel or act superior, or believe one is imposing one's ethos or values on others, since one senses naturally that others cannot doubt the emancipator's righteous cause any more than his capacities. In this respect, the American role as superpower, particularly in the early postwar years, is very analogous to the role that can be attributed to a professor, mentor, or other type of emancipator.

Thus, "the professor is obviously capable" and "he is clearly disinterested." "Moreover, like the American superpower, the professor does not control the lives or destinies of his students; they remain free to come or go," just like the peasants of South Vietnam or the Guazapa mountains in El Salvador. "It will help us understand America's performance and psychology as a superpower, and the whys and wherefores of its Indochina involvement, if we bear in mind this analogy of the American performance in the superpower role with that of the benevolent but clearly egocentric professor, dispensing emancipation through knowledge of both righteousness and the right way to the deprived students of the world."

The reader must bear in mind that this is not intended as irony or caricature, but it is rather presented seriously, is taken seriously, and is not untypical of what we find in the literature, not at the lunatic fringe, but at the respectable and moderately dissident extreme of the mainstream spectrum.

The standard drivel about Wilsonian principles of self-determination—unaffected by Wilson's behavior, for example in Hispaniola, or in succeeding to eliminate consideration of U.S. domination in the Americas from the Versailles deliberations—by no means stands alone. Kennedy's Camelot merits similar acclaim among the faithful. In a fairly critical study, Robert Packenham writes that Kennedy's policies toward Latin America in 1962–1963 "utilized principally diplomatic techniques to promote liberal democratic rule," and cites with approval Arthur Schlesinger's comment that the Kennedy approach to development, based on designing aid for "take off" into self-sustaining economic growth, was "a very American effort to persuade the developing countries to base their revolutions on Locke rather than on Marx."[43] In the real world, the Kennedy administration succeeded in blocking capitalist democracy in Central America and the Caribbean and laying the basis for the establishment of a network of National Security States on the Nazi model throughout the hemisphere; and the aid program, as the facts of aid disbursement make clear, was designed largely to "improve the productivity of Central America's agricultural exporters and at the same time to advance the sales of American companies that manufacture pesticides and fertilizer," which is why nutritional levels declined in the course of "economic miracles" that—quite predictably—benefitted U.S. agribusiness and their local associates.[44] Locke deserves better treatment than that. But these again are mere facts, not relevant to the higher domains of political commentary.

Open the latest issue of any major journal on U.S. foreign policy and one is likely to find something similar. Thus, the lead article in the current issue of *Foreign Affairs*, as I write, is by James Schlesinger, now at Georgetown University after having served as Secretary of Defense, Director of Central Intelligence, and in other high positions.[45] He contrasts the U.S. and Russian stances over the years. "The American desire was to fulfill the promise of Wilsonian idealism, of the Four Freedoms, . . . The themes of realpolitik remain contrary to the spirit of American democracy," while the Russians, so unlike us, are guided by "deep-seated impulses never to flag in the quest for marginal advantages." The United States seeks all good things, but "almost inevitably, the Polands and the Afghanistans lead to confrontation, even if the Angolas and the Nicaraguas do not"—and most assuredly, the Guatemalas, Chiles, Vietnams, Irans, Lebanons, Dominican Republics, etc., do not have the same effect; indeed, the idea would not be comprehensible in these circles, given that in each such case the United States is acting in defense against internal aggression, and with intent so noble that words can barely express it. True, one is not often treated to such delicacies as Huntington's Ode to the Holy State cited earlier, but it is, nevertheless, not too far from the norm.

The official doctrine as propounded by government spokesmen, the U.S. media, and a broad range of scholarship is illustrated, for example, in the report of the National Bipartisan (Kissinger) Commission on Central America: "The international purposes of the United States in the late twentieth century are cooperation, not hegemony or domination; partnership, not confrontation; a decent life for all, not exploitation." Similarly, Irving Kristol informs us that the United States "is not a 'have' nation in the sense that it exercises or seeks to maintain any kind of 'hegemony' over distant areas of the globe. Indeed, that very word, 'hegemony,' with all its deliberate vagueness and ambiguity, was appropriated by latter-day Marxists in order to give American foreign policy an 'imperialist' substance it is supposed to have but does not." Among these "Marxists," he fails to observe, are such figures as Samuel Huntington, who, accurately this time, describes the 1945–1970 period as one in which "the U.S. was the hegemonic power in a system of world order."[46] And again, the idea that the United States does not exercise or seek any kind of "hegemony," alone among the great powers of history, requires no evidence and stands as a Truth irrespective of historical facts.

Similar thoughts are familiar among the culturally colonized elites elsewhere. Thus, according to Michael Howard, Regius Professor of Modern History at Oxford, "For 200 years the United States has preserved almost unsullied the original ideals of the Enlightenment: the belief in the God-given rights of the individual, the inherent rights of free assembly and free speech, the blessings of free enterprise, the perfectibility of man, and, above all, the universality of these values." In this nearly ideal society, the influence of elites is "quite limited." The world, however, does not appreciate this magnificence: "the United States does not enjoy the place in the world that it should have earned through its achievements, its generosity, and its goodwill since World War II"—as illustrated in such contemporary paradises as Indochina, the Dominican Republic, El Salvador, and Guatemala, to mention a few of the many candidates, just as belief in the "God-given rights of

45

the individual" and the universality of this doctrine for two hundred years is illustrated by a century of literal human slavery and effective disenfranchisement of blacks for another century, genocidal assaults on the native population, the slaughter of hundreds of thousands of Filipinos at the turn of the century and millions of Indochinese, and a host of other examples.[47]

Such commentary, again, need not be burdened by evidence; it suffices to assert what people of power and privilege would like to believe, including those criticized, e.g., the "left isolationists" of Krauthammer's fancies, who are delighted to hear of their commitment to Wilsonian goals. Presupposed throughout, without argument or evidence, is that the United States has been committed to such goals as self-determination, human rights, democracy, economic development, and so on. It is considered unnecessary to demonstrate or even argue for these assumptions in political commentary and much of scholarship, particularly what is intended for a general audience. These assumptions have the status of truths of doctrine, and it would be as pointless to face them with evidence as with doctrines of other religious faiths.

The evidence, in fact, shows with considerable clarity that the proclaimed ideals were not the goals of Woodrow Wilson, or his predecessors, or any of his successors.[48] A more accurate account of Wilson's actual goals is given by the interpretation of the Monroe Doctrine presented to him by his Secretary of State, Robert Lansing, an argument that Wilson found "unanswerable" though he thought it would be "impolitic" to make it public: "In its advocacy of the Monroe Doctrine the United States considers its own interests. The integrity of other American nations is an incident, not an end. While this may seem based on selfishness alone, the author of the Doctrine had no higher or more generous motive in its declaration."[49] The category including those who function as "an incident, not an end" expanded along with U.S. power in subsequent years. How planners perceived the world, when they were not addressing the general public, is illustrated in a perceptive and typically acute analysis by George Kennan, one of the most thoughtful and humane of those who established the structure of the postwar world:

> We have about 50% of the world's wealth, but only 6.3% of its population. . . . In this situation, we cannot fail to be the object of envy and resentment. Our real task in the coming period is to devise a pattern of relationships which will permit us to maintain this position of disparity without positive detriment to our

national security. To do so, we will have to dispense with all sentimentality and day-dreaming; and our attention will have to be concentrated everywhere on our immediate national objectives. We need not deceive ourselves that we can afford today the luxury of altruism and world-benefaction. . . . We should cease to talk about vague and—for the Far East—unreal objectives such as human rights, the raising of the living standards, and democratization. The day is not far off when we are going to have to deal in straight power concepts. The less we are then hampered by idealistic slogans, the better.[50]

The subsequent historical record shows that Kennan's prescriptions proved close to the mark, though a close analysis indicates that he understated the case, and that the United States did not simply disregard "human rights, the raising of the living standards, and democratization," but evinced a positive hostility towards them in much of the world, particularly democratization in any meaningful sense, any sense that would permit genuine participation of substantial parts of the population in the formation of public policy, since such tendencies would interfere with the one form of freedom that really counts: the freedom to rob and to exploit. But again, these are only considerations of empirical fact, as little relevant to political theology as is the fact that the United States attacked South Vietnam.

Given these lasting and deep-seated features of the intellectual culture, it is less surprising perhaps—though still, it would seem, rather shocking—that the man who is criticized for his extreme devotion to human rights should say that we owe Vietnam no debt because "the destruction was mutual," without this evoking even a raised eyelid.

The reasons for the rather general and probably quite unconscious subordination of large segments of the educated classes to the system of power and domination do not seem very difficult to discern. At any given stage, one is exposed to little that questions the basic doctrines of the faith: that the United States is unique in the contemporary world and in history in its devotion to such ideals as freedom and self-determination, that it is not an actor in world affairs but rather an "emancipator," responding to the hostile or brutal acts of other powers but, apart from that, seeking nothing but justice, human rights and democracy. Intellectual laziness alone tends to induce acceptance of the doctrines that "everyone believes." There are no courses in "intellectual self-

47

defense," where students are helped to find ways to protect themselves from the deluge of received opinion. Furthermore, it is convenient to conform: that way lies privilege and power, while the rational skeptic faces obloquy and marginalization—not death squads or psychiatric prison, as elsewhere all too often, but still a degree of unpleasantness, and very likely, exclusion from the guilds. The natural tendencies to conform are thus refined by institutional pressures that tend to exclude those who do not toe the line. In the sciences, critical thought and reasoned skepticism are values highly to be prized. Elsewhere, they are often considered heresies to be stamped out; obedience is what yields rewards. The structural basis for conformity is obvious enough, given the distribution of domestic power. Political power resides essentially in those groups that can mobilize the resources to shape affairs of state—in our society, primarily an elite of corporations, law firms that cater to their interests, financial institutions, and the like—and the same is true of power in the cultural domains. Those segments of the media that can reach a large audience are simply part of the system of concentrated economic-political power, and naturally enough, journals that are well-funded and influential are those that appeal to the tastes and interest of those who own and manage the society. Similarly, to qualify as an "expert," as Henry Kissinger explained on the basis of his not inconsiderable experience in these matters, one must know how to serve power. The "expert has his constituency," Kissinger explained, "those who have a vested interest in commonly held opinions: elaborating and defining its consensus at a high level has, after all, made him an expert."[51] We need only proceed a step further, identifying those whose vested interest is operative within the social nexus.

The result is a system of principles that gives comfort to the powerful—though in private, they speak to one another in a different and more realistic voice, offering "unanswerable" arguments that it would be "impolitic" to make public—and is rarely subjected to challenge. There are departures, when segments of the normally quiescent population become organized in efforts to enter the political arena or influence public policy, giving rise to what elite groups call a "crisis of democracy" which must be combated so that order can be restored. We have recently passed through such a crisis, which led to an awakening on the part of much of the population to the realities of the world in which they live, and it predictably evoked great fear and concern, and a dedicated and committed effort to restore obedience. This is the source of the reactionary jingoism that has misappropriated the term "conservatism" in recent years, and of the general support for its major goals on the part of the mainstream of contemporary liberalism, now with a "neo" affixed. The purpose is to extirpate heresy and to restore domestic and international order for the benefit of the privileged and powerful. That the mainstream intelligentsia associate themselves with these tendencies while proclaiming their independence and integrity and adversarial stance vis à vis established power should hardly come as a surprise to people familiar with modern history and capable of reasoned and critical thought.

### NOTES

Some of these remarks here are adapted from my articles in *Granta* (1985), 15; and *In These Times*, May 15, 1985.

1. News conference, March 24, 1977; *New York Times*, March 25, 1977.

2. Zbigniew Brzezinski, "Afghanistan and Nicaragua," *The National Interest* (Fall 1985), Premier Issue.

3. Bernard Gwertzman, "The Debt to the Indochinese is Becoming a Fiscal Drain," *New York Times*, March 3, 1985.

4. *New York Times*, March 18, 1968; Noam Chomsky, *American Power and the New Mandarins* (New York: Pantheon, 1969), p. 14.

5. "A Vietnam War Board Game Created by Princeton Senior," *New York Times*, April 1, 1984; *Far Eastern Economic Review*, January 30, 1981.

6. Barbara Crossette, *New York Times*, November 10, 1985.

7. For documentation and further discussion of the interesting concept of "internal aggression" as developed by U.S. officials, see my *For Reasons of State* (New York: Pantheon, 1973), pp. 114f.

8. Francis Jennings, *The Invasion of America* (Chapel Hill: University of North Carolina Press, 1975), p. 6.

9. Alexis de Tocqueville, *Democracy in America*, vol. 1 (New York: Knopf, 1945); General Andrew Jackson, General Orders, 1813; cited by Ronald Takaki, *Iron Cages* (New York: Knopf, 1979), pp. 80–81, 95–96.

10. Daniel Boone Schirmer, *Republic or Empire* (Cambridge, Mass.: Schenkman, 1972), p. 231; Stuart Chreighton Miller, *Benevolent Assimilation* (New Haven: Yale University Press, 1982), pp. 78, 213, 220, 248f., 255, 269; David Bain, *Sitting in Darkness* (Boston: Boston University Press, Houghton Mifflin, 1984), p. 78.

11. Samuel Huntington, "American Ideals versus American Institutions," *Political Science Quarterly* (Spring 1982); and subsequent correspondence (Winter 1982–83). On Wilson's achievements, see Lester Langley, *The Banana Wars* (Lexington: University Press of Kentucky, 1983); Bruce Calder, *The Impact of Intervention* (Austin: University of Texas Press, 1984).

12. For extensive discussion of these matters and their sources in U.S. planning, see my *Turning the Tide* (Boston: South End, 1985), and sources cited there.

13. For references to material not specifically cited, here and below, and

discussion in more general context, see my *Towards a New Cold War* (New York: Pantheon, 1982), *Turning the Tide,* and sources cited there.

14. Norman Podhoretz, "Proper Uses of Power," *New York Times,* October 30, 1983.

15. Mark McCain, *Boston Globe,* December 9, 1984; memo released during the Westmoreland-CBS libel trial.

16. Bernard Fall, *New Society,* April 22, 1965; Paul Quinn-Judge, *Far Eastern Economic Review,* October 11, 1984.

17. John Corry, *New York Times,* April 27, 1985.

18. *Time,* April 15, 1985.

19. *Wall Street Journal,* April 4, 1985. An exception was *Newsweek,* April 15, 1985, which devoted four pages of its thirty-three-page account to a report by Tony Clifton and Ron Moreau on the effects of the war on the "wounded land."

20. Walt W. Rostow, *The View from the Seventh Floor* (New York: Harper & Row, 1964), p. 244. On the facts concerning Indochina, see the documentation reviewed in *For Reasons of State.* Rostow's account of Mao and North Korea is also fanciful, as the record of serious scholarship shows.

21. Cited in Chomsky, *American Power and the New Mandarins,* pp. 238, 253.

22. *New Republic,* October 9, 1965.

23. James Reston, *New York Times,* February 26, 1965.

24. Bernard Fall, *Last Reflections on a War* (New York: Doubleday, 1967), pp. 33, 47; James Reston, *New York Times,* November 24, 1967.

25. Allan E. Goodman and Seth P. Tillman, *New York Times,* March 24, 1985.

26. Chomsky, *At War with Asia* (New York: Pantheon, 1970), p. 286.

27. Charles Krauthammer, *New Republic,* March 4, 1985.

28. *New York Times,* March 31, 1985.

29. *Far Eastern Economic Review,* August 16, 1984, and November 1, 1984.

30. Douglas Pike, *St. Louis Post-Dispatch,* November 29, 1979; *Christian Science Monitor,* December 4, 1979. Cited by Michael Vickery, *Cambodia* (Boston: South End, 1983), pp. 65–66.

31. On Lebanese opinion and the scandalous refusal of the media to consider it, and the general context, see my *Fateful Triangle* (Boston: South End, 1983).

32. Noam Chomsky and Edward S. Herman, *Political Economy of Human Rights,* vol. 1, ch. 4 (Boston: South End, 1979).

33. The major scholarly study of the Pol Pot period, Vickery's *Cambodia,* has been widely and favorably reviewed in England, Australia, and elsewhere, but never here. The one major governmental study, by a Finnish Inquiry Commission, was also ignored here: Kimmo Kiljunen, ed., *Kampuchea: Decade of the Genocide* (London: Zed Press, 1984). See Kiljunen in *Bulletin of Concerned Asian Scholars* (April-June 1985), for a brief account of the Finnish study, and my "Decade of Genocide in Review," *Inside Asia* (February 1985), for review of this and other material. Note that the Finnish study is entitled *Decade of the Genocide,* in recognition of the fact that killings during the U.S.-run war were roughly comparable to those under Pol Pot. The facts are of little interest in the United States, where the Khmer Rouge have a specific role to play: namely, to provide justification for U.S. atrocities.

34. William Shawcross, in David Chandler and Ben Kiernan, eds., *Revolution and Its Aftermath in Kampuchea* (New Haven: Yale University Press, 1983); see my "Decade of Genocide" for further discussion.

35. See Chomsky and Herman, *Political Economy of Human Rights;* and Edward S. Herman, *The Real Terror Network,* for extensive evidence.

36. In Chandler and Kiernan, *Revolution and Its Aftermath* and William Shawcross, *Quality of Mercy* (New York: Simon and Schuster, 1984); see my "Decade of Genocide" for discussion. Perhaps I may take credit for suggesting

this clever idea to him. In a 1978 essay (reprinted in my *Towards a New Cold War*, p. 95), I wrote that "it is not gratifying to the ego merely to march in a parade; therefore those who join in ritual condemnation of an official enemy must show that they are engaged in a courageous struggle against powerful forces that defend it. Since these rarely exist, even on a meager scale [and in the case of Khmer Rouge, were undetectable outside of marginal Maoist groups], they must be concocted; if nothing else is at hand, those who propose a minimal concern for fact will do. The system that has been constructed enables one to lie freely with regard to the crimes, real or alleged, of an official enemy, while suppressing the systematic involvement of one's own state in atrocities, repression, or aggression." These comments accurately anticipate the subsequent antics.

37. On Shawcross' fabrication of evidence in support of his thesis, see my "Decade of Genocide" and Christopher Hitchens, "The Chorus and Cassandra; What Everyone Knows about Noam Chomsky," *Grand Street* (Autumn 1985), pp. 106–31.

38. *Nation*, June 25, 1977.

39. John Holdridge of the State Department, Hearing before the Subcommittee on Asian and Pacific Affairs of the Committee on Foreign Affairs, House of Representatives, 97th Congress, second session, September 14, 1982, p. 71.

40. Cited by Ben Kiernan, *Tribune* (Australia), March 20, 1985.

41. Norman A. Graebner, *Cold War Diplomacy* (New York: Van Nostrand, 1962).

42. Paul M. Kattenburg, *The Vietnam Trauma in American Foreign Policy, 1945–75* (New Brunswick, N.J.: Transaction Books, 1982), pp. 69ff.

43. Robert A. Packenham, *Liberal America and the Third World* (Princeton: Princeton University Press, 1973), pp. 63, 156.

44. Lester Langley, *Central America: The Real Stakes* (New York: Crown, 1985), p. 128; see my *Turning the Tide* for discussion and further sources on these matters.

45. *Foreign Affairs* (Summer 1985).

46. Irving Kristol, *The National Interest* (Fall 1985); Samuel Huntington, in M. J. Crozier, S. P. Huntington, and J. Watanuki, *The Crisis of Democracy* (New York: New York University Press, 1975).

47. Michael Howard, "The Bewildered American Raj," *Harper's* (March 1985).

48. For a review of the facts of the matter, see my *Turning the Tide* and sources cited.

49. Gabriel Kolko, *Main Currents in American History* (New York: Pantheon, 1984), p. 47.

50. Policy Planning Study (PPS) 23, (February 24, 1948, *FRUS 1948*, vol. 1, pt. 2; reprinted in part in Thomas Etzold and John Lewis Gaddis, *Containment* (New York: Columbia University Press, 1978), pp. 226f.

51. Henry Kissinger, *American Foreign Policy* (New York: Norton, 1969), p. 28.

T W O

# America's "Enemy": The Absent Presence in Revisionist Vietnam War History

## STEPHEN VLASTOS

The revolutionary upsurge throughout the developing world that followed America's defeat in Indochina produced profound apprehension on the political right. The Vietnam War represented an unparalleled commitment of military resources and prestige to containing revolution in the third world, and defeat appeared to confirm the worst fears of the war's advocates. Not only did the U.S. withdrawal from Indochina in 1973 lead to the collapse two years later of client regimes in South Vietnam, Laos, and Cambodia. Before the end of the decade, from Central America to the Middle East radical governments seized power in countries that had been Western colonies or rightwing dictatorships loyal to Washington.[1]

The "tragic legacy" of the Vietnam War, as viewed by the American right, was the opening to third world revolution created by America's humiliating defeat in Indochina. In a seminal essay published in *Harpers* magazine in 1981, Professor Robert W. Tucker declared the fracturing of the cold war domestic political consensus in support of military intervention abroad to be the "spoils of defeat" in Vietnam.[2] Since 1947 liberal Democrats had loyally supported global counterrevolution, but after the "trauma" of Vietnam and Watergate Congress passed legislation that limited the capacity of the Nixon and Ford administrations to intervene militarily in regional conflicts. The Case-Church amendment of 1973 prohibited future U.S. air operations over Indochina, and the landmark War Powers Act was passed later the same year. Two years later, Congress placed limits on CIA military operations in Angola and Mozambique. Even more alarming, the Carter administration eschewed direct military intervention in Nicaragua and Iran: longstanding regional client states whose strategic importance—unlike Vietnam's—was universally acknowledged.[3]

The root cause of the break of the cold war consensus, Tucker argued, was the "Vietnam syndrome": a view of the Vietnam War as morally suspect and geopolitically mistaken which directly led to the "contraction of our power." While not discounting other factors, Tucker linked the revolutions of the late 1970s to a failure of will in Washington.[4] Because in Tucker's opinion the left-liberal view of the Vietnam War as a moral and intellectual failure became the orthodox view during the Carter administration, "the highest goal of the Carter foreign policy—particularly as conceived by its high priest, Cyrus Vance—was avoiding any action that might incur the risks of using military power, because any use of military power raised the prospects of another Vietnam."[5]

Nevertheless, Tucker took heart from the emergence of a "second wave of Vietnam revisionism" most notable in the pages of *Commentary* magazine and Ronald Reagan's campaign speeches that unapologetically endorsed the war. Undertaken to contain communism, the Vietnam War was indeed a noble cause; measured against the global ramifications of defeat, in retrospect it must also be deemed a rational exercise of U.S. global power. To Tucker, Vietnam revisionism held the key to reversing the foreign policy setbacks of the late 1970s. "Should the conservative revisionism of yesterday, even today, become the conventional view of tomorrow," Tucker wrote, "we might be looking toward a new era in the nation's relations with the world."[6]

In analyzing revisionist Vietnam history, I am especially interested in rhetorical strategy. Writ large, revisionist historiography reproduces familiar, pre-1965 justifications of U.S. intervention: America intervened against expansionist, totalitarian Communism in defense of Free World interests and values. Not so obvious, however, are the discursive strategies that produce historical narratives justifying America's war in Vietnam.

Four of the most contentious issues in Vietnam War historiography are analyzed, principally with reference to three texts. The issues are the war's origins, the Geneva Accords of 1954, the resistance movement in South Vietnam, and America's defeat. The texts discussed below were selected not only because they are widely read and cited, but also because stylistically they span the gamut of historical writing on the Vietnam War. Richard Nixon's book *No More Vietnams* (1985) is a mass-marketed and self-promoting polemic which makes not the slightest gesture to objectivity. Guenter Lewy's massively documented *America in Vietnam* (1978) is cast in the mold of disinterested academic scholarship; reissued as a paperback in 1980 it is widely used on college campuses.[7] Analytic rather than empirical and read by scholars as well as the general public, Harry Summer's *On Strategy* (1982) was first published by the Army's Presidio Press and reissued in 1984 as a mass-circulation paperback.

The analysis will show that despite great stylistic and formal difference, these (and other) revisionist texts share a distinctive syntax of historical representation, one which marginalizes the historical experience of America's Vietnam "enemy": the millions of Vietnamese North and South who opposed U.S. intervention. Admitted to the discourse only as abstract agents of "external aggression" and expansionist international Communism, Vietnamese who resisted U.S. efforts to dominate the political life of Vietnam are the "absent presence" in revisionist history. Ironically, in denying "enemy" Vietnamese subject status in their own history the revisionists recapitulate the fundamental intellectual error of the planners of the war: the utter failure to take measure of very historical forces in Vietnam whose life and death resistance would defeat America's imperial agenda for postcolonial Vietnam.

## Origins of the War

Revisionist historiography locates the origins of the Vietnam War in the post-World War II confrontation in Asia between international communism, the aggressor, and the United States, the defender of the Free World. This, the principal narrative strategy, finds model expression in the opening paragraph of Guenter Lewy's *America in Vietnam.*

> The decision of the Truman administration in early 1950 to provide financial aid to the French military effort in Indochina was taken against the background of the fall of Nationalist China and the arrival of Communist Chinese troops on the Indochina border in December 1949. The Ho Chi Minh regime had just been recognized as the government of Vietnam by the Soviet Union and Communist China. Mao's government provided sanctuary, training and heavy arms to the Viet Minh (Revolutionary League for the Independence of Vietnam) which, despite the trappings of a mere nationalist movement, was increasingly evolving into a party openly committed by organization and ideology to the

communist sphere. On 6 March 1950 the U.S. secretary of defense informed the president: "The choice confronting the United States is to support the legal government in Indochina or to face the extension of Communism over the remainder of the continental area of Southeast Asia and possibly westward."[8]

Lewy's beginning conceals the colonial origins of the Vietnam War and obfuscates two critical historic associations: Vietnamese communism with anticolonial nationalism and the United States with foreign domination.

The Vietminh, whom Lewy narrowly describes as "a party openly committed by organization and ideology to the communist sphere," was founded by the Vietnamese Communist Party in 1941 after the Japanese occupation of French Indochina, and rapidly developed into a mass, multiparty and multiclass movement of national liberation. Capitalizing on the power vacuum that attended Japan's surrender, and on generations of anti-French sentiment, in August 1945 Vietminh revolutionary committees took over government offices and functions throughout most of the country. So great was the national euphoria that Emperor Bao Dai abdicated, and on September 2, 1945, Ho Chi Minh proclaimed Vietnam's independence. When France moved to reimpose colonial authority, the Vietminh again led the nationalist struggle in opposition. France enlisted support from many Catholics, the Southern religious sects, and the wealthy, particularly large landlords; but the majority of Vietnamese joined the Vietminh or aided the war effort. Mobilizing their vast popular base, the Vietminh defeated France's technologically superior army in the savage eight-year war of independence often called the First Indochina War.[9] It was a truly epoch-making event: the first outright military victory by indigenous people in a modern war against a major colonial power.

The Truman administration responded to the Vietminh's "August Revolution" by aiding France's bid to reimpose colonial rule: affirming French sovereignty over postwar Indochina; permitting the diversion of military equipment authorized for Europe to the Indochina campaign; and from 1950, directly subsidizing France's war. When the war ended in 1954, the United States was paying 80 percent of the costs. Throughout the First Indochina War, the United States urged France to make concessions to Vietnamese nationalism—but did not directly link aid to independence. France's aims remained restorationist and colonial. In financing the war, the Truman administration aligned the United States with colonialism and against a broadly supported, and Communist-led, movement of national liberation.[10]

Ideologically committed to a cold war narrative which portrays the United States as defender of World Freedom, Lewy elides colonialism from the history of the Vietnam War. The exclusion occurs in the first sentence, where France's colonial war becomes the ambiguous "French military effort in Indochina." Next, he denigrates the government that led the independence struggle. Not only does Lewy refuse to acknowledge the historic identity of the Democratic Republic of Vietnam (DRV) as Vietnam's first post-colonial state. He signals its illegitimacy by reducing an entire political formation to the person of a single Communist leader in the phrase "the Ho Chi Minh regime."

Obfuscating the respective historic roles of the Vietnamese Communist Party and the United States in the first phase of Vietnam's struggle for independence, the initial strategy, is reinforced by a second: inundating the reader with referents which superimpose on Vietnam images of worldwide Communist expansion. In a veritable avalanche of cold war signifiers, we read of the *fall of Nationalist China, Communist Chinese* troops positioned along the Indochina border; *Soviet* and *Communist Chinese* recognition of the Vietminh; *Mao's* government providing sanctuaries and material aid; and the Vietminh's organizational and ideological commitment to the *Communist sphere.* They function, of course, to foster the illusion of a "free" country threatened by (external) Communist aggression—the paradigmatic cold war moral justification of U.S. military intervention. Because Lewy has systematically suppressed contrary facts, the naive reader is likely to swallow it whole.

The paragraph closes with a quotation that completes the task of building an ideological defense of U.S. military intervention into an apparently purely factual account of the war's origins. The United States must support the "legal government," we are warned, or face the extension of Communism throughout southeast Asia, perhaps to our very shores. The key assertion embedded in the quotation, that Vietnam already possessed a "legal" national government attacked by Ho Chi Minh's Communist "regime," provides a clear moral justification. If the Truman administration responded to aggression against the *legal* government of Vietnam, however one judges the wisdom of military intervention, the Vietnam War can be equated with the "good war," World War II. We should also note that Lewy introduces a critically important claim by way of quotation, which absolves him of the responsibility of substantiating the truth claims.

Lewy never explains the origins of this "legal government"—and with good reason. Their war already faltering by 1947, French leaders sought a strategy to counter the nationalist appeal of the Vietminh. A willing collaborator was found in former Emperor Bao Dai, who from March to August 1945 had served as titular head-of-state of the regime established by the Japanese military at the end of the Pacific War. In March 1949 Bao Dai signed agreements authorizing an "independent" Associated State of Vietnam within the French Union, which were ratified by the French Parliament early the next year. Constitutionally, Bao Dai's government lacked sovereign powers; personally, he lacked legitimacy. Even anti-Communist Vietnamese were alienated by its collaboratist character. Yet the United States immediately extended diplomatic recognition.[11]

Lewy's revisionist history, we have seen, hinges on selectively presenting facts, superimposing cold war images, and obfuscating indigenous conflicts. It is a pure rhetoric of bipolar cold war ideologies that allows no other description. Thus, in the example we just considered, U.S. recognition suffices to establish the legality of Bao Dai's government—even though spurned by most Vietnamese; and by the same logic, Soviet and Communist Chinese recognition of the Democratic Republic of Vietnam signifies illegality, despite its broad popular base. How Vietnamese may have regarded these rival political formations cannot be queried in this totalizing cold war discourse.

Cold war discourse requires that the Soviet Union, China, and all other Communist movements be the initiators of post-World War II hostilities. Not merely totalitarian, everywhere the Communists rejected peaceful coexistence. Thus, we also see that Lewy's account of the war's origins strongly implies that the Vietminh provoked American intervention; that they wanted to be our enemy.

A dramatically different picture emerges in the following description of ceremonies in Hanoi that marked the birth of the DRV.

> When Ho Chi Minh proclaimed the independence of Vietnam from French rule on September 2, 1945, he borrowed liberally from Thomas Jefferson, opening with the words "We hold these truths to be self-evident. That all men are created equal." During independence celebrations in Hanoi later in the day, American warplanes flew over the city, U.S. Army officers stood on the

reviewing stand with Vo Nguyen Giap and other leaders, and a Vietnamese band played the "Star-Spangled Banner." Towards the end of the festivities, Giap spoke warmly of Vietnam's "particularly intimate relations" with the United States, something, he noted, "which is a pleasant duty to dwell upon."[12]

If Lewy suppresses troublesome facts about the origins of the Vietnam War, Richard Nixon goes one step further. In *No More Vietnams* Nixon turns the historical relationship between anticolonialism and Communism in Vietnam upside down.

> The great powers were totally at odds on the future of the European empires. President Roosevelt insisted on rapid decolonization. Prime Minister Churchill and General de Gaulle demanded a return to the status quo *ante bellum*. General Secretary Stalin, while talking of national independence for the colonies, consolidated his grip on Eastern Europe and began scanning the world for possible Communist conquests like a vulture searching for fresh carcasses.[13]

Nixon inverts the actual roles of the great powers in postwar Indochina by raising the specter of Stalin and transforming Ho Chi Minh into an agent of Soviet expansionism. In fact, the Soviet Union barely took notice of events in Vietnam before 1950, when, five years into the First Indochina War, Stalin finally recognized the DRV. England and the United States, on the other hand, actively aided the reimposition of French colonial rule. British troops under the command of General Douglas Gracey sent to Saigon in September 1945 to oversee the Japanese surrender, not only rearmed French forces in Indochina but also the Japanese to expel the Vietminh from Saigon and reinstate the colonial administration. Despite Ho Chi Minh's desperate appeals for friendly relations, Truman allowed France to use Lend-Lease war supplies to rebuild its military power in Indochina and launch a full-scale war against the Vietminh.[14]

Nixon's rhetoric is crude while Lewy's is sophisticated but the syntax is the same. Representing conflict in Vietnam exclusively in terms of Cold War oppositions (East vs. West, Totalitarianism vs. Freedom, Aggression vs. Defense of the Status Quo) preempts a historical assessment of the *Vietnamese* dimension of the conflict. The exclusion of native points of view is total.

## The Geneva Accords

Interpretation of the Geneva Accords of 1954 directly bears on the question of the legality of American military intervention. If international agreements negotiated at Geneva ending the First Indochina War in fact authorized establishment of a separate non-Communist state south of the seventeenth parallel, one of two minimal conditions needed to establish the legality of U.S. intervention is satisfied. (A historically related but quite separate question is the legitimacy of the Saigon government: degree of dependence on a foreign power, of popular support, etc.) If, on the other hand, the Geneva Accords affirmed Vietnam's status as a unitary and sovereign state, the de facto North-South division enforced by the United States lacked legal basis, as did American military intervention to sustain the government of South Vietnam.

The Vietminh, we have seen, won the First Indochina War despite massive American military aid to the opposition. By the end of the war, with the exception of the major cities the Vietminh controlled most of north and central Vietnam and large portions of the southern countryside. Negotiated after the French defeat at Dienbienphu, the Geneva Accords of 1954 contained an armistice which terminated military hostilities and a "Final Declaration of the Conference" which addressed the political situation in Indochina. Signed by France and the Democratic Republic of Vietnam, the armistice required French forces and their allies to regroup south of the seventeenth parallel and the Vietminh to regroup to the north, pending a final political settlement. We note, however, that the language of the armistice affirmed the territorial integrity and sovereignty of Vietnam. The "Final Declaration of the Conference," which was not signed but orally affirmed, explicitly stated that "the military demarcation line is provisional and should not in any way be interpreted as constituting a political or territorial boundary," and stipulated that elections be held in July 1956 to decide the governing authority of the newly independent nation.[15]

The Geneva Accords are a considerable embarrassment to defenders of the American war in Vietnam, for it was the United States and Bao Dai's successor, Ngo Dinh Diem, that refused to allow the people of Vietnam to vote their own future, and the Communists who clamored for elections. While the Vietminh generally observed the terms of the armistice, the U.S.-backed government of Ngo Dinh Diem immediately declared South Vietnam a sovereign state and refused to permit national elections in violation of key provisions of the Accords.

Militarily and politically the internal balance of power dictated unification under the Vietminh. France was a spent force and without foreign support, the Associated State of Vietnam simply could not challenge the Democratic Republic of Vietnam. Although segments of the Vietnamese population were anti-Communist, the Communist-led Vietminh enjoyed immense prestige as victors over the hated French. It was widely acknowledged (even by the CIA) that on the strength of nationalism alone, Ho Chi Minh would win any freely and openly contested election.[16] Most revisionist do not dispute Ho Chi Minh's popularity and nationalist stature.[17] They argue, rather, that the Geneva Accords authorized permanent division into Communist North Vietnam and non-Communist South Vietnam.

Appearances to the contrary, the revisionists contend, the provision for elections written into the Final Declaration did not express the intent of the Conference. In a highly revealing passage Nixon writes: "Nor did any of the participants expect elections to occur. The Geneva Conference was intended not to establish peace for all time through the ballot box but rather to create a partition of Vietnam similar to that of Korea. Partition was formally treated as a temporary expedient, but all major participants expected it to be permanent."[18]

A cogent argument can be made that both China and the Soviet Union, the Vietminh's nominal allies at Geneva, viewed elections as a face saving device and expected the division to be long lasting. Prior to the opening of the Conference on Indochina, U.S. Secretary of State John Foster Dulles repeatedly threatened unilateral U.S. military action in Vietnam in the absence of some arrangement for a non-Communist government in the south. Backed by the United States, France insisted on an armistice and regroupment of the Vietminh army to the north before agreeing to a political settlement. Confounding cold war alignments, China and the Soviet Union supported the French position. Having just extricated itself from the Korean conflict, China wanted to avoid confrontation with the United States on its southern border; hoping to dissuade France from joining the European Defence Community, the Soviet Union went along. At Geneva, then, both Communist powers put national geopolitical interests above international socialist solidarity, and later failed to respond to the DRV's many protests of violation of the Accords by Saigon and Washington.[19]

But note how in characterizing intent and expectation, Nixon uses totalizing nominatives to exclude the DRV from the discourse: first, "The Geneva Conference ... was intended ... to create a partition of Vietnam similar to that of Korea"; followed by, "all major participants expected it to be permanent." (The expectations of parties who sign a contract constitute a mitigating factor; in an extreme case of variance, as Nixon here contends, a written agreement can lose its legal force.)

The exclusion is crucial. Quite obviously, the Vietminh never *intended* the Geneva Conference to yield a "Korea-type solution." As victors, they went to Geneva to negotiate independence, the surrender of French forces, and the conditions under which political unification would take place. When Diem blocked the elections they fought on, eventually forcing the American army into a costly stalemate. Not even Nixon could contend that the Vietminh intended the Geneva Conference to produce permanent division.

Here we again encounter the refusal of revisionist history to admit to the discourse the voice of Vietnamese who opposed America's intentions and expectations. It is an exclusion that enacts the revisionists' imperial cold war vision: the Vietminh as mere proxies of International Communism. Thus, in Nixon's world view, the tacit agreement among the Great Powers at Geneva on a Korea-style division of Vietnam is none other than the intent of *all parties* to the Geneva Accords.

The same imperial syntax governs Guenter Lewy's discussion of the Geneva Accords. The government of South Vietnam, Lewy argues, was not legally bound by obligations assumed on its behalf by France, even though at the time of the Geneva Conference France formally controlled the foreign relations of the Associated State of Vietnam.

> There is no suggestion in the record of the Geneva Conference that in accepting the final declaration France sought to bind South Vietnam. Quite the contrary, on 14 May French foreign minister Georges Bidault stated at the fourth plenary session that France considered the Government of Vietnam, recognized by 35 states, "fully and solely competent to commit Viet Nam." Moreover, there is no agreement in international law on the extent to which a newly independent state must be regarded as bound by

> political obligations accepted prior to full independence by the state responsible for the conduct of its foreign affairs. Thus, whatever the degree of sovereignty possessed by the government of South Vietnam in July 1954, the refusal of the Diem government to hold elections cannot be said to have violated international law. Still less can this refusal be held a justification for the North's employment of force against the South.[20]

We begin by observing the blatant double standard. The armistice is legally binding, the Final Declaration is not; the United States is free to violate international agreements, the enemy must obey the letter of the law. More interesting, in a mirroring Nixon's exclusion of the Vietminh, Lewy wills into existence "a newly independent state" of South Vietnam.

Sovereignty is commonly understood as the possession of supreme power within a body politic, or at the least controlling influence; because a government controls the internal political process within its borders, other nations extend diplomatic recognition. In Lewy's discourse, however, the signification process is reversed and sovereignty is imposed from the outside. The Associate State of Vietnam is a sovereign state, Lewy tells us, because "Free World" nations recognize its existence.

Did Vietnamese view their country as one nation or two? How many regarded the Democratic Republic of Vietnam as the legitimate national government? How many the Associated State of Vietnam, or its post-1954 incarnation, the Republic of Vietnam? Did Ngo Dinh Diem, Bao Dai's successor, command loyalty or respect even from Vietnamese living south of the seventeenth parallel? Did anti-Communist Vietnamese in South Vietnam constitute a viable political community? These questions which speak directly to native points of view are excluded from the discourse.

Nor should we be surprised. To frame the historical issue of the refusal of the Diem regime to hold elections in terms of the sentiments, views, values, and allegiances of the Vietnamese themselves is to acknowledge the right of Vietnamese freely to choose socialism. And the United States, as guardian of the "Free World," historically has not acknowledged this right.

The sole Vietnamese voices admitted are the anti-Communist. The Geneva Accords permitted free movement of the civilian population during the 300-day period of military regroupment, and vastly larger numbers moved from north to south than from south to north. On this basis, Nixon argues "The Vietnamese people voted with their feet, and it was a landslide against the Communists."[21]

Indeed, the fact that as many as 900,000 Vietnamese living north of the seventeenth parallel moved into South Vietnam attests to their anticommunism—even if the CIA pulled out all stops to maximize the flow.[22] But first, who were the Northern refugees? By and large they were landlords, urban elites, soldiers, and functionaries of the Associated State of Vietnam and, most of all, Catholics who since the French occupation had long looked to the colonial authorities for protection from the sometimes hostile non-Catholic majority.[23] Second, why should the flow of population constitute a referendum when only a small minority of the total population moved? The Geneva Accords stipulated elections by July 1956 and explicitly ruled out permanent political division; Vietnamese who accepted the Vietminh vision of a unified country under Ho Chi Minh had good reason to stay put. Relocating acquired urgency only for anti-communist Vietnamese who believed that the partition would turn into permanent division. Yet in revisionist historiography, it is this minority whose political allegiances are totalized as representative of the collective will of the Vietnamese people.

### The Southern Resistance

The third issue in revisionist Vietnam War history we shall examine is resistance to the U.S.-supported government of South Vietnam (GVN). Founded in December 1960, the National Liberation Front of South Vietnam (NLF) militarily and politically contested the authority of the GVN. Building on Vietminh networks and prestige, the NLF expanded rapidly and, by the early 1960s, functioned as the government in large areas of rural South Vietnam.[24] At first strictly a guerrilla movement, with aid from North Vietnam the NLF developed main force units, which by 1963 decimated the Army of the Republic of Vietnam (ARVN) in battalion-size engagements. Only the intervention of half a million U.S. soldiers beginning in March 1965 prevented the NLF from achieving early victory.[25] Later in the war, the NLF suffered heavy losses during the Tet Offensive in 1968 and its political apparatus was weakened by the CIA Phoenix Operation, which between 1968 and 1971 abducted or killed approximately 45,000 suspected NLF supporters.[26]

Nevertheless, until the late 1960s the NLF carried the burden of the fighting against the U.S. and the ARVN forces.[27]

To Richard Nixon, the National Liberation Front was merely the first stage of North Vietnam's invasion of South Vietnam "shrewdly camouflaged . . . to look like a civil war."[28] The invasion, according to Nixon, was both military and political, coming "under and around the border instead of over it. By 1963, North Vietnam had infiltrated more than 15,000 troops or advisers into the South, most of them southerners trained by the Communists in the North. Subsequently, the infiltration became predominantly northern. . . . It sent 12,000 troops in 1964, 36,000 in 1965, 92,000 in 1966 and 101,000 in 1967."[29]

Politically, Nixon contends, the NLF was Hanoi's fifth column:

> He had ordered thousands of Communist Viet Minh to stay in the South after the 1954 partition in anticipation of his push to conquer the whole of Vietnam. They organized the National Liberation Front, a coalition of political groups opposing the South Vietnamese government. These included idealistic youths, peasants in areas where land reform had failed, Saigon intellectuals, and victims of Diem's anti-Communist campaigns. It was a classic example of the Communist tactic of the united front. Though some non-Communist groups gathered under this umbrella organization, the Communists always dominated it.[30]

Nixon next asked whether the NLF was an indigenous political movement and whether it represented the legitimate aspirations of the South Vietnamese. The NLF was neither, he contends, because it had only the appearance of an independent movement. "Communist leaders went to elaborate lengths to maintain this illusion. But Hanoi's hand was hidden only from those who chose not to see it."[31]

Unlike Nixon who presents "facts" without citation, Guenter Lewy's discussion of the National Liberation Front is extensively documented. On certain points Lewy is circumspect and acknowledges distinctions elided by Nixon between political and military cadres and between "infiltrators" who entered the NLF and People's Army of Vietnam (PAVN) regulars. While Nixon claims infiltration constituted a camouflaged invasion only marginally supported in South Vietnam, Lewy acknowledges broad support. Lewy even acknowledges the deliberate misrepresentation of the NLF as a "creation of Hanoi" in official reports issued by the U.S. Department of State—views Nixon reproduces without qualification. Perhaps to reassure the reader of evenhanded treatment of all the evidence, Lewy quotes from a secret CIA report of October 1961 that called the NLF "still largely a self-supporting operation in respect to recruitment and supplies."[32]

Nevertheless, Lewy's use of evidence is highly selective—as it must be to add weight to the contention of North Vietnamese "aggression." On the issue of infiltration, for example, not just in 1961, as Lewy implies, but as late as 1964 U.S. intelligence reported the overwhelming majority of NLF soldiers to be local recruits and NLF military units self-sufficient in most respects. A comprehensive CIA report prepared in December 1964 confirmed the indigenous origins of NLF fighting forces, with the qualification that infiltrators provided valuable services as specialists in communications, logistics, heavy weapons, and training of newly recruited battalions."[33] Even at this late date, the majority of their arms had been captured or purchased in South Vietnam, which caused much embarrassment to Johnson Administration officials as they tried to justify U.S. military intervention. As late as February 1965, U.S. officials in Saigon were able to produce only four weapons of Chinese manufacture in addition to the ten shown previously to Secretary of Defense Robert McNamara.[34]

Both Lewy and Nixon assume that, on their own the people of South Vietnam lacked the will and capacity to threaten the GVN. Nixon, we saw, portrayed southerners as witless dupes. Always more careful, Lewy's argument hinges on the qualitative judgment that North Vietnam's assistance transformed the NLF. Citing what he calls "very conservative" estimates of 28,000 infiltrators from North Vietnam between 1959 and 1964, Lewy asserts that infiltration "built the VC into a highly disciplined and effective military force." Thus, he defends the dramatic escalation of the U.S. war that began in late 1964 under President Johnson as justified by North Vietnamese "aggression."[35]

Revealed in the revisionist discourse on Northern "aggression" is the by now familiar imperial syntax. Presupposing as universally recognized fact the "Korean-type solution" imposed by United States and the GVN, the very vocabulary of "infiltration" reifies the political division of Vietnam into two states. Because "international borders" are crossed, an act of aggression has occurred. Thus, already encoded in the "facts" adduced by the revisionists as evidence of Northern "aggression" is the U.S. agenda for postcolonial Vietnam: permanent division. Truly imperial it preempts the very questions which directly address the indigenous roots of the conflict: did Vietnamese want one country or two? did they want Ho Chi Minh or Ngo Dinh Diem as their leader?

The mirror image of this imperial discourse on Northern "aggression" is the presumed legitimacy of U.S. "assistance" that maintained the government of South Vietnam in power. Beginning in 1954 the United States officially stationed over 600 "non-combat" advisors in Vietnam on a permanent basis and by 1960 they had grown to 875. When President Kennedy took office, tens of thousands U.S. soldiers were sent both as advisers and combatants: 3,164 in 1961; 11,326 in 1962; 16,263 in 1963; 23,310 in 1964. Between 1962 and 1964 the United States Air Force flew over 15,000 sorties in support of the ARVN.[36] If one includes CIA operatives, mercenaries paid by the United States, and American civilians employed by the U.S. government, the U.S. military role vastly exceeded that of North Vietnam. Yet none of this, of course, constitutes aggression.

On the basis of aid from North Vietnam, Nixon and Lewy declared the NLF a creature of Hanoi and illegitimate. Indeed, the NLF partially depended on aid from the North; the GVN, however, entirely dependent on vastly greater aid from a distant superpower. Here, too, revisionists fail to extend the logic of their own argument to the GVN, an obvious client regime with little claim to legitimacy.

Revisionist history focuses on the role of the Vietnamese Communist Party in organizing the NLF to the exclusion of all other considerations. Lewy quotes an NLF defector who revealed to his interrogators that the appeal for armed struggle against the Diem regime issued in March 1960 was "simply the product of a meeting called in accord with Central Committee policy, with the dual purpose of arousing internal support for the new phase of the revolution and of misleading public opinion about the true leadership of the revolution." He also quotes a key passage of a resolution passed by the Third Congress of the Vietnamese Communist Party in September 1960: "To ensure the complete success of the revolutionary struggle in South Vietnam, our people must strive to . . . bring into being a broad National United Front directed against the U.S. and Diem and based on the worker-peasant alliance." Finally, he traces the political platform of the NLF, a 10-point program published in December 1960, back to Secretary General Le Duan's speech before the same Third Congress.[37]

Clearly, Lewy's sources provide evidence of political direction from Hanoi. However, it is one thing to argue outside political direction of the NLF and quite another to write off the mass movement in South Vietnam. In classic misuse of metonymy, Lewy takes one aspect of a complex historical movement (that is, political control) to signify the whole, a reduction that marginalizes all other aspects of the movement and precludes consideration of what motivated hundreds of thousand NLF supporters. Omitted from revisionist discussion of the NLF is the social revolutionary dimension of the southern resistance: land distribution, rent reduction, progressive taxes, literacy and health campaigns, greater sexual equality, promotion of the low status peasants, and so forth.[38] But we should not be surprised by these omissions, for by writing off the NLF as mere "symptom of North Vietnamese aggression," revisionist history need not examine either the revolutionary program of the NLF or the reasons why the GVN could not enlist the support of the population it purportedly "represented."

## America's Defeat

The final issue we consider is the revisionists' explanations of America's defeat in Vietnam. For three decades Republican and Democratic administrations had made the preservation of a non-Communist regime in South Vietnam the cornerstone of America's Southeast Asian policy; yet in 1973 Nixon signed a treaty with the Democratic Republic of Vietnam which merely provided a "decent interval" between the U.S. withdrawal and the defeat of the GVN. The United States, a country with seemingly unlimited military and economic resources, was humbled by a country Washington considered a "third-rate military power with a fourth-rate economy." Revisionist historians are unmoved by the death of several million Vietnamese, the uprooting of one-third of the population of rural South Vietnam, and destruction of the region's ecology and productive resources. Yet they lament the loss of prestige and self-doubt brought on by America's first defeat in a foreign war. Explaining why America lost the Vietnam War (but need not lose the next time around) is central to the revisionist project.

While there is broad agreement on all other issues relating to U.S. intervention, revisionist historians cannot agree on why America lost. In fact, there are as many explanations as there are authors.

Nixon actually claims that the United States had won the war in 1973. "When we signed the Paris peace agreements in 1973, we had won the war. We then proceeded to lose the peace. . . . Defeat came only when the Congress, ignoring the specific terms of the peace agreement, refused to provide military aid to Saigon equal to what the Soviet Union provided for Hanoi." [39]

Many on the right blame the media, especially television reporting. Produced by Reed Irvine's organization Accuracy-in-Media and dutifully aired nationally by the Corporation for Public Broadcasting, "Television's Vietnam: The Real Story" predictably lays the blame at the door of the media. After exposing alleged liberal bias in the thirteen-part television series "Vietnam: A Television History" produced by WGBH, Boston, Charlton Heston, the engaging on-camera narrator, concludes the program by intoning "In the end words—disinformation, deception—were the deciding factors in the Vietnam War." [40] Norman Podhoretz delivers much the same message in *Why We Were in Vietnam*, although he directs his fire mainly at fellow East Coast intellectuals Francis FitzGerald, Susan Sontag, Harrison Salisbury, and Mary McCarthy, "apologists for the Communist side in the Vietnam War" whose journalism persuaded many that the U.S. cause was not just. [41]

The explanation of defeat salient in "Rambo" genre movies holds that the government did not let our boys win. In *Strategy For Defeat* Admiral U.S. Grant Sharp, the former commander of U.S. naval forces in the Pacific, blames President Johnson and civilian advisers for preventing U.S. military commanders from moving "decisively with our tremendous air and naval power." [42] Sharp believes that by 1966 the United States had assembled sufficient ground and air power to have "forced Hanoi to give up its efforts to take over South Vietnam." The interdiction of Soviet and Chinese aid to North Vietnam by mining the port of Haiphong and destroying the overland routes from China, Sharp argues, would have crippled the war in the South. In Sharp's scenario, once deprived of outside military supplies, enemy forces would be ground down in the "big unit war" of U.S. and ARVN search-and-destroy operations. The Johnson administration fatally erred, Sharp concludes, in adopting a strategy of gradual escalation of the air war against North Vietnam which not only failed to produce a negotiated settlement but allowed the enemy to defend against the escalation of the air war.

Thus, timorous civilians in the White House and Pentagon para-
lyzed by fears of provoking China and the Soviet Union ultimately
caused America's defeat in Vietnam.

To a people whose self-identity is so closely bound up with
illusions of America's omnipotence, explaining defeat in terms of
limited deployment of military power salves wounded national
pride. It also appears to resolve the paradox of the world's richest
and most powerful country failing to compel a populous but very
poor Asian nation to cry uncle. In the final analysis, the cause of
failure is easily remedied: to win the next one, send packing the
unmanly Washington bureaucrats and politicians who chose the
path of gradual escalation; put real men in charge who will go in
big, hard and fast. With his uncanny sense of the lowest common
denominator in the popular culture, Ronald Reagan early endorsed
this view. On the campaign trail in August 1980, Reagan declared,
"Let us tell those who fought in that war that we will never again
ask young men to fight and possibly die in a war our government is
afraid to let them win."[43]

Revisionist explanations of defeat need not be polemical. In *On
Strategy*, Colonel Harry G. Summers, Jr. develops a theoretically
grounded analysis of what went wrong. Along the way, Summers
explicitly rejects stab-in-the-back theories: he denies that the reporting of the war by the U.S. media was in any fundamental sense
"biased" or untrue and disputes the notion so dear to many on the
right that how the war was reported was of greater consequences
than what actually transpired on the battlefield. Because the Joint
Chiefs of Staff failed in their advisory capacity, Summers contends,
the military establishment contributed to defeat in Vietnam.

Summers begins his book by reporting an exchange he had in
Hanoi with a North Vietnamese colonel in April 1975:

> "You know you never defeated us on the battlefield," said the
> American colonel.
> The North Vietnamese colonel pondered this remark a mo-
> ment. "That may be so," he replied, "but it is also irrelevant."[44]

The anecdote serves to introduce Summers' thesis that tactical
success is meaningless without a winning strategy. The fundamental strategic error, Summers contends, was misunderstanding the
enemy's strategy and especially the role of guerrilla warfare. "Judged
by the results of the war, the basic mistake ... was that we saw
their guerrilla operations as a strategy in itself: Because we saw it

69

as a strategy, we attempted to understand it in terms of 'people's war' theories of Mao Tse-tung, and devised elaborate theories of counterinsurgency."[45] In the 1960s, Summers argues, counterinsurgency became a virtual "dogma" and victory in Vietnam was equated with winning the village war against the NLF. This, Summers insists, was a fatal mistake. Not only did the American army expend vastly superior manpower and firepower in inconclusive search-and-destroy operations whose very nature aroused public controversy. The U.S. military acquired a new and entirely inappropriate mission of nation building. According to Summers, the U.S. army should have strictly adhered to the pre-Vietnam doctrine of defeating the enemy "by application of military power directly or indirectly against the armed forces which support his political structure."[46] The enemy's "center of gravity" was the North Vietnamese army, population, and political structure; the NLF mere "partisans," irregulars incapable of achieving decisive results on their own. The mission of the U.S. army, Summers concludes, "should have been focused on protecting South Vietnam from outside aggression, leaving the internal problems to the South Vietnamese themselves."[47]

All that was needed to win the war, if one grants Summers' analysis, was to prevent the NVA and arms shipments from entering South Vietnam. Summers raises the possibility of carrying the land war into North Vietnam World War II-style, destroying the enemy's army, occupying its capital, and thereby eliminating its capacity to continue the war in the south. But he does not advocate invasion, presumably because of very high U.S. casualties and adverse reaction at home and abroad. Instead, he endorses General Bruce Palmer's much more modest strategy of constructing a defensive line extending across Laos just below the DMZ permanently to block the Ho Chi Minh trail. Just eight combat divisions would be needed, Summers optimistically predicts, with additional divisions deployed "to stabilize the situation in the central highlands and in the Saigon area."[48] Keeping the NVA out of South Vietnam, he concludes, would allow the ARVN to contain the insurgency. Quoting General Palmer, Summers offers the following prediction: "Cut off from substantial out-of-country support, the Viet Cong was bound to wither on the vine and gradually become easier for the South Vietnamese to defeat."[49]

Conceptually, Summers' analysis turns on a highly contrived distinction between revolutionary and conventional warfare: "it is essential to distinguish the First Indo-China war between France and the Viet Minh from the Second Indo-China war between North Vietnam and South Vietnam. The first was a revolutionary war. The second was not. The forces that besieged Dien Bien Phu grew out of the guerrilla movement; the forces that captured Saigon did not grow out of the Viet Cong but were the regular armed forces of North Vietnam."[50]

In Summers' formulation, unless the guerrillas achieve "decisive result on their own" the entire war was conventional rather than revolutionary.[51] Because the Vietnam War ended with a largely conventional military offensive by the North Vietnamese army in the spring of 1975, Summers reduces the entire conflict to a conventional military contest.

The obvious problem with Summers' definition is that it collapses the distinction between necessary and sufficient conditions of victory in order to write off the NLF. (If winning "on their own" is the sole criterion of a revolutionary war, the American War of Independence becomes a mere conventional war won by French army and navy regulars at Yorktown.) In point of fact, by pushing the GVN to the brink of collapse in 1964 the NLF produced the necessary condition for the victory in 1975. The dramatic escalation of the U.S. war in Vietnam prevented the NLF from achieving victory "on their own"; but their near success forced the United States to take over the ground war from the ARVN. It was not some trendy fascination with counterinsurgency, as Summers implies, but imminent defeat of the GVN that compelled the Johnson administration to throw the U.S. army into the village war—the very decision which Summers identifies as fatal to successful prosecution of the war. Once the United States had committed half a million ground troops and deployed the most intensive firepower in the history of modern warfare, the NLF could not, of course, win the war "on their own." But compelled to fight the "dirty" village war, the American army sustained several hundred thousand casualties, consumed billions upon billions of dollars, engaged in tactics that caused many Americans to question the morality of U.S. intervention, and brought sufficient dissension and insubordination within the army's ranks to persuade many it would be better to lose the war than lose the American army. The guerrillas, whom Summers denigrates as "mere partisans," never permitted U.S. war planners the luxury of deploying the U.S. forces solely against North Vietnam.

The revisionists' explanations of defeat in Vietnam differ on the question of what America did wrong. What is most striking in this discussion, however, is the utter lack of interest in what motivated the millions of Vietnamese—Southerners and Northerners, political cadres and soldiers, regulars and guerrillas, women and men, old and young—who willingly sacrificed their lives and livelihood in resisting America's imperial agenda for postcolonial Vietnam. Revisionist historians acknowledge the need to "know thy enemy" but none seriously asks why "their" Vietnamese fought so hard and so long and for so little material reward. In revisionist discourse, America lost the war because of our mistakes; all the answers can be found within ourselves.

Writing history necessarily involves not only the inclusion but the exclusion of social facts; not only the affirmation but the devaluing of themes and viewpoints. Nevertheless, historical explanations which by necessity will be partial stand or fall to the extent that they engage the external reality they purport to describe and explain. Our conclusion, therefore, is not that revisionist historiography is biased or lacking in objectivity—for this goes without saying. Rather we should note how its very syntax uncannily mirrors that of the war planners: America always the subject, Vietnam the object. Even "our" Vietnamese, the anti-Communists, were marginal. Despite pious pronouncements about protecting the "freedom" of the people of South Vietnam, in internal documents the harsh realities of U.S. war aims were spelled out—none more succinctly than a memorandum prepared by Assistant Secretary of Defense John McNaughton for Secretary McNamara (with an eyes-only copy to McGeorge Bundy) on U.S. war aims: 70 percent to preserve our national honor; 20 percent to keep South Vietnam territory from being occupied by the Chinese; and 10 percent to the South Vietnamese to enjoy a better and freer way of life.[52]

NOTES

I gratefully acknowledge the helpful comments and criticisms of Mary Ann Rasmussen, Sheldon Pollock, Will Swaim, Allan Megill, Donald McClosky, John Nelson, the University of Iowa POROI seminar, George McT. Kahin, Stefan Tanaka, Irwin Scheiner, Bill Billingsley, Arjo Klamer, and Spencer Olin.

1. See Fred Halliday, *The Making of the Second Cold War* (London: Verso, 1983), p. 81–104.

2. Robert W. Tucker, "Spoils of Defeat," *Harpers* (November 1981), 263:85–88.

3. Halliday, *Second Cold War*, pp. 105–33.

4. Few of the Vietnam revisionists are as circumspect. More typical is Norman Podhoretz's polemical assessment in the concluding chapter of his book: "Thus, no sooner had Vietnam fallen than Soviet proxies in the form of Cuban troops appeared in Angola to help the Communist faction there overwhelm its pro-Western rivals in a civil war. With local variations, the same pattern was repeated over the next few years in Ethiopia, Mozambique, South Yemen, and Afghanistan, all of which were taken over by Communist parties subservient to or allied with the Soviet Union with the help of Soviet proxies or massive infusions of Soviet arms." Norman Podhoretz, *Why We Were in Vietnam* (New York: Simon and Schuster, 1982), pp. 176–77.

5. Tucker, "Spoils of Defeat," p. 86.

6. Ibid., p. 85.

7. On the rhetoric of "objective" Vietnam war history, Stephen Vlastos, "Teaching the Vietnam War: Objectivity in the Classroom?" *Bulletin of Concerned Asian Scholars* (1984) 16(4):52–54.

8. Guenter Lewy, *America in Vietnam* (New York: Oxford University Press, 1978), p. 3.

9. For a detailed discussion of these events, William J. Duiker, *The Communist Road to Power in Vietnam* (Boulder, Colo.: Westview Press, 1981), pp. 91–168.

10. For the most complete account of the Truman and Eisenhower administrations' policy, George McT. Kahin, *Intervention* (New York: Knopf, 1986), pp. 3–65.

11. Duiker, *Communist Road*, p. 137.

12. George C. Herring, *America's Longest War* (New York: Wiley, 1979), p. 1.

13. Richard Nixon, *No More Vietnams* (New York: Avon Books, 1985), p. 24.

14. Kahin, *Intervention*, pp. 7–8.

15. For complete text of the "Final Declaration," see Gareth Proter, ed., *Vietnam: A History in Documents* (New York: New American Library, 1979), pp. 159–61.

16. For extract of "National Intelligence Estimate 63–5–54 On the Post-Geneva Outlook in Indochina" see Porter, *Documents*, pp. 162–64.

17. Norman Podhoretz concedes the point but still argues "If in the name of democracy, elections had been forced on Diem and the Communists had won, the result would have been not the extension of democracy to the South but the destruction of any possibility of a development in the direction of democracy there." Norman Podhoretz, *Why We Were in Vietnam*, pp. 41–42.

18. Nixon, *No More Vietnams*, p. 41.

19. Stanley Karnow. *Vietnam: A History* (New York: Viking Press, 1983), pp. 198–205.

20. Lewy, *America in Vietnam*, pp. 9–10.

21. Nixon, *No More Vietnams*, p. 35.

22. See Neil Sheehan et al., *The Pentagon Papers as Published by the New York Times* (New York: The New York Times, 1971), pp. 16–18.

23. Kahin, *Intervention*, pp. 75–77.

24. Although a regional study, the most thoroughly documented study of the political ascendancy of the NLF in the South Vietnamese countryside is provided in Jeffrey Race, *War Comes to Long An* (Berkeley: University of California Press, 1972), pp. 105–40.

25. An exhaustive and well-documented account of the battle of Ap Bac, generally regarded as the turning point in the war up to that point, and of the

cover-up by the American military command in Vietnam, is related in Neil Sheehan, *A Bright and Shining Lie* (New York: Random House, 1988), pp. 203–65.

26. Lewy, *America in Vietnam*, p. 281.

27. The October 1967 MACV (Military Assistance Command, Vietnam) estimate of Communist forces listed 175,612 Viet Cong (62,852 regulars, 37,587 guerrillas, and 75,173 Self Defense and Secret Self Defense); 53,700 NVA (North Vietnam Army); 25,753 Administrative Service (northerns and southerners); and 39,175 Viet Cong/NVA Infrastructure. Thomas C. Thayer, *War Without Fronts* (Boulder, Colo.: Westview Press, 1985), p. 31.

28. Nixon, *No More Vietnams*, p. 47.

29. Ibid., pp. 47–48.

30. Ibid., p. 48.

31. Ibid.

32. Lewy, *America in Vietnam*, p. 23.

33. Larry E. Cable, *Conflicts of Myths* (New York: New York University Press, 1986), p. 225.

34. Ibid., p. 245.

35. Lewy, *America in Vietnam*, pp. 40–41.

36. Ibid., p. 24.

37. Ibid., pp. 15–17.

38. The social revolutionary dimension of the NLF's program is exhaustively documented in Race, *Long An.*

*39. Nixon, No More Vietnams, p. 18.*

40. For discussion of "Television's Vietnam: The Real Story" see Stephen Vlastos, "Television Wars: Representations of the Vietnam War in Television Documentaries," *Radical History Review* (1986), 36:115–32.

41. Podhoretz, *Why Vietnam*, p. 99.

42. U.S. Grant Sharp, *Strategy for Defeat* (San Rafael, Calif.: Presidio Press, 1978), p. 2.

43. Quoted in "Vietnam: A Television History" 101 produced by WGBH Boston.

44. Col. Harry G. Summers, Jr., *On Strategy* (New York: Dell, 1984), p. 21.

45. Ibid., p. 125.

46. Ibid., p. 116.

47. Ibid., p. 115.

48. Ibid., p. 171.

49. Ibid., p. 172.

50. Ibid., p. 122.

51. Ibid., p. 113.

52. Quoted in Kahin, *Intervention*, p. 313.

# Missing In Action: Women Warriors in Vietnam

## CAROL LYNN MITHERS

For years after the American military defeat in Vietnam, the war vanished below the surface of a country that wanted only to forget it. It did not go away. Nearly a decade after the last American troops left Southeast Asia, Vietnam resurfaced in a cathartic flood of memoirs, novels, poems, songs, studies, analyses, and films, all seeking to explain, understand, or in some way come to terms with what had happened there. Vietnam veterans, once reviled as "baby-killers," or feared as men of uncontrolled and unpredictable violence, reemerged as heroic Christlike figures who paid for the sins of an entire nation. Yet, even as Vietnam-related material poured out (at times threatening to turn the war into a small cottage industry), one important group of war stories remained untold. Virtually all Vietnam memoirs and novels were written by men. All war analyses and studies were written *about* men. But men were not the only ones who went to war.

About ten thousand women served with the U.S. military in Vietnam. The vast majority were nurses, low-ranking officers, but there were also enlisted women working as communications, intelligence, and language specialists, air-traffic controllers, and aerial reconnaissance photographers. As a group, they were different from the men who carried the guns, on the average several years older and more educated. They were overwhelmingly white and middle-class; idealistic, often deeply religious "good girls" for whom the admonition to "ask what you can do for your country" was not political rhetoric but a moral imperative. All had volunteered to join the military; many specifically requested assignment to Vietnam.

Like the men with whom they served, however, most knew nothing about the country of Vietnam, the politics of the war raging there, or the realities of war in general. Introduction was immediate and brutal, the first sight, for instance, of a "typical patient: a double amp. No legs, the bones and muscles and everything showing, like a piece of meat in a butcher shop."[1]

That introduction set the tone for the year to come, a time one woman later likened to "a fast forward on a tape."[2] On the one hand, Vietnam offered women the kind of intense comradeship and community that makes so many men recall war with nostalgia:

> There was no place to go . . . so you always met outside your hooches and you'd sit in the quadrangle and you'd watch the stars. And everybody was there together, there with maybe popcorn; or maybe it wouldn't be everybody, it would be just one or two people and everything would come out because there was time for you to talk about everything, and you talked about everything from the time when you were small till you were old. . . .
>
> It's hard to explain how everybody felt about everybody. We would sit around and we would just sort of be amazed at how close we all were and we knew it would never happen again. Most of us would never have this experience again.[3]

Moreover, for women raised in an era when women lived within narrow, rigidly prescribed boundaries, a year in Southeast Asia promised a rare chance for independence and adventure. For nurses, it also offered an opportunity to escape the subservient roles they had always played in civilian life. Treated by doctors as fully valued medical team members, constantly called on to master new skills and put everything they already knew into practice, Vietnam became what almost every nurse would recall as the absolute peak of her professional career.

But service in a war that had no front and was everywhere also meant fear and danger. Although women in Vietnam were classified as "noncombatants," the cities and hospital compounds where they worked received their share of mortar and rocket attacks. The red crosses on the hospitals, commented one nurse, "just gave [the enemy] something to shoot at."[4] The war's massive number of casualties—some 58,000 dead and at least 300,000 wounded—and one of the best medical evacuation systems in history (bringing men from combat to emergency room in half an hour) brought nurses an endless horror show of death and mutilation. Seventy-hour operating room shifts were spent patching bodies blown apart by mines, ripped by bullets and shrapnel and burned by napalm;

helicopters came in "filled with hundreds and hundreds of body parts, arms, legs, heads. . . ."[5] Every nurse had one case she couldn't forget, one man who symbolized for her all the war's waste and carnage: the shrieking, traumatized GIs who arrived at the emergency room carrying the headless body of a friend; the man so incinerated he was "just a lump, like a burned marshmallow, and there was a tube at one end and this rasping breathing—aaaah!— like that";[6] the man carried into the E.R., "just the trunk of a guy, no arms, no legs, not a spot on him where there's not a frag wound, blinded, but he still has his nose and mouth and he's screaming that he wants to die. . . ."[7]

Perhaps anyone who witnesses such scenes is left with indelible emotional scars. But it's one of war's central requirements, particularly for those who must deal with its casualties, that it be fought for a purpose so clear and important that people can bear sights like an armless, legless man begging to die because they are able to attach some meaning to his suffering. In Vietnam, it often seemed there was none. Not only did the reasons offered for U.S. involvement appear too flimsy to support the weight of so much pain and death, the day-to-day reality of the war itself seemed insane and out of control. There were the dead civilians and children, the atrocity stories told by both sides. There were the GIs dead from drug overdoses and from "friendly fire," and soldiers' stories of their leaders' deadly ineptitude. Nurses often treated both Vietnamese civilians and POWs, and, to their own dismay, many found themselves coming to share the GIs' open racism against the "gooks"— "we'd take some Vietnamese guy who was really injured and give him an extra hard ride over to the operating room table, really give him a hard jolt when we dropped him down. . . .[8] And the jarring disjunction between the war as publicly reported and personally experienced suggested that either the U.S. government had no idea what was going on or was deliberately lying.

Male soldiers dealt with the war's unacceptable contradictions by using drugs, striking out against the Vietnamese and each other, and, ultimately, refusing to fight. Women drank, smoked, "partied hard," and had affairs that too often just brought more grief. Some nurses, forbidden to fraternize with enlisted men, became involved with doctors, most of whom were older and married, in relationships that ended abruptly and painfully when the men's tours of duty were up; others saw men they'd been dating brought into the emergency room in body bags. Some became cynical, some became bitter, many—like one nurse at the 27th Surgical Hospital in Chu Lai—learned to stop feeling anything at all:

> The first three months, I'd get off work and write letters home describing what I'd seen, and cry while I wrote. After three months, I realized I couldn't keep allowing myself to be open to that kind of emotional trauma or I wasn't going to make it. I pulled up the barriers around myself. I stopped crying and I stopped writing letters home. I really numbed out.
>
> What was so hard to take was a sense of tremendous helplessness about an absolutely insane situation. I almost think if I hadn't had that, I could've remained open to some degree, allowing myself to grieve, because then the grieving would have had some meaning. But this was going on just because no one had a sane handle on it. That's what was so devastating. I saw this stupid thing happening, and there wasn't anything I could do to make it change. All I was doing was picking up the pieces.[9]

Like male GIs, women finished their tours of duty and were abruptly dropped back into civilian life. The adjustment was, at best, difficult. Women who'd been dealing nonstop with life and death had no patience for the more trivial concerns of normal American life. Nurses had "attitude problems" when it came to resuming their old "handmaiden" relationships with doctors, and missed being as needed as they had been in Vietnam. The continuing debate about the war raised conflicting emotions. Hardest of all, there was no way for a woman to come to grips with, or even acknowledge, what she had been through because it seemed that no one wanted to hear. Brush-offs, whether intentional or not, came from friends and family, from male vets who were absorbed with their own problems, and from the Veterans Administration, whose hospitals often lacked the facilities to give women the most basic health care. Isolated from each other, reluctant to identify themselves as veterans because the public image of a military woman was a lesbian, a whore, or a loser looking for a husband, the women tried to go on with their lives, and waited for the war to go away.

It didn't. Exposure to injury and death is one of the best predictors for Post Traumatic Stress Disorder (PTSD).[10] And although those beginning to acknowledge PTSD as a problem for male veterans ignored "noncombatant" women, and nurses themselves often opted for denial "because it's sort of a thing with health people

never to cop to any of your own problems,"[11] still, the problems
were there. Some women found themselves having olfactory hallucinations of the smell of pseudomonas, an infection common among
burn patients. Others had nightmares of being shot at while running across a field or of being sought out and hurt by badly wounded
men. Still others had flashbacks:

> At first it was as though I was daydreaming. What scared me to
> death was that I couldn't turn it off. . . . The cow grazing in the
> field became a water buffalo. Fields marked off and cross-sec-
> tioned became cemeteries. We flew over this tent . . . and sud-
> denly it became the 18th Surg. . . . I started to cry, I couldn't
> control myself. I saw blood coming down onto the windshield
> and the wiper blades swishing over it. There was blood on the
> floor, all over the passenger area where we were sitting. The
> stretchers clicked into place had bodies on top of them.[12]

In 1982, the first study of women's experiences in Vietnam and
their aftereffects showed what several other studies and individual
accounts would later confirm: that this was a group of people
seriously, often permanently, affected by their Vietnam service.
Significant percentages had suffered anxiety and depression, in-
somnia, nightmares, war flashbacks, thoughts of suicide. Nearly
half felt some emotional numbness; over half an inability to trust
or become close to others. Sixty-five percent said they felt alienated
from the government, and 57 percent felt they had been used by it.
Included in those "symptoms" reported as still present in their
lives by over half the responding women were: alienation; hyper-
sensitivity to issues of fairness, justice, and legitimacy; cynicism
and mistrust of government; and ideological changes and confusion in value systems.[13] "I don't believe anything I'm told by the
government now," said one nurse who returned from a year in the
busy operating room of the 12th Evacuation Hospital in Cu Chi
with "an explosive temper" and the ability to hear a helicopter
coming long before anyone else in the room.

> There's something all of us know who've been to Vietnam. It's
> not particularly how we were victimized. I guess it's being de-
> mythed. Pretty painful to go through. See, everybody else is real
> comfortable with their lives. We're all pretty much haunted by
> what happened to us, what we saw, what went on, why it hap-
> pened. Maybe I could live a more peaceful life not knowing the
> things I found out.[14]

The experiences that women had in Vietnam were profound and painful; the stories that women Vietnam veterans have to tell are powerful, compelling, and add a new dimension to what we know about the war. In fact, once one becomes aware of them, there comes an inevitable question: why did they remain unheard for so long? To be sure, over the years, women's presence in Vietnam merited occasional notice. Two novels called *Vietnam Nurse* were published in 1966; "the view of the Vietnam war as the locale for a sort of extended prom date is certainly unusual," commented one later reviewer.[15] A third with the same title, published in 1984, was also a "romance," this one an attempt at soft-core pornography, although its descriptions of female sexual response are so strange they suggest the book was written by a male virgin.

An episode of the old "Quincy, Medical Examiner" television show dealt with a Vietnam nurse suffering from PTSD; the film "Purple Hearts" was a love story set around a Vietnam hospital. The oral histories in *Nam*, by Mark Baker (1981), and *Everything We Had*, by Al Santoli (1981), contained some women's stories. In 1982, Patricia Walsh, who worked for the U.S. Agency for International Development as a civilian nurse-anesthetist in Danang, published *Forever Sad the Hearts*, the story of a civilian nurse in Vietnam; in 1983, Lynda Van Devanter's *Home Before Morning* became the first autobiographical account of an army nurse's Vietnam experience. But such books and accounts—even the ludicrous ones —comprised but a negligible percentage of Vietnam literature, and never really penetrated the public consciousness. As late as 1981, a chapter entitled "Women and the War," written by a respected journalist for a mainstream Vietnam book, confined itself to feminism and the antiwar movement; women who went to Vietnam were never even mentioned.[16]

This silence becomes more understandable, however, when one looks beyond Vietnam. Few women's voices have been heard in the history of *any* war. That is not because they haven't been present in those wars, haven't suffered and died. Women were found among the slain at Waterloo,[17] women served as seamstresses, spies, and soldiers during the American Revolutionary War,[18] and as nurses during the American Civil War. (Louisa May Alcott, best known for the sentimental *Little Women*, first made her reputation with *Hospital Sketches*, an account of her time as a Civil War nurse.[19] The experience was deeply traumatic—while in Fredericksburg, Alcott caught typhoid pneumonia and was sent home "hallucinating and furious much of the time, plagued by scenes from the hospital. . . . From time to time she would say, 'If you will only take that man away, I can bear the rest'.")[20]

During World War II, more than 800,000 Soviet women and girls served at the front,[21] and 100,000 Yugoslavian women fought after their country's regular army was destroyed; 25,000 died. In Italy, 25,000 women fought as partisans; 624 were killed or wounded. Fifteen—most of whom had been caught by the Germans and tortured to death—were awarded Italy's Gold Cross for Military Valor.[22] Sixty-seven Army nurses survived the defeats of Bataan and Corregidor and spent nearly three years in a Japanese POW camp in the Philippines.[23] Army nurse Genevieve de Galard spent weeks stranded in the French garrison during the battle of Dien Bien Phu, the only woman and nurse to care for the 6,000 soldiers wounded and killed.[24] Eight American women died in Vietnam; by 1968, according to the North Vietnamese government, 250,000 Vietnamese women fighters had been killed and 40,000 disabled.[25] And when women have written of their wartime experiences, as did Vera Brittain, who served as a nurse during World War I, they have been movingly eloquent:

> "The strain all along," I repeated dully, "is very great . . . very great." What exactly did those words describe? The enemy within shelling distance—refugee Sisters crowding in with nerves all awry—bright moonlight, and aeroplanes carrying machine-guns —ambulance trains jolting noisily into the siding, all day, all night—gassed men on stretchers, clawing the air—dying men, reeking with mud and foul green-stained bandages, shrieking and writhing in a grotesque travesty of manhood—dead men with fixed, empty eyes and shiny, yellow faces. . . . Yes, perhaps the strain all along *had* been very great. . . .[26]

Women's Vietnam stories remained unheard and untold for so long because what women have to say has *never* been considered a legitimate part of war's history. Women who went to Vietnam shared with men the horror, contradictions, and aftereffects specific to this particular war and, with earlier generations of women, an exclusion specific to their sex: there has always been a place for women to serve in war, but there is no place for them in its mythology.

The terrible truth about war is that for all its horror it is powerfully appealing. The visual allure of war's spectacle, the passionate feelings of comradeship engendered in those who defy danger to work towards a common goal, the intensity of coming face-to-face with death, and the opportunity to "escape [from] the cramping restrictions of an unadventurous civilian existence"[27] often seem much more exciting and meaningful than what peace can provide. The promise of transcending ordinary existence makes war mythical; within that mythology, those who've experienced the war are forever set apart and made special: they have proved themselves in a war as civilians have not, they know something civilians never will. War stories, wrote former Marine and *Newsweek* editor William Broyles, are "not meant to enlighten but exclude. ... I suffered, I was there. You were not. Only those facts matter."[28]

War's attractions call out to women as well as to men—certainly women historically have had far more "cramping restrictions" and "unadventurous existences" from which to want escape. The physical ability to *be* in a war, to endure hardship and danger, to kill or be killed, has no gender requirements. Being admitted to the inner circle of the war's elite, however, is a very different story.

Throughout history, cultures and societies have assigned men and women very different social roles. Men, by "nature" harsh, aggressive, and violent, take as their province the dangerous "outside" world of politics and marketplace, while women, compassionate, nurturing, and fragile, are keepers of the "inner" arena of heart, hearth, and home. War not only extends those roles, with men fighting "as avatars of a nation's sanctioned violence" and women acting as "the collective 'other' to the male warrior,"[29] it becomes an arena for *proving* them. The standards for being a "real" soldier—"courage, endurance and toughness, lack of squeamishness when confronted with shocking or distasteful stimuli, avoidance of display of weakness in general, reticence about emotional or idealistic matters"[30]—are identical to those of stereotypical "real" masculinity. Going to war, then, is not simply a test of "courage" or "endurance" (or even patriotism) but of *manhood:* someone who becomes a warrior has become a "real" man.

"Real" men, of course, are the opposite of women; the imagery of sexual domination and women as inferior "other" permeates all levels of war's mythical universe. "Pussy!" the drill sergeant shouts at the recruit who isn't making it, *"Woman!"* "I didn't just screw Ho Chi Minh," Lyndon Johnson said after the passage of the Gulf of Tonkin Resolution in 1964, "I cut his pecker off."[31] Although women require the presence and attention of men to "prove" their femininity, men cannot become men except in the *absence* of women. If combat is to "make" men, women cannot be included. "War," said General Robert H. Barrow, Commander of the U.S. Marines, in 1980, "is man's work."

> Biological convergence on the battlefield would not only be dissatisfying in terms of what women could do, but it would be an enormous psychological distraction for the male who wants to think that he's fighting for that women somewhere behind, not up there in the same foxhole with him. It tramples the male ego.[32]

War mythology does, of course, assign women a place. As civilians, points out Jean Bethke Elshtain, they stand on the sidelines as goads to action, weepers over war's tragedies, male surrogates mobilized to meet manpower needs, and witnesses to male bravery. On or near the battlefield, they may be healers, reminders of home, pure incarnations of all that men must fight to protect, or sexual objects—whores, rape victims, battle "spoils."

In Vietnam, military women might be assigned to any or all of these categories. Wearing perfume and hair ribbons to remind men of gentleness and femininity, they were sometimes idealized. "Someone wakes up on your O.R. table and says 'Oh my God, I've died and gone to heaven and you're an angel'," recalled one nurse.[33] Such "canonization" had its drawbacks.

> If the guys wanted to . . . screw ninety-seven prostitutes in a day, it was to be expected. "Boys will be boys." Every PX stocked plenty of GI issue condoms and according to the grapevine, some commanders even went so far as to bus in Vietnamese girls for hire to keep morale high. However if we wanted to have a relationship, or to occasionally be with a man we cared deeply about, we were not conducting ourselves as "ladies should." And if we might be unladylike enough to want birth control pills, which were kept in a safe and rarely dispensed, we could expect the wrath of God, or our commander, to descend upon us.[34]

As the only "round-eye women" around, they also were descended on by American men wherever they went, a deluge in which the difference between flattering popularity and sexual harassment often became blurred. Over half of the 135 former Vietnam nurses surveyed in a Northwestern State University study reported having suffered sexual harassment ranging from simple insult to rape. One nurse was offered a Bronze Star to sleep with her commander; another, who was threatened by a patient, was scolded for being "seductive."[35] One nurse who had gone with friends to a pilots' party learned that the men had plans for them.

> I said, "Hey, you know there's a room full of mattresses back there and some of the guys are getting the girls pretty drunk." There was also a lot of opium and a lot of dope. "We got to get out of here."
>
> We tried to put up a united front. Those of us who were reasonably sober practically carried the drunk ones to the chopper pad and tried to get someone to give us a ride home. The guys were furious. We thought it was going to be a gang rape, that's how bad it was. The GIs called the nurses "round-eye tail," and suddenly that's exactly what we were.[36]

Within such traditional categorizing, however, what women were really doing in Vietnam got lost. Certainly the gap between myth and reality was most dangerous where it concerned women's role as "noncombatants": according to one article in the military paper *Stars and Stripes*, a Harris poll found that 75 percent of women veterans had been "in or exposed" to hostile fire and combat.[37] Noncombatant status, said one nurse, simply meant that "we couldn't shoot back."[38] Added another, "I realized that [GIs] were trained to survive in a war zone but that I was not—that I could get killed. . . . The Army never taught me anything—I mean anything. Nothing. Everything I learned about surviving I learned from the men."[39]

But similar contradictions could be found everywhere. In *Home Before Morning*, Lynda Van Devanter describes a nurse's rescue of a wounded man from a flaming helicopter. Afterwards, the head nurse puts in her name for a Bronze Star with a "V" for valor. The Star comes, but without the "V"—it cannot, says the commanding officer, be awarded to a nurse.[40] And just as Vera Brittain discovered in 1918 that her devastating experiences as a combat nurse in France made her "merely the incompetent target for justifiable criticism, since a knowledge of surgical nursing did not qualify me for housekeeping,"[41] women who returned from Vietnam were told that what they had seen, felt and done did not really "count." Lynda Van Devanter described trying to join a veterans' antiwar march:

> When we moved outside to line up, I took a place near the front. However one of the leaders approached me. "This demonstration is only for vets," he said apologetically.

"I am a vet," I said. "I was in Pleiku and Qui Nhon."

"Pleiku!" he exclaimed. "No shit! I used to be with the 4th infantry. You must have been at the 71st Evac. . . . You folks saved my best friend's life. . . ."

"Do you have a sign or something I can hold?" I asked.

"Well," he said uncomfortably, "I . . . uh . . . don't think you're supposed to march."

"But you told me it was for vets."

"It is," he said. "But you're not a vet."

"I don't understand."

"You don't look like a vet," he said. . . . "You can't be a member of our group. I'm sorry."[42]

Another nurse, who had served at Cu Chi and Danang, got the same message from different sources.

For the past twelve months I'd made decisions about whether someone was going to live or die. I got into this [county] hospital and was told I could not hang a pint of blood unless a doctor was standing there. I kept getting called in by the head nurse: "You've really got an attitude problem. You're no longer in Vietnam." Like, who do you think you are? I went through a severe depression in 1978 and I remember telling the shrink I had been in Vietnam and he just brushed that over and said "Tell me about your childhood." Just brushed it aside as if it wasn't important at all.[43]

If post-Vietnam America did not want to deal with men who symbolized a lost war, it did not know *how* to deal with women who simply could not be made to fit into any of women's traditional wartime categories. Women who'd spent a year in combat boots and mud- and blood-stained fatigues working at or near the front weren't clichéd, self-sacrificing Florence Nightingales or breathy, bouncing Hot Lips Houlihans. One name that might have suited them was "soldier"—certainly someone who'd worked around the clock in an operating room that was sometimes under fire, numbing her emotions while piecing together burned and mangled bodies had exhibited strength, courage, endurance, toughness, and lack of squeamishness in large measure.

But if being a man was the antithesis of being a woman, and if one *became* a man by becoming a soldier, how could soldiers be anything but men? If going to war was, "for those men trying to fulfill society's expectations, part and parcel of displaying their male identity and thus qualifying for the privileges it bestows,"[44] by definition, warriors simply *could not be women.* To close the gap between the myth and reality of what women do in war, writes Cynthia Enroe, "would require that military officials resolve their own ideological contradictions." [45] Instead,

> women *as women* must be denied access to "the front," to "combat" so that men can claim a uniqueness and superiority that will justify their dominant position in the social order. And yet because women are in practice often exposed to frontline combat, the military has to constantly redefine "the front" and "combat" as wherever "women" are not. [46]

And if that meant that ten thousand women were left with bad dreams, problems they were told they had no right to have, and experiences they were informed did not "count," then that was something they would have to work out themselves.

During the mid 1980s, the silence surrounding women veterans seemed to break. A flurry of newspaper and news magazine articles introduced America to its "forgotten vets." The House of Representatives instructed the Veterans Administration to provide for an epidemiological study of the effect of herbicides on women who had served in Vietnam. Colonel Mary Stout, a former Vietnam nurse, was elected head of Vietnam Veterans of America. Although a movement to place the statute of a nurse next to Frederick Hart's three male soldiers at the Vietnam Memorial Wall in Washington, D.C. was thwarted by the Federal Commission on Fine Arts, three women's oral history collections (incorporating the testimonies of combat nurses, enlisted women, and civilian volunteers for organizations like the Red Cross, USO, and American Friends Service Committee) were published during that same year by the mainstream press.

Hollywood, too, which had preciously shied away from Vietnam nurse features and movies-of-the-week (perhaps because multiple amputations and third-degree body burns were considered problematic in terms of entertainment value) began to discover women. Patricia Walsh's *Forever Sad the Hearts* went into development at Paramount as a feature film for Cher, and Lynda Van Devanter's *Home Before Morning* went into development as a possible CBS miniseries. Ironically both quickly became embroiled in the kind of political infighting familiar to male veterans. Walsh, claiming that Van Devanter "portrayed medical teams in an utterly disgusting fashion," formed a group called Nurses Against Misrepresentation, whose efforts were centered around preventing *Home Before Morning* from reaching the small screen.[47] (So far, neither film has been made.) And 1988 marked the premier season of "China Beach," a television series set at a large medical evacuation and R&R area, whose main characters were a combat nurse, a USO entertainer, a Red Cross "donut dolly," and a prostitute/black marketeer.

Certainly much of this burst of attention was attributable to the war's sudden emergence as a "hot" (i.e., eminently saleable) commercial and cultural topic. "China Beach," for instance, came on the heels of the series "Tour of Duty," itself spawned by the success of the feature film "Platoon."

Perhaps equally important, according to Joan Bethke Elshtain, was the *way* the War was increasingly coming to be viewed: once a reminder of national shame and defeat, Vietnam was "being reconstructed as a story of universal victimization."[48] Of course, women as victims was an image America could accept with no trouble at all.

Embracing the notion that everyone suffered and no one is to blame for what happened in Vietnam has been a way for this country to avoid facing the truth about the war and the challenges which defeat poses to our most basic assumptions about ourselves and the world. Similarly, portraying women Vietnam veterans *only* as victims (as most book and magazine articles have done), or trying to fit their wartime experiences into male war movie genre conventions, as "China Beach" almost always does, is just another way of ignoring the more complex reality of who such women were, what they did, and what it meant. Moreover, such an approach virtually guarantees that women's accounts of military service will not endure beyond a brief existence as novelty byproducts of Vietnam's currently "fashionable" status. In *The Perfect War,* James William Gibson points out that because they have regarded only high-level "official" accounts as sources of information and ignored the stories of men who actually fought, conventional assessments of what happened in Vietnam have been both skewed and incomplete. True understanding of the war, he says, requires accepting the validity of what he calls "the Warrior's knowledge."

Women's voices can complete that understanding. First, however, women must be accepted as warriors. Their knowledge of war must come to be considered legitimate. Most of all, their accounts of Vietnam must be viewed as *war stories*—stories that are *different* from those of men but no less valid, stories that, like men's, both constitute a war's history and create its mythology. "Writing women's history," points out one writer, ". . . involves much more than digging up some little-known facts; it means redefining historical categories like war."[49]

That, of course, is not easily done. One can't redefine war to legitimize women's experiences without confronting, on a number of levels, its social and sexual mythology. Feminists remain divided by conflicting beliefs about war, uncertain if women are inherently pacifist and war itself is a masculine creation or if true equality means allowing women to pick up weapons and join men on the battlefield. The belief that only war can "make" a man continues to haunt men who escaped service in Vietnam only to suffer "Viet Guilt" (or, more accurately, "Viet Envy") years later:

> Like 17 million other men who came of age during Vietnam, I did not serve in the armed forces. It was a blessing, then, to have escaped; it is a burden now. I find there is something missing in me. . . . Those like me, who, for one reason or another, did not serve, suffer because we chose not to perform a primary and expected rite of passage. We were never inducted, not merely into the Army, but into manhood.[50]

The old belief that war imparts some mysterious, specifically masculine, knowledge lingers in the mind of women like the writer whose short story appeared in a 1985 issue of *Mademoiselle:*

> Ellen sees her brother, separated from his unit. She tries to imagine his being ambushed by the two Vietcong in the jungle, as Warren explained matter-of-factly he had been, how they had damaged his spine with his own hand grenade, attempting to set it off between his legs. She cannot, she doesn't have the words or the understanding, not a metaphor, to describe it to herself. No wonder men seldom spoke in intimacy; the things they needed to air were unspeakable.[51]

The old belief that women can't know war silences even women who should know better, women who *do* have the words and understanding and metaphor to describe a man crippled by a grenade. In a documentary aired in 1985, one nurse recalled being caught in the rain on a gunboat in Vietnam. "I was thinking," she said, "this is what *real war* [my emphasis] must be like."[52]

As long as the old war mythology holds, the experiences of women will never have legitimacy. But a male-dominated culture of war, especially one that seeks to perpetuate itself, has nothing to gain and everything to lose by acknowledging and incorporating the experiences of women Vietnam veterans. To admit that women serve and suffer in war is to destroy the claim to special male knowledge and all the privileges it brings. To admit that they have been in danger and acted heroically is to contradict the myth that they need to be protected.

Most of all, to hear the stories of women whose intimate knowledge of war is of its wreckage is to contradict the most basic myth of war's glory—to change forever a tradition in which we hear about those who have gained manhood from war, not those who've been castrated by it; in which we identify only with the victors; in which the camera quickly pans over the dead to focus on the survivors. "War," wrote William Broyles in *Esquire*, "may be for men, at some terrible level, the closest thing to what childbirth is for women: the initiation into the power of life and death."[53] Within the mythology of war, the warrior, a man who kills, who sees himself holding "the power of life and death," can imagine himself a god. The woman who has seen warriors weeping and calling "Mommy!", who knows that in the end war comes down to blood, pain, and broken bodies, can only remind him that he is not.

## NOTES

1. Kathryn Marshall, *In The Combat Zone* (New York: Little, Brown, 1987), p. 214.

2. Ibid., p. 134.

3. Dan Freedman and Jacqueline Rhoads, *Nurses in Vietnam: The Forgotten Veterans* (Austin: Texas Monthly Press, 1987), pp. 129, 135.

4. Author's interview with Pamela White, 1984.

5. Author's interview with Chris McGinley-Schneider, 1984.

6. Marshall, *In The Combat Zone*, p. 133.

7. Interview with Pamela White.

8. Ibid.

9. Author's interview with Pat Miersma, 1984.

10. John P. Wilson and Gustave E. Krauss, "Predicting Post-Traumatic Stress Syndromes Among Vietnam Veterans," *Proceedings* of the twenty-fifth Neuropsychiatric Institute Conference, Veterans Mental Center, Coatesville, Pennsylvania, October 25, 1982), 37.

11. Interview with Pamela White.

12. Freedman and Rhoads, *Nurses in Vietnam*, p. 22.

13. Jenny Ann Schnaier, "Women Vietnam Veterans and Mental Health Adjustment: A Study of Their Experiences and Post-Traumatic Stress," Master's thesis, University of Maryland, 1982.

14. Interview with Pamela White.

15. John Newman, *Vietnam War Literature* (Metuchen, N.J.: Scarecrow Press, 1982), p. 44.

16. Susan Jacoby, "Women and the War," in A. D. Horne, ed., *The Wounded Generation: America After Vietnam* (New York: Prentice-Hall, 1981).

17. Helen Rogan, *Mixed Company: Women in the Modern Army* (New York: G. P. Putnam's Sons, 1981), p. 81.

18. Ibid., pp. 120–23.

19. Louisa May Alcott, *Hospital Sketches* (Cambridge: Belknap Press, 1960), introduction.

20. Martha Saxton, *Louisa May: A Modern Biography of Louisa May Alcott* (Boston: Houghton Mifflin, 1977), p. 255.

21. Shelley Saywell, *Women In War* (Penguin Books Canada, 1985), p. 131.

22. Rogan, *Mixed Company*, p. 85.

23. Ibid., p. 258.

24. Saywell, *Women In War*, p. 193.

25. Ibid., p. 321.

26. Vera Brittain, *Testament of Youth* (New York: MacMillan, 1933), p. 423.

27. J. Glenn Gray, *The Warriors: Reflections on Men in Battle* (New York: Harcourt, Brace, 1959), p. 29.

28. William Broyles, Jr., "Why Men Love War," *Esquire*, November 1984, p. 61.

29. Jean Bethke Elshtain, *Women and War* (New York: Basic Books, 1987), p. 3.

30. Samuel A. Stouffer et al. *The American Soldier: Combat and Its Aftermath*, vol. 2 of *Studies in Social Psychology in World War II*, edited by Samuel A. Stouffer et al. (Princeton: Princeton University Press, 1949), p. 179.

31. David Halberstam, *The Best and the Brightest* (New York: Random House, 1972), p. 414. Cited in James William Gibson, *The Perfect War: The War We Couldn't Lose and How We Did* (New York: Vintage Books, 1988), p. 435.

32. Michael Wright, "The Marine Corps Face the Future," *New York Times Magazine*, June 20, 1980, p. 73. Cited in Cynthia Enroe, *Does Khaki Become You? The Militarization of Women's Lives* (Boston: South End Press, 1983), p. 154.

33. Author's interview with Lynda Van Devanter, 1983.

34. Lynda Van Devanter, with Christopher Morgan, *Home Before Morning: The Story of an Army Nurse in Vietnam* (New York: Beaufort Books, 1983), p. 122.

35. Vincent Coppola, "They Also Served," *Newsweek*, November 12, 1984, p. 36.

36. Mark Baker, *Nam: The Vietnam War in the Words of the Men and Women Who Fought There* (New York: Morrow, 1981), p. 228.

37. Elizabeth Hess, "Statute of Limitations?" *Village Voice*, July 15, 1986.

38. Marshall, *In The Combat Zone*, p. 132.

39. Ibid., p. 213.

40. Van Devanter and Morgan, *Home Before Morning*, p. 195.

41. Brittain, *Testament of Youth*, p. 430.

42. Van Devanter and Morgan, *Home Before Morning*, p. 213.

43. Author's interview with Rose Sandecki, 1984.

44. Enroe, *Does Khaki Become You?*, p. 13.

45. Ibid., p. 107.

46. Ibid., p. 15.

47. "Nurses At War!" *Los Angeles Times* "Calendar" section, 1987.

48. Elshtain, *Women and War*, p. 218.

49. Karen Rosenberg, "Peaceniks and Soldier Girls," *Nation*, April 14, 1984, pp. 453–54.

50. Edward Tick, "Apocalypse Continued," *New York Times Magazine*, January 13, 1985, p. 60.

51. Linsey Abrams, "Secrets Men Keep," *Mademoiselle*, August 1985, p. 283.

52. "A Time to Heal," by Gary Gilson, St. Paul: KTCA Television, a Twin Cities Production, 1985.

53. Broyles, "Why Men Love War," p. 61.

# PART TWO

# The Vietnam War
# and Mass Media

# FOUR

# Military Propaganda: Defense Department Films from World War II and Vietnam

## CLAUDIA SPRINGER

During the Vietnam War, the American military was faced with the difficult task of instilling enthusiasm in its recruits, many of whom had been drafted unwillingly. Previous American wars had not prepared the Department of Defense for the resistance they encountered in the 1960s and 1970s, not only from antiwar civilians but also from some members of the armed forces. The job of selling a war had never been more difficult. How the Defense Department represented the war in Vietnam and American involvement to the GIs, by contrast with World War II strategies, is the subject of this essay.

The American military has a long history of devising persuasive strategies to motivate its troops. During World War II, the War Department brought in Hollywood directors, most notably Frank Capra, to inject a sense of drama into documentary film formats, conveying the sense of mission that infused government rhetoric about the war. World War II propaganda films exhibit a style that has become immediately identifiable: dramatic, hyperbolic, dependent on montage techniques that incorporate footage from a variety of sources, with an authoritative narration accompanied by a rousing score. National solidarity in opposition to fascism made it easy for the films to adopt a confident style that presupposed viewers who shared their values, goals, and interpretation of events. Although there had been widespread isolationism during the 1930s and in 1940–41, after the Japanese attack on Pearl Harbor it had dissipated and support for American involvement in the war had become strong.[1]

During the Vietnam War, American military propaganda films underwent a shift in purpose as well as in style. One purpose of both the World War II and Vietnam films was identical—to motivate and educate the troops—but they diverged in their relationship to civilians. The World War II films were distributed not only to the troops but to public movie theatres where their purpose was to rally civilian support around the war.[2] In contrast, the Vietnam films were shown almost exclusively to the troops and not to civilians, with a few noteworthy exceptions: the distribution of *Why Vietnam?* (1965) to high schools and colleges, and TV broadcasts of a series of Defense Department films on the *Big Picture* program.[3]

How the films' creators envisioned their goals during World War II and Vietnam suggests that the term "propaganda" carried different connotations during the two wars. During World War II, the word "propaganda" had not yet acquired the completely pejorative meaning it carries today. Propaganda was a useful, even necessary, weapon in the war of ideas being waged against fascism.[4] American government officials and scholars studied Nazi propaganda in part to learn how to produce their own equally persuasive material.[5] War Department personnel were frank about their goal—to educate the armed forces and the American public about the reasons for the war and the necessity for American involvement. What made it possible for officials to speak openly of "propaganda" was their belief in American consensus around a cause—an end to the spread of fascism—presumed to be above propaganda. It is when ideological divisions exist that opposing sides tend to accuse each other of using propaganda to propagate lies. A P. Foulkes makes a useful point when he writes that we recognize propaganda as a result of our ideological distance from it. He continues, "It is all too easy to 'detect' propaganda when we are distanced, not historically but politically, from acts of communication, and from modes of perception which we attribute to speakers and hearers. . . . The propaganda which is most elusive, and which for that reason is most in need of detection, is not the one we observe but the one which succeeds in engaging us directly as participants in its communicative systems."[6]

By the time of the Vietnam War, consensus had been replaced by conflict and the term "propaganda" had acquired a wholly negative connotation, perhaps largely as a result of the mounting cold war, revelations about Nazi atrocities, and growing public cynicism about official rhetoric. It had come to mean any material intended to persuade people to adopt incorrect, dangerous viewpoints, and it was attributed to those with opposing viewpoints—the enemy—rather than to oneself, but by this time many Americans who were opposed to the war considered the enemy to be their own government.[7]

Not only had the concept of propaganda, and potentially all persuasive discourse, fallen into disfavor after World War II, the role of the military in providing information to the general public had also changed. During World War II, Defense Department films playing in local movie theatres were important sources, along with newsreels, for learning about the war, but by the time of Vietnam, TV had appropriated the function of disseminating war-related information.[8] In addition, the general impression that TV provided objective, unbiased accounts of the war, or at least provided "both sides of the issue," relegated other, more partisan, sources of information, including even the Defense Department, to the marginalized realm of "one-sided" points of view. Presumably it would have been difficult for the Defense Department to alter public opinion substantially about the Vietnam War by distributing films to movie theaters, or even by expanding their TV broadcasts, since their material would automatically have been contrasted with TV news coverage and would have been regarded more suspiciously than it had been in the 1940s, for resistance to the Vietnam War gave rise to skepticism about official versions of events. In fact, when the Defense Department released *Why Vietnam?* (1965) to schools and colleges, critics attacked it for its many falsifications, indicating to the Defense Department that they could no longer count on widespread approval.[9] Instead of increasing the distribution of their films to the public to try to persuade skeptics, the Defense Department chose to limit civilian viewing and concentrate on their military audience.

It seems apparent that TV also influenced the stylistic shift undergone by the Defense Department films by setting the standard for what was accepted as plausible representation. TV helped to establish a camera crew's presence on location as the primary requirement for documentary realism, so that studio-produced compilation and animation techniques from World War II seemed outmoded by the time of Vietnam. The shift from highly manipulated images during World War II to on-location immediacy during Vietnam was accompanied by a corresponding shift in tone. The Vietnam films abandoned the bombast and drama characteristic of World War II films in favor of a quieter, more restrained tone, perhaps in an effort to imitate the restrained tone of "objective"

TV coverage and to heighten the sense that the information was factual ("real") rather than fabricated. The Vietnam films replaced the structuring principle of montage in the World War II films with a style closer to Bazinian realism, which, in the intervening years, had become associated with believability, although since both types of films contain elements of realism and montage, the dichotomy between formalist montage and Bazinian realism would be too simple to fully explain the difference.[10] In general, the Vietnam films used longer takes, footage from a single source rather than combinations of found footage, and the illusion of verisimilitude instead of the obviously constructed images, including animation, found in the World War II films.

Military films are not designed to be equivocal; their purpose is to present a war in the best possible light and to prepare soldiers for their tours of duty. To this end, the Vietnam films contained important and appropriate information. At the same time, they evaded certain questions or answered them in ways that were designed to elicit GI enthusiasm. These textual practices reveal ideology at work in a situation where there was an immediate goal: to persuade GIs to adopt the administration's viewpoint on Vietnam. This sometimes required turning losses into victories, brutality into beneficence, and suffering into enjoyment. Also inscribed in the films is the lack of clarity in official Washington policy around several questions: who was the enemy in Vietnam? Why were Americans fighting them? Were the Americans fighting with the Vietnamese, helping them achieve self-determination, or against the Vietnamese, fighting instead for American self-interest?

My analysis of the Vietnam propaganda films is hindered by the fact that many of the films are classified and unavailable for public viewing. This study, then, is based on a limited sample determined by the Defense Department.

To set the stage for the Vietnam films, it is necessary to briefly describe World War II propaganda techniques. The "Why We Fight" series, in particular, is well known for its rousing tone, appeals to the emotions, and (if nothing else) its Walt Disney animation sequences. The seven films comprising the series were directed by Frank Capra under explicit orders from Army Chief of Staff General George C. Marshall who was dissatisfied with existing methods of educating troops.[11] At the time, the dominant method of education was the lecture, which paled in comparison to Leni Riefenstahl's *Triumph of the Will* (1935), a film that single-handedly jarred the

American military into taking film seriously.[12] Upon their completion in 1942, the seven "Why We Fight" films became mandatory viewing for all military personnel. Three were subsequently released commercially to movie theatres in the United States and abroad.

Technically superb, the "Why We Fight" films blend music, direct address narration, production footage, newsreel footage, and animation. They create dramatic dichotomies between right and wrong, good and evil, and the "free world versus the slave world" with sweeping generalizations. Most importantly for our comparison with Vietnam films, these World War II films focus on the enemy, especially on Hitler's stated desire to conquer the world.

My examples are taken not from a "Why We Fight" film but from *Know Your Enemy—Japan* (1945), one of Capra's last troop indoctrination films for the government. It exemplifies his formulaic pattern and warrants examination for its attempts to rouse American wrath against an Asian nation. All of the film's assertions as well as its cinematic techniques were designed to instill distrust of the Japanese in its American viewers. Capra typically attributed the characteristics of fascism—repression, authoritarianism, brutality—to national traits rather than to a political ideology. In other words, instead of providing an analysis of how Japan had come to be governed by a fascist system, Capra's films implied that fascism was a biological trait inherent in Japanese people. He thereby naturalized fascism, caricatured the Japanese, and avoided substantive historical analysis. When he attempted to give historical proof for the Japanese desire to dominate the world, Capra turned to animation, which allowed him, with the help of the Disney Studio, to exert maximum control over his images of Japanese people without any semblance of an actual Japanese profilmic presence. Capra apparently assumed that audiences would agree with his premises or, if not, that skeptics could be convinced of Japanese fanaticism by watching studio-produced line drawings. The presence of so many animated sequences in the Capra films supports the observation that different conventions of documentary realism prevailed in the 1940s than in the 1960s and 1970s.

One of the film's animated sequences shows the earth under Japanese domination as a roof under the massive figure of Jimmu, the first God-Emperor, who holds a scroll stating his divine command: "Let us extend the capital and cover the eight corners of the world under one roof." In another animated sequence, a modern

Japanese soldier is dwarfed beneath his monstrous samurai ancestor to suggest a genetic lineage for Japanese militarism. Quotes from Japanese officials are printed onscreen as firsthand evidence of Japanese motives. One such example from near the film's beginning reads "the sword is our steel bible." Printing the letters in a Walt Disney version of Japanese calligraphy is presumably motivated by the same impulse that has the quotes spoken in English with a heavy Japanese accent: to infuse everything Japanese with an aura of danger.

Nonanimated images are also highly manipulated when otherwise innocuous images of Japanese people are made sinister by the film's reliance on narration. A group of soldiers, for instance, is used to illustrate the statement that "he and his brother soldiers are as much alike as photographic prints off the same negative" (figure 4.1). A fisherman in his boat is implicated as an officer of the imperial Japanese navy masquerading as a fisherman off the coast of California. Capra's version of history implicates Japanese tourists and Japanese-Americans as enemy agents when the narrator states: "Other Japanese traveled widely as tourists photographing the sights of Honolulu and Seattle. Something to show the folks back home. Still others went to work in barber shops, strange barbers who didn't talk. This information was collected, studied, filed away in Tokyo, ready for the day the army decided to go into action" (figure 4.2).

Capra frequently used images of children to evoke feelings of pity and outrage in the viewer. Schoolteachers are seen patrolling the aisles to ensure that children do not stray from the correct lessons, and children who have learned their lessons well bear witness to Japanese militarism by standing at attention wearing military uniforms and holding rifles. Japanese mothers are accused of lacking maternal feelings as they "accept the ashes of their dead soldiers without grief or sorrow," an insidious notion that resurfaced during the Vietnam war.

Just in case the message that the Japanese are "hellbent to rule the world" has not been conveyed, Capra uses animation to represent Japan in the form of a voracious octopus wrapping its tentacles around nearby countries (figure 4.3). The narrator declares that "defeating this nation is as necessary as shooting the mad dog in your neighborhood." After the Japanese threat has been built to a fever pitch, American force is introduced as the savior with images that were to become iconic: troops hitting the beach and soldiers raising the flag at Iwo Jima. What makes America unique? A previous image contains the film's answer in one tidy shot: FREEDOM (figure 4.4). *Prelude to War*'s division of the world into a free half and a slave half is recalled, but it is no longer necessary to explain; it has already become a shorthand message that vaguely stands for everything opposed to fascist regimentation. As military propaganda increasingly relied on "freedom" to justify American intervention in other countries, the word's meaning became increasingly obscure. Never defined in the first place, perhaps it was meant to take on meaning through sheer repetition.[13] Emotionalism and fear tactics can sway audiences, but when called upon to justify a war, the old standby "freedom" is dusted off and paraded across the screen once again.

Capra's films received a great deal of attention and were highly touted as trend-setters. Although acclaimed as successful, they proved not to have a lasting effect on military films. The last Defense Department film to use the hyperbolic World War II style was *Why Vietnam?* (1965), which resembles "Why We Fight" in ways other than its title. Like Capra's films, it covers a wide range of issues and attempts to encapsulate the entire Vietnam conflict and American involvement in thirty-two minutes. It relies on emotional appeals and a turgid orchestral score to persuade its viewers, and it mirrors official Washington rhetoric: it is virtually a position paper structured around a speech given by President Johnson.

*Why Vietnam?* has fewer images than Capra's films of the enemy, relying instead on the narration to accuse aggressive, unscrupulous Communists in South Vietnam of receiving orders from China and North Vietnam to subjugate the people of Southeast Asia through random terrorist acts. In keeping with Washington rhetoric, the film obscures the differences between the Russians, Chinese, North Vietnamese, and the National Liberation Front (which it calls "Vietcong"), and relies on the term "Communist" with all its negative associations, many of them transferred from World War II era antifascist imagery, already embedded in the public imagination. As F. M. Kail writes, "The refusal to tolerate the expansion of Communist power was couched not in terms of opposition to Communist social, economic, or political theory, but in terms of opposition to Communist methods. The enemy in Asia was in this respect the same enemy the United States had found in Europe

101

twenty-five years earlier. It was called Communism now and had been called fascism then, but the differences were largely semantic."[14]

The film's infrequent representations of the enemy consist of analogies and inferences. An analogy to Hitler and Mussolini carries instant associations as it equates the Geneva Agreement of 1954 with the Munich Pact of 1938. Posters of Mao and Ho Chi Minh are also ideologically loaded, but some of the film's images depend entirely on the narration for their intended significance, and they may even undermine it. A sequence showing Ho surrounded by a group of children is accompanied by the narrator's assertion that "in the north, Ho Chi Minh, Communist leader of North Vietnam, plays the kindly, smiling grandfather. But behind the smile is a mind that is planning a reign of terror in Vietnam, in which children and adults alike will be the victims" (figure 4.5). GIs may have been puzzled by the distinction made between this image and one of an American soldier carrying two Vietnamese children, accompanied by the statement: "We are committed to helping a free people defend their sovereignty" (figure 4.6). Both images convey compassion, but they are used to illustrate opposing concepts. American concern for children is indisputable, while the enemy is assumed to be incapable of such emotions.[15] The confusion is heightened by an image of a GI training a Vietnamese child, meant to represent America's advisory role in Vietnam, but also possibly raising a question about whether Americans were performing a valuable service by teaching children to wear fatigues and fire weapons. Capra's use of children to evoke an emotional response remains, and childhood innocence is used as a metaphor for the Vietnamese people who, according to the film, were in danger of being corrupted by Ho but would be assured of "freedom" under paternalistic American guidance.

*Why Vietnam?* ends with a Capraesque finale that depicts Americans arriving to save the day. American military might is once again mythologized with iconic images such as troops hitting the beach. The tone of the ending expresses the same uplifting patriotic sentiments as *Know Your Enemy—Japan*, with Johnson making a token acknowledgment of pacifism: "I do not find it easy to send the flower of our youth, our finest young men into battle. . . . But as long as there are men who hate and destroy, we must have the courage to resist. We did not choose to be the guardians at the gate, but there is no one else." Johnson neglects to explain who chose for us, but his reference to a greater force guiding American destiny recurs in other military films to be discussed later. The Defense Department distributed *Why Vietnam?* to "the flower of our youth" in high schools and colleges as well as in the armed forces. Opponents to American intervention in Vietnam were quick to see the falsehoods contained in the film and criticized it for its fabrications and "brainwashing" techniques.[16] How the film was received was perhaps partly responsible for the Defense Department's shift to a less aggressive style and its decision to deemphasize civilian viewing.

Subsequent Vietnam propaganda films rejected dramatic techniques introduced by Hollywood directors and turned instead to TV-inspired documentary realism to persuade GIs. In the following discussion, I have divided the Vietnam films into three broad categories for organizational reasons (the Defense Department does not make these distinctions): films designed to teach GIs about the Vietnamese country and people; training films; and military history films.

The first group of films can best be described as resembling the *National Geographic* type of ethnographic film, in which deep focus long shots predominate and a narrator provides a commentary "explaining" the habits and customs of a group of people. Converting from Hollywood to a *National Geographic* style was not done in a vacuum but during a time when anthropologists were going to work for the American government in Southeast Asia. For example, in 1967 an American specialist in Thailand told the *New York Times:* "The old formula for successful counterinsurgency used to be ten troops for every guerrilla. Now the formula is ten anthropologists for each guerrilla."[17] Defense Department filmmakers appropriated formal devices of ethnographic films—long and medium shots and long takes—but their films' narrations and structuring principles were always motivated by the military's purpose—to teach the troops about the war (figure 4.7).

With the switch to an ethnographic film style, the Defense Department shifted attention from the enemy to South Vietnam's need for American assistance. During World War II, Capra could rely on public agreement when he described Germany, Italy, and Japan as enemy countries. But Vietnam presented a much more complicated situation where, as GIs discovered, it was difficult to tell Vietnamese enemies from friends. Defense Department films no longer focused their attention on the enemy or represented them as Capraesque monsters. Instead, the films emphasized America's obligation to help the South Vietnamese, as if military service in Vietnam were comparable to joining the Peace Corps. Johnson's administration relied on goodwill rhetoric more often than others, as if he were simply exporting his Great Society to Southeast Asia.[18] Nixon could no longer sustain Johnson's argument once it became common knowledge that the United States was intentionally destroying villages and relocating villagers to refugee camps, not to mention devastating the countryside with massive bombings.

*The Unique War* (1966) illustrates the new use of ethnographic imagery. South Vietnamese people, seen "working and playing" in their "villages and hamlets," are portrayed as simpleminded, mired in tradition, and dependent on American aid. The narrator, Glenn Ford, instructs GIs on the importance of a benevolent attitude toward the Vietnamese: "In this kind of struggle, whoever has the people wins the war, so we have to deny the enemy the popular support he has to have in order to survive. And more than that, we have to enlist that popular support behind our own effort." What Ford's statement reveals is that Americans did not have, but thought they could still win, the South Vietnamese people's support. Yet the film undermines its commitment to winning South Vietnamese loyalty when it chooses images that misrepresent Vietnamese culture in order to emphasize similarities between Americans and Vietnamese, such as sequences showing a statue of the Virgin Mary and children crossing themselves in church. The narrator states that although some Vietnamese villages, like this one, are Catholic, the majority are Buddhist, but only images of Catholicism are shown, suggesting that the Defense Department thought American soldiers could sympathize only with people similar to themselves.[19]

*Vietnamese Village Reborn* (1967) goes even further than *The Unique War* in belaboring American benevolence to the Vietnamese. It is an example of a joint American and South Vietnamese operation designed to "end the nightmare" of Communist presence in a Vietnamese village. Troops move in and while the village men are driven away in trucks for interrogation, the remaining villagers are distracted from a house to house search for "Vietcong" by a festival complete with a clown, rock and roll bands, and party favors (figure 4.8). The film represents the Vietnamese people as children and then assumes that they enjoy childlike pleasures. The narrator's condescension knows no bounds: "The ARVN troops also furnish a good deal of the talent for the festival. And while this particular group may never make the top 40, the villagers seem to eat it up. And speaking of eating, there's good food and plenty of it." This paternalism derives from a long tradition of colonial discourse that creates an analogy between colonialism and the relationship between adults and children. Colonial powers tried to justify their colonies by suggesting that colonial control constituted assistance to less "developed" cultures, analogous to adults assisting children. The Vietnam films sustain the analogy with frequent Capraesque images of Vietnamese children accompanied by solicitous American soldiers while the narration refers to the American role in Vietnam.

Both *The Unique War* and *Vietnam Village Reborn* emphasize American aid to the Vietnamese with depictions of medical, technical, and educational assistance and self-congratulatory rhetoric about American generosity.[20] Intrinsic to the films' argument is that there is a distinction to be made between the South Vietnamese people and the enemy. GIs could not be expected to watch ethnographic films about a nation's people and then destroy those people. However, although the narrators do not directly address it, the films exhibit an underlying ambiguity about enemy identity, exposing the difficult situation that would confront GIs. For example, in *The Unique War* Glenn Ford states that "circumstances call for an exercise of restraint beyond that normally required on the battlefield. . . . For the blunt truth is that death or injury to helpless civilians even when it is unavoidable works against us." He continues: "To the people in the villages, there might well be little difference between the calculated cruelty of Communist forces and the fire which rains on them and their families from an American rifle or an American plane." At the same time, he warns that American servicemen should never jeopardize their own lives through excessive caution. Since the identity of the enemy is never clarified, GIs might reasonably, and accurately, have wondered how to attack the enemy without harming civilians and still protect themselves. The images heighten this confusion, particularly when they are intended to illustrate American friendship toward the Vietnamese. A soldier who "must face his personal responsibility through the sights of his personal weapon" is seen in close-up glaring down the barrel of his rifle at the viewer before sneaking

Claudia Springer

through high grass toward a village (figure 4.9). The film's message
—that Americans come as friends—is hard to reconcile with this
soldier's approach to the village.

In another instance, Ford says that the Communists resorted to
terrorism once the buildup of American forces thwarted their efforts to persuade the people by pretending to befriend them. Images of American planes dropping bombs illustrate American military buildup, followed by images of injured people and a town in
flames, supposedly the aftermath of "Vietcong terrorism." But in
terms of narrative logic, image progression argues that bombs
dropped by American planes caused the destruction on the ground.
The images call into question Ford's assertion that there is no
danger of Americans ever using terrorism as a weapon.

Another ambiguous sequence from *Vietnam Village Reborn* shows
a man who reportedly has been so frightened by "Vietcong terror
tactics" that he distrusted the American and South Vietnamese
soldiers who came to "liberate" his village. He is discovered hiding
by a South Vietnamese soldier who is seen checking his identity
papers (figure 4.10). Rather than depict the compassion of the
American and South Vietnamese forces, the image shows a man's
fear at being held at gunpoint and forced to prove his identity.

One film does deal directly with the enemy and borrows Capra's
technique of using enemy footage. *Know Your Enemy—the Viet
Cong* (1968) is a series of NLF newsreels introduced and described
by a stern narrator who is surrounded by film reels and moviolas
to signify his expertise. His presence shows that when the NLF are
represented in Defense Department films, American government
officials control the ideological apparatus, as Rick Berg writes in
essay 5. The Defense Department must have feared that the newsreels could sway GIs to the NLF cause; the narrator cautions the
audience before each newsreel that this is Communist propaganda
that is only being shown to provide insights into the "motives and
methods of the enemy" (figure 4.11). *Know Your Enemy—the Viet
Cong* does not, however, discuss NLF motives, only their methods.
No reasons are offered for the NLF activities shown: preparing an
ambush, taking prisoners, planting explosives, transporting supplies, and touring a printing press and underground hospital with
visiting Chinese and North Vietnamese dignitaries.

The NLF made predominantly silent newsreels; lecturers in the
field provided spoken commentary suited to their audience.[21] The
Defense Department narration attempts to sound purely descrip-

106

tive as it explains the NLF's activities, but many images, such as American planes flying overhead, are left unexplained. NLF methods include transporting supplies on their bicycles while the narrator describes the special reinforcement that allows each bike to carry up to five hundred pounds. They are seen gathering American weapons and dismantling unexploded bombs in order to use every piece of available material. Their "destructive raids" consist of planting explosives on bridges and derailing trains (figure 4.12). Juxtaposed with films that display American weaponry, *Know Your Enemy—the Viet Cong* highlights the discrepancy between American and NLF strength. The narrator downplays the discrepancy by emphasizing that the "Vietcong" are resourceful, highly skilled, and well prepared after undergoing grueling physical training. Not as blatantly racist as Capra's films, *Know Your Enemy—the Viet Cong* in fact attempts to impress the NLF's strength upon GIs to dispel the irony that American B-52s oppose NLF bicycles.

A second type of film, the training film, is designed to brief soldiers on their tours of duty. Most of the Vietnam training films are classified, so my discussion is limited to one example, *Your Tour in Vietnam* (1970). Unconventional warfare is its theme, with distinctions made between "normal" warfare with its battle lines, advances, and retreats, and the new guerrilla warfare. New iconic images were created for the new warfare, such as GIs piling out of a helicopter. The film contains tough talk from narrator Jack Webb, who appeals to the GIs' desire for adventure, excitement, and male bonding: "You'll learn the deep bonds that develop between men who share danger and ideals. You won't talk about it much, but it'll be there." Webb addresses all his comments to "you," thereby heightening the intimacy already promoted by direct address narration. "You" are invited to share the fun of playing with sophisticated military equipment: "Maybe you'll fly a big jet tanker rock-steady through the stratosphere," or "maybe you'll do your damage from high up in the big B-52s that deliver a couple carloads at a time." A rapid montage sequence shows aerial views of bombs exploding in rhythm with upbeat jazz. "You" are also invited to "learn about a culture far different from your own," with visual evidence in the form of a soldier learning to eat with chopsticks. Finally, "you" will experience the satisfaction of defending freedom, for "one day, the advice you gave may be the important factor in aiding the Vietnamese gain the practical know-how to forge freedom." "Freedom" is a carryover from the World War II films, and this last claim highlights the fundamental contradiction that the film seeks to conceal: were Americans defending freedom in Vietnam, as the majority of the narration asserts, or were they "forging" freedom, in other words, imposing an American form of government onto the Vietnamese? Helping people in need and having fun with military hardware at the same time is an attractive notion that helps mask the film's major omission: who were the Americans fighting in Vietnam and why?

A third type of military film recounts victorious episodes from the history of American presence in Vietnam to convince GIs that they would meet with the same success. *The First Infantry Division in Vietnam: 1965–1970* (1971) is a paean to the Division known as The Big Red One, referring reverently to its Revolutionary War origins and summarizing its five years in Vietnam in chronological order. The film is interesting for two reasons: it includes references to American casualties, and it is edited at breakneck speed. These two features are in fact related; the rapid pace prevented GIs, who did not need to be reminded that war can kill, from contemplating the casualties too long before moving on to the Division's next victory. The narrator glosses over American defeats to emphasize that the Vietcong suffered much greater losses: "There were American casualties, but the Vietcong left 198 dead. . . . It was proof they (the Division) could win against the hard-fighting enemy on his own terrain;" or to praise American technology: "The Big Red One had its losses, but Medivac Ambulance helicopters flew in and saved many lives."

*The First Infantry Division in Vietnam* precludes any historical analysis in its representation of events by suggesting that the First Infantry inevitably won all its battles: "There were casualties and destruction, but the inevitable result was annihilation of the insurgent force"; "The result was inevitable—smashing victories"; "The results were always the same . . . victory." By claiming that victory was always inevitable, the narrator dispenses with the need for providing either the specific details of each battle or the historical roots of the conflict. The rhetorical advantage of deferring to destiny is to deny any responsibility for one's actions; the film suggests that Americans were fulfilling their predetermined role rather than constantly formulating and reformulating aggressive foreign policies. What it implied for the GI viewers was that destiny inevitably would guarantee their victory.

Another film that praises American performance in Vietnam is

*The Battle of Khe Sanh* (1969). It interprets the siege of Khe Sanh between January and March 1968 as a resounding victory for the United States, and attempts to disprove those who question its strategic importance by answering the question: "Was Khe Sanh worth it?" The answer is asserted with the help of maps, statistics, technical jargon, and experts, primarily Khe Sanh's Commanding Officer, Colonel David Lownds, presumably by virtue of his having been there in a position of authority. (See John Carlos Rowe's discussion, essay 6 in this volume, of the tendency in American documentary representations of Vietnam to rely on personal testimony as a substitute for analysis.) The other expert who provides occasional voice-over commentary is General Westmoreland. The film appears to have been an attempt to counteract negative impressions that the media might have given GIs about Khe Sanh.

The film combines actual footage from the battle, shot with a cinema verité hand-held camera, with a topographical map (reminiscent of the tabletop map of Khe Sanh that President Johnson installed in the White House to monitor the battle's progress) to explain the circumstances of the siege.[22] Tiny numbered flags label each strategic hilltop on the map and Colonel Lownds gestures with a pointer while providing commentary.

The film introduces the narrative as an underdog story by asserting that at Khe Sanh, 6,000 Marines and support troops held out for seventy days against a besieging force of 20,000 North Vietnamese. The underdog stance is set up with a flashback to Dien Bien Phu in 1954 early in the film, just after the narrator states that intelligence reports revealed a North Vietnamese buildup in the area: "It looked like the Vietcong wanted another Dien Bien Phu."[23] Actual black and white footage from Dien Bien Phu shows French soldiers under heavy fire while the narrator describes how the French were "surrounded, cut off," and "the end was inevitable; the French were overrun." The narrator continues: "The Russian Communists were quick to congratulate the victors." Black and white footage shows Ho Chi Minh and "brilliant General Giap" standing on a stage receiving accolades from the Soviet Union for their victory over the French. The narrator brings GIs up to date: "the same General is now hoping to repeat his victory at Dien Bien Phu." The impression is that of a match between two football teams, with the Vietnamese coach hoping to repeat his success against the French as he prepares to meet the American team on the field. Colonel Lownds furthers the analogy when, just minutes

109

later, he describes how his men had been "banging head on" with the enemy.

An American underdog stance is maintained throughout the first part of the film with its concentration on small-scale clashes between the Americans and Vietnamese, but a turning-point occurs when the Vietnamese surround the base, forcing the Marines to cease running patrols. After the siege begins, the Americans shift their effort to the air, where B-52 bombers pelt the earth with 110,000 tons of bombs, making fifty bomber runs a day. Once the enormity of American bombing is revealed, the narrative shifts to a show of massive strength and the underdogs start to emerge as winners. Footage from a bomber's point of view shows a steady stream of bombs descending to earth. The narrator boasts: "The North Vietnamese had to dig in to avoid being scorched by napalm or pulverized by bombs" which "literally destroyed the area."

In an attempt to depict Khe Sanh as a resounding American victory, the film suggests that conditions during the siege were not unpleasant for the American troops. Colonel Lownds criticizes the American media for having misrepresented conditions as worse than they were while a montage shows soldiers on the base reading, relaxing, playing basketball, and eating food that a cook describes as "quite tasty."

The film concludes by insisting that Khe Sanh did indeed have strategic importance. President Johnson stands at a podium delivering a speech about the significance of Route 9 and Khe Sanh: "Some have asked, what did we accomplish? ... We pulled down and decimated two North Vietnamese divisions. ... Our mission toward talks with the North Vietnamese is closer, because we proved to the enemy the utter futility of his attempts to win a military victory in the south. ... Brave men will continue to fight for freedom in Vietnam, and soon, God willing, they will come home. We would like nothing more than to see that day." The narrator adds: "Historians will call it the single most important battle of the Vietnam War. Only time can determine that." What the film tried to convey to GI viewers was that, even in dire circumstances, they would be provided for (with air support and livable conditions) and they ultimately would be victorious.

A third film structured around a particular wartime episode, *Mission in Action* (1971), represents the yearlong stint in Vietnam of members of the U.S. Army Reserve. Like other Vietnam films, this one avoids providing reasons for American intervention except to refer to it as a job that needs to be done. ("When you want a job done, you choose a man of responsibility to do it.") There is some confusion over whether this job is a defensive or an offensive one; shots of servicemen kissing their families farewell before flying to Vietnam are followed shortly after by the narrator referring to the "American defense posture." In this way, the film narrativizes the servicemen's departure using the convention of men bidding farewell to their families before marching off to defend their homeland. However, the nature of the threat to the United States from Vietnam remains unexplained.

Static talking-head interviews with Army Reserve personnel and still photographs in montage showing them on the job sorting mail, pumping gas, navigating ships, and giving medical assistance, give the film the appearance of a low-budget educational filmstrip. The interviews in this film are rare instances of military personnel having individualized identities (their names are given) and a voice in the Vietnam propaganda films, but their voices are constrained by the formal, rehearsed nature of their statements. A records clerk in Vietnam shown sitting in an office stares down at his desk, apparently reading a prepared statement, as he describes his daily routine. An orthopedic doctor in an evacuation hospital (one of the few women in the military shown in any of the films) is asked, "Do you find your work here in Vietnam different from your work at home?" She responds that, "It is in some ways" and goes on to elaborate that she treats more open fractures than closed fractures in Vietnam, as if in all other ways the jobs are identical. If she had been given time to continue, she might have explained who 'she was treating and the nature and severity of injuries resulting in so many open fractures, injuries not often found with equal frequency outside a war zone.

Direct address statements continue after the Army Reserve units return to the States. The narrator suggests that the war, despite its hardships, could evoke pleasant memories after the troops came home: "Yes, it's tough sometimes to assume responsibility. The rewards are only the satisfaction of knowing you've done important work and done it well. When it's over, it's great to come home. And it's fun to remember and talk about your experiences." Two members of the reserve units address the camera: "I feel I was lucky and I'm very proud;" "It wasn't that bad, really. . . . I'd do it again." Their statements cannot be characterized as wildly enthusiastic; in fact, their restraint casts doubt on the narrator's enthusiasm. GIs might also have wondered whether the servicemen who sustained open fractures found it fun to talk about their experiences.

The film's contradictory messages are heightened by its title, *Mission in Action*, which sounds remarkably like "missing in action," a condition that hardly qualifies as desirable. This title might have been intended to lend a new, positive connotation to the original meaning, but it nevertheless throws into question the narrator's cheerful talk of coming home. Yes, "it's great to come home," but what about those who don't make it?

Unlike Capra's belligerent accusation that the enemy wanted to march down Pennsylvania Avenue, the Vietnam films evoked hostility with the catchwords "Communists," "aggressors," "terrorists," and "insurgents" while they stressed American generosity and the exciting opportunities awaiting GIs in Vietnam. Between World War II and Vietnam, cultural and technological changes ushered in a new era in propaganda: the Defense Department was no longer an important source of wartime images since TV brought the war into American homes every day; Americans became increasingly opposed to their country's involvement in Vietnam and regarded official pronouncements about the war with skepticism; and the Johnson administration responded to growing antiwar sentiment by choosing to downplay the war, from calling it "limited" to making increasingly defensive comments, and by focusing propaganda efforts on the armed forces rather than on the public. Military propaganda reflected administration defensiveness with its new, more subtle and evasive rhetorical strategy. While the aggressive World War II approach constructed a clear-cut vision of good vs. evil and "us" vs. "them," the contradictions in the Vietnam War were so pervasive that even the military propaganda machine could not generate precise reasons for why we fought.

NOTES

Thanks to Rick Berg, David James, Gerald Graff, and Mimi White for their helpful editorial comments.

1. For discussions of American isolationism during the early years of World War II, see Wayne S. Cole, *America First: The Battle Against Intervention 1940–41* (Madison: University of Wisconsin Press, 1953); Robert A. Divine, *The Reluctant Belligerent: American Entry into World War II* (New York: Wiley, 1965); and William L. Langer and S. Everett Gleason, *The Challenge to Isolation 1937–1940* (New York: Harper, 1952).

2. William Thomas Murphy, "The Method of 'Why We Fight'," *Journal of Popular Film* (Summer 1972), 1(3).

3. The U.S. Army's Big Picture television series circulated Defense Department propaganda films about Vietnam. The films were "donated by the federal government for so-called public service programming via the many independent commercial and noncommercial television stations throughout the country—stations that don't originate or acquire sufficient alternative programs of their own." *Film Comment* (Spring 1969), 5:81.

4. The introduction to Harold Lavine and James Wechsler's, *War Propaganda and the United States,* published for the Institute for Propaganda Analysis (New Haven: Yale University Press, 1940) is an example of World War II-era attitudes toward propaganda: "We live in a propaganda age. . . . Every articulate person with a purpose is a propagandist. . . . The task of the thoughtful citizen, who still believes that it is his responsibility to formulate the principal ends of life, then becomes that of distinguishing and choosing between rival propagandas. And the task of the propaganda analyst is to assist the citizen in this performance. Propaganda is a method, a device for conditioning behavior."

5. The text cited in note 4 is just one example of how Americans studied Nazi and Allied propaganda.

6. A. P. Foulkes, *Literature and Propaganda* (London: Methuen, 1983), p. 107.

7. Ibid., p. 2.

8. David Culbert suggests that "editing techniques in "The March of Time" obviously influenced Capra. The extensive narration and the recreation of historic events within what purported to be a factual presentation encouraged Capra to find his own style of filmmaking in which many of the distinctions between documentary and fiction film were blurred." David Culbert, " 'Why We Fight': Social Engineering for a Democratic Society at War," in K.R.M. Short, ed., *Film and Radio Propaganda in World War II,* (Knoxville: University of Tennessee Press, 1983), p. 180.

9. Henry Steele Commager, Professor of History at Amherst College, attacked *Why Vietnam?* for being "well below the standards of objectivity, accuracy, and impartiality which we are accustomed to in newspapers and on television; needless to say, as scholarship it is absurd. In simple, uncritical, and one-dimensional terms it presents the official view of the war in Vietnam with never a suggestion that there is or could be any other view. When Communists sponsor such propaganda, we call it brainwashing." Henry Steele Commager, "On the Way to 1984," *The Saturday Review,* April 15, 1967, p. 68.

10. For a discussion of how Frank Capra appropriated Eisensteinian montage in his fiction films, an influence that is even more pronounced in Capra's government propaganda films, see Paul Warren, "The Influence of the Frontier Myth (the Move West) on Commercial American Cinema," presented at the Society for Cinema Studies conference, Concordia University, Montreal, May 21–24, 1987.

"Why We Fight," in turn, was praised by V. I. Pudovkin, the Soviet filmmaker and theorist, who, along with Eisenstein, promoted montage techniques, in "The Global Film," *Hollywood Quarterly,* (July 1947), 2:327–32.

11. Culbert, "Social Engineering," p. 175.

12. Ibid.

13. F. M. Kail, *What Washington Said: Administration Rhetoric and the Vietnam War: 1949–1969* (New York: Harper & Row, 1973), p. 16.

14. Ibid., p. 12.

15. For a discussion of how Americans misinterpreted as insincere Ho Chi Minh's identifying with the ordinary people and playing with children, see Frances Fitzgerald, *Fire in the Lake* (New York: Vintage Books, 1972), pp. 38–39.

16. Commager, "On the Way to 1984," p. 68.

17. Gerald D. Berreman, *The Politics of Truth: Essays in Critical Anthropology* (Atlantic Highlands, N.J.: Humanities Press, 1982), p. 80.

18. Kail, *What Washington Said*, pp. 82–83.

19. For a discussion of how the Vietnamese converted to Catholicism because Catholic villages received the most American relief aid and benefited most under the Diem regime, see Fitzgerald, *Fire in the Lake*, p. 139. Fitzgerald also describes American misunderstanding of Vietnamese religious beliefs on page 18.

20. For the falsity of administration claims that Americans were bringing economic and other humanitarian assistance to Vietnam, see Kail, *What Washington Said*, p. 83, and Fitzgerald, *Fire in the Lake*, p. 161–62.

21. "Films in Vietnam: USIS Film Officer interviewed by Film Comment," *Film Comment* (Spring 1969), 5:58.

22. Stanley Karnow, *Vietnam: A History* (New York: Penguin Books, 1983), p. 541.

23. Michael Herr discusses how, during the siege, the analogy between Khe Sanh and Dien Bien Phu was popular but faulty, in *Dispatches* (New York: Knopf, 1977), pp. 99–101.

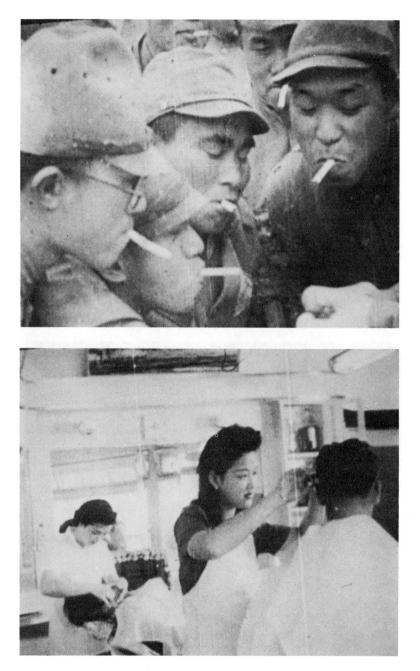

From *Know Your Enemy—Japan* (1945). (above)
From *Know Your Enemy—Japan* (1945). (below)

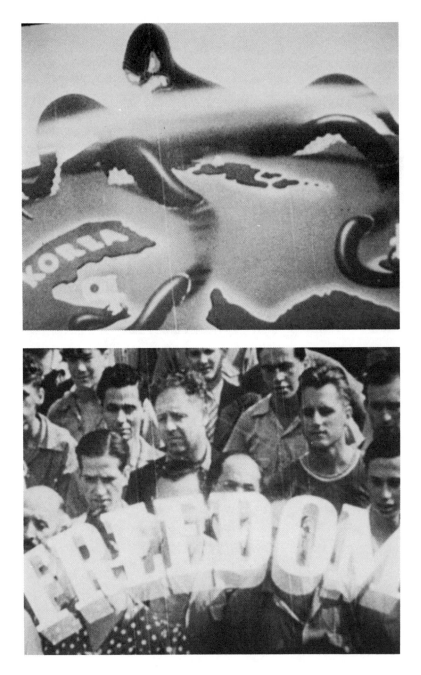

From *Know Your Enemy—Japan* (1945). (above)
From *Know Your Enemy—Japan* (1945). (below)

From *Why Vietnam?* (1965). (above)
From *Why Vietnam?* (1965). (below)

**From a Defense Department "teach the troops about the war" film. (above)
From *Vietnamese Village Reborn* (1967). (below)**

From *The Unique War* (1966). (above)
From *Vietnam Village Reborn* (1967). (below)

From *Know Your Enemy—the Viet Cong* (1968). (above)
From *Know Your Enemy—the Viet Cong* (1968). (below)

# Losing Vietnam: Covering the War in an Age of Technology

## RICK BERG

*What does it mean to win or lose a war? How striking the double meaning is in both the words! The first, manifest meaning, certainly refers to the outcome of the war, but the second meaning—which creates that peculiar hollow space, the sounding board in these words—refers to the totality of the war and suggests how the war's outcome also alters the enduring significance it holds for us. This meaning says, so to speak, the winner keeps the war in hand, it leaves the hands of the loser; it says the winner conquers the war for himself, makes it his own property, the loser no longer possesses it and must live without it. And he must live not only without the war per se but without every one of its slightest ups and downs, every subtlest one of its chess moves, every one of its remotest actions. To win or lose a war reaches so deeply, if we follow the language, into the fabric of our existence that our whole lives become that much richer or poorer in symbols, images, and sources.*
*—Walter Benjamin, "Theories of German Fascism"*

America won no hearts or minds in Vietnam—it lost them. They went the way of the war and the country. After April 30, 1975, when the NVA unfurled a flag from what had once been the presidential palace in what had once been Saigon, Vietnam became part of our past. Our history inherited the ever-escalating incident, and Vietnam, which for the United States had always been more a war than a country, faded from our national, collective attention. Little remained of the war that was an enduring aspect of many lives during the 1960s and early 1970s. Still less remained of the country we wasted to preserve. For Americans, the experience of Vietnam was one of loss. We lost the war in 1973 and the country in 1975. This loss haunts us.[1]

But the absence that haunted us in the 70s is lost to the 80s. The war's remains have been resurrected, and like Frankenstein's monster, given new life. Ten years after Saigon's fall and liberation,

115

Vietnam has become, if not a commodity, then a resource for the American culture industry. Publishers and producers are working it for all it is worth. Books on Vietnam, once almost impossible to find in any major chain, are now almost impossible to avoid. New books appear regularly; older works, long out of print, have reappeared with glossy new covers, and mass-market publishers distribute them nationwide.

Nor have TV and film producers been slow to exploit the resource. Although TV has been unable to find an agreeable fictional format for the Vietnam War, other than the thinly veiled *M\*A\*S\*H*, it has, since 1975, aired a number of documentaries and news specials. But while it waits for the right fictional vehicle, TV has added the Vietnam vet to its lineup. Via the magic of the flashback, TV heroes from *Miami Vice* to *Magnum P.I.* have gained a past as well as a quick justification for mayhem and irreverence. There is even, thanks to Coors Beer, a television commercial for those "who paid the price."

Film producers are also cashing in on the expanding market. Hollywood is no longer looking away. Capitalising on the synonymity of "lost" and "missing," *Uncommon Valor* (1983), *Missing in Action* (1984), and *Rambo* (1985), have recovered Vietnam, and film audiences everywhere have discovered that what they once imagined lost was only MIA. Hollywood has even recalled the veterans. But, as the recently proposed sequel for *Billy Jack* (1971) implies, the ones they remember are their own. The vets in such films as *Search and Destroy* (1981), *First Blood* (1982), *Exterminator I* (1983), and *Fleshburn* (1983) favor only the vets of earlier films like *The Losers* (1970) or *The Visitors* (1972).

Even music producers have joined in.[2] Although no Britten or Penderecki has composed a *Vietnam Requiem*, Country, Rock, Punk, and New Wave have all made their contributions. From The Clash's "Charlie Don't Surf," to Paul Hardcastle's "19," from Charlie Daniels' ode to the flashback, "Still in Saigon," and Billy Joel's "Goodnight Saigon," to Stevie Wonder's embittered "Front Line," the music industry sings its sad song of Vietnam to a generation that, because of a long silence, knows little more of Vietnam and its victims than the media's revised images. And often the music seems to sing that with the dependence on past media images. Other media and their images are the subject of the music and their videos. The subject of Paul Hardcastle's "19" video, for example, is just this interdependence of past and present representations of the war, and not age.[3] The subject of John Sayles' video for "Born in the USA" negates the media-made myths, and supports Springsteen's lyric by wrenching an image of Vietnam away from the former media-made doxa, and wedding it to a class perspective.

*In Country*,[4] the most recent addition to the growing body of fiction on Vietnam, exploits this awareness of our dependence on the media. Samantha Hughes, the seventeen-year-old heroine, finds herself trying to come to terms with a Vietnam that she only experiences as a loss. Almost twenty years after, like a female Telamachus, she attempts to find her lost father and his war, but ends, like Penelope, weaving and unravelling her inherited texts. Like the child in *Tender Mercies* (1983), Sam Hughes has a dead father (KIAed in his irresponsible adolescence), a disturbed Uncle Emmett ailing from the probable affects of Agent Orange, an impotent vet lover, and representations like *In Country* speaking of one generation's desires to another. She knows nothing of Nam other than the multitude of representations that signify our loss: her father's letters and his journal, Springsteen's lyrics and their accompanying video. Nothing is authentic. Even the *M\*A\*S\*H* episodes are reruns. She is the subject of distances and displacements. When Emmett finally tells her a war story—one of those ever-present horror stories authenticating the vet while it drives a wedge between him and the community—Sam can respond only by comparing it to pictures she has seen. In short, Sam Hughes is today's child suffering yesterday's trauma. She suffers a modernist nostalgia for authentic experience. She desires to know and experience the lost war, and she remains unsatisfied with her representations. Mason has bequeathed our desire for Nam to the next generation.

Vietnam remains, then, regardless of the ritual cleansings and willed suspensions of memory, regardless of the many memorials for the unknown dead and the parades for the soldiers who should have known better. While it remains, it stays a problem, or to be more precise the remains of Vietnam are problematic. What is left of the war, its fragments and its ruins, stays unrepressible and endlessly recuperable. The many mutations mark not merely the continuing effort to misrepresent what has been lost as merely missing and possibly recoverable. They also mark the failure of our modes of cultural representation. None of the transformations satisfies. The illusion, so necessary to particular production values, fails. Vietnam succeeds in challenging and foiling the ideological

apparatus' modes of production. These ruins and fragments of Vietnam—these mutable, protean images—compose a history of recu-
peration. This history signifies not only our desperate desire to win
the lost war, to conquer and possess it, to make it our own property, as Benjamin suggests, but also Vietnam's continuing liberation. Our fetishized desire to win defeats us. With each imagined
success, we only picture our loss.

At first America took her loss on the chin, recovering with the
slogan "peace with honor." As we watched the POWs emerge from
the planes in 1973, no one even noticed that America had lost her
first war. Like the POWs, the country was released, and the release
signified an end, not a loss. The country, war-weary (like the returning vets and POWs), needed to heal its wounds and forget the
trauma—or so the official and popular rhetoric ran. For the national health and welfare, Vietnam and its effects, the war and its
remains, were to be decently repressed and forgotten, buried like
the $300 aluminum coffins.[5]

At this time, and it seems peculiar now, the war's loss was
marked by its absence from the marketplace. Vietnam was gone. It
was unavailable in either of the two contending clearinghouses of
information: neither the academy nor the culture industry, neither
pedagogues nor producers, classrooms nor TV recalled Vietnam.
Whether because of a lack of commitment on the part of the culture
industry or because of a sense of "good taste" on the part of the
academy, information about Vietnam prior to 1980 was spotty.
What had been all too present, almost omnipresent, seemed to
disappear. Vietnam's apparent absence from both markets, the
sign of its end, became a simulacrum of its loss.

For years, homes all over the country had been flooded with
scenes from Vietnam.[6] TV news shows like *ABC Scope*, NBC's *Vietnam Weekly Review*, and CBS' *Vietnam Perspective* brought the war
home.[7] It rushed into living rooms. But wars in the living room are
not unusual. World War II had been a radio war,[8] and (like radio)
TV brought the war home, but (unlike radio) it did not so much
report the war or even dramatize it; rather, TV witnessed the event
actually happening. The family at home watched the front (not
altogether a negligible, geographic metaphor, since it displays our
desire to map the war even as we blocked and subdivided the
country), and witnessed the firefights. Parents had the pleasure of
seeing their children or the children of others blown away right

before the weather and just after the sports roundup (or so we who were fighting the war often imagined this grotesque evening ritual). The family had what appeared to be an intimate acquaintance with Vietnam, even though the correspondent's reportage (which would change during the course of the war) mediated it all.

But what the viewer saw on the nightly news only passed itself off as direct and objective, hence, by the logic of association, unmediated and real. The medium of television journalism, with its quality of self-effacement, created an illusion of reality (an illusion so stylized that it could be recreated for the TV film *Special Bulletin* [1983]).[9] The trick is in the photography. The photographer's *cinema verité*[10] style effaces its technology and intervention, thus translating the production of the "real," the real production, into a "capturing of reality." By means of this TV magic (which conjured up and transmitted the "real" war to the "world"), Vietnam, the war, and the country became for the American viewer a set of transparent signs, signifying at one and the same time "reality" and "Vietnam." They were interlocked, especially when TV's master authorized each evening's fare with his signature—"and that's the way it was."[11]

After 1973, Vietnam faded from the screen. The living-room war was gone. The major networks took it off the air. It was as if TV canceled the war, and then the president recalled the actors. Between 1973 and 1977, a respectful silence seemed to reign. At this time, journalists wrote a number of articles about the forgotten war. According to many, the culture industries seemed to have called a moratorium on works dealing with Vietnam, unless they dealt with the fact that it was forgotten. Vietnam, however, made a brief return on April 29, 1975 when the three networks aired *Vietnam: A War That Is Finished; Special Report: Seven Thousand, Three Hundred Eighty-Two Days in Vietnam;* and *Vietnam: Lessons Learned, Prices Paid.* They were received, however, as interesting, but unwarranted interruptions.

In 1985, the crews returned. Ted Koppel, perched on a balcony overlooking Ho Chi Minh City, attempted to interview Le Duc Tho. The TV cameras watched the troops parade down a major thoroughfare, and newscasters, those insipid heros of Vietnam, continued to exploit the Vietnamese. Between commercials, television even touted its own technological achievements, showing the viewer how they were receiving a direct and immediate image from Vietnam via the miracle of satellites, while showing those who were

119

looking how television was again selling itself as an unmediated, therefore objective, window onto the world. Not many troubled to look, least of all newsmen.

Nor did it seem to trouble newscasters, during most of the ten-year anniversary news specials, that although there seemed to be a major revision of the history of the war, the war we saw "beneath" all those omniscient "voice-overs" was the same war we had always seen. The same nameless man was summarily executed on the same nameless street in Saigon. The same nameless bodies were dragged by their heels from the Embassy, and the same nameless Marines fought in the streets of Hue. While the words of the faceless narrators declared a new understanding, it was obviously one that had little to do with how the cameras saw and defined the war. According to TV's revisions, the correspondents might have misunderstood the war, but they understood brilliantly the nature of representations. In the process, TV displayed yet another forgotten lesson, learned by Michael Herr, who like other journalists had gone to Nam to "watch": "you were as responsible for everything you saw as you were for everything you did." [12]

If the television news has attempted to rewrite its original take on Vietnam, TV has not. TV producers seem unable to come up with the right formula for fictionalizing the "Living Room War," even though *M\*A\*S\*H* kept the war on TV ten years after it was lost. Films like *A Rumour of War* (1980) and *Friendly Fire* (1979) [13] were made for TV and aired, but network shows concerning Vietnam have been scarce. In 1985, for example, CBS spent a million dollars attempting to turn Anthony Grey's *Saigon* into a miniseries before they cancelled the project, even as in the early 80s the networks toyed with projects for sitcoms. But little came of them. Nam is still an anathema.

During the war, programs like *Combat, The Rat Patrol, Garrison's Gorillas*, and *Gomer Pyle, U.S.M.C.*, plus the usual fare of World War II flicks aired nightly. Only such a rare exception as *The Final War of Ollie Winter* (1967) dared compete with the nightly news' version of the war in Vietnam, and it flopped. [14] TV, then, took a lesson from Hollywood. Instead of airing Nam directly, it pictured Vietnam by representing the veteran. For instance, in 1969 ABC aired the TV film *The Ballad of Andy Crocker*, [15] a story about a returning vet who discovers the "world" has changed. The film was unpretentious but unusual. Unlike the POW (Martin Landau) in

*Welcome Home Johnny Bristol* (1971) or the three crippled veterans in *Beg, Borrow, or Steal* (1974) who pull off the perfect heist, Andy Crocker was neither psychotic nor criminal, merely alienated and marginalized.

For a number of years that was the TV vet. Like his film counterpart, he would play a strung-out, criminal psychotic who could go off at the sound of a backfire. During the 1974 TV season, for instance, the vet was seen as a hired killer on *Colombo*, as a drug-dealing sadistic murderer on *Mannix*, as a suspected (yet innocent) murderer on *The Streets of San Francisco*, as a shakedown artist on *Cannon*, and, on *Hawaii Five-O*, "a returned hero blew up himself, his father and a narcotics lab."[16] In each instance, the vet threatens law and order with a criminality founded on his tour in Nam. Some time would elapse before veterans' groups persuaded TV to stop confusing the veteran with the war; even as the more offensive aspects were muted in the media, the character of the Vietnam vet had been drawn and determined.

Where the early 70s had depicted him—never her—as a mad threat to law and order, the late 70s turned him into an always irreverent, slightly crazed, eccentric, subject to the occasional flashback. The professional soldiers of a film like *Welcome Home, Soldier Boys* (1971), who massacred the town of Hope, New Mexico, became the *A-Team*. Now the TV vet works either as a cop, a private eye, or (in the case of *Lou Grant)* as a photographer for a large metropolitan newspaper—where, disguised as the mild-mannered "Animal," he photographs the "world." The former object of representation has become the representer. *Simon and Simon* can even turn the original crazed vet stereotype into a plot device: the "Phantom" vandalising an American theme park is not a crazed vet carrying out a psychotic vendetta against his old commanding officer—on the contrary, the phantom vet has good reasons for destroying the park. The criminal threat to law and order of the early 70s has, by the early 80s, become a vigilante hero, a true "Victor" Charlie, committed to truth and justice.

By the late 70s, TV's attitude toward Nam had waffled. The networks even considered projects for sitcoms.[17] MTM developed *The Bureau*[18] for CBS, which had been interested in an earlier such project, *Mike Freit*.[19] NBC developed *The 6:00 Follies*, and ABC tried with *Bringing it Home*, which went nowhere, and again with *Fly Away Home*, which ended as a summer movie.[20] These projects have a number of similarities. With one exception, *The 416* ("a comedy pilot about a group of misfit reserves called to active duty in Vietnam"), none dealt with troops fighting the war.[21] When it came time to find a pilot for a Vietnam sitcom, TV turned (in narcissitic fashion) to the makers of the living-room war. Most of the pilots, besides including a major black character *(Mike Freit* and *The 6:00 Follies)*, included several photojournalists *(Mike Freit* and *Fly Away Home)*, or news service reporters who were "a conduit for getting the word out." What doctors had done for Korea, journalists would do for Vietnam—display the unvarnished, liberal truth.

But the initial paradox, the ground for all of *M\*A\*S\*H*'s liberal outrage, is not present. It is one thing to be a doctor in the service of the military: saving lives and taking them are at odds. It is another thing to be a correspondent in the service of a war, where newsmen made reputations reporting that truth had become the "first casualty." For instance, the central character in the pilot *Fly Away Home*, Carl Danton (Bruce Boxleitner), a newsreel cameraman, is told: "Forget the big picture. We're into miniatures. Combat footage is a cinch for the 6 o'clock news."[22] Besides the obvious reference to TV's displacement of film (big picture by miniatures) or even the implied critique of military propaganda ("The Big Picture"), there is also a recognition that TV news produced a vision of the Vietnam War. Once TV began to represent that what was being reported in Vietnam was untrue, the stereotype of the committed war correspondent began to unravel.

But for all their failures, these shows offer an insight into TV's understanding of its relation to Vietnam and its participation in the war. In these shows, we see TV defining its own flaws, creating its own dimensions, signifying its own place in history, willing to picture itself as a technology of production, but not as a site of distribution, or an intrusion into living rooms where participants become passive viewers and eyewitnesses. *The 6:00 Follies*, for instance (a sitcom about the Armed Forces TV network in Saigon), is about television watching itself. It is TV seeing itself covering Vietnam and being covered by the war. According to the show's writers: "The characters opposed the war, but their opportunities to express that opposition on the air are limited. They're generally confined to reporting the Army point of view, even when they know the truth. They do manage to get off a word now and then but generally their conduit for getting the truth out will be a news service reporter."[23] In this case, TV pictures itself as a maligned and manipulated technology sending out a version of the war, but not to some estranged public back "in the world," fixed by TV's evil eye and turned into voyeurs, but to those "in country." The misinformed viewers become those fighting the war, already understood as uninformed: "The soldiers could actually get instant replay. They could fight in a battle and see it on the news that night" (occasionally true, but hardly the rule, a situation more relevant to antiwar demonstrators than combat troops). By 1979, TV tried to rewrite the war, its combatants, and its role. The theatre of war ironically became the living room, an inversion that David Rabe already exploited in *Sticks and Bones*. And the dirty work of war was lost in its spectacle.

If television producers floundered and quit, film producers fared somewhat better. During the war they seemed unwilling to compete with the nightly news. Unlike World War II, when the film industry could serve both itself and the country by placing a screen between the war and the viewer—a screen which veiled the war as it displayed it—Vietnam could not be readily accommodated by such a framing. Television had apparently eliminated the distance between the "world" and the war, rending the veil so necessary for the producing and screening of war films, rescinding the license for fictional recreation.[24]

Throughout the war, film companies and publishers seemed to follow TV's example, or at least its impulse toward documentary realism. A number of books, for instance, published during and just after the War bear the imprint of either a diary or a simple chronology. Their titles give the impression that they are catalogues of events recorded as they occurred : *365 Days, Vietnam Diary,* and *The War Year.* A reading proves the first impression wrong. Film producers, also appearing to compete with television's realistic version, invested in documentaries. Some, like the *Anderson Platoon* (1966), were shown on TV. Others, like the fictional *P.O.W.* (1973), used a documentary style. Still others, like *A Face of War* (1967) and *Hearts and Minds* (1975), revealed television's influence because they insisted on documenting the real war, the one seen on TV, whether it was the big picture—the history of American involvement in Vietnam—or the day-to-day grind of a Marine grunt company.

But unlike the nightly news, *A Face of War* (1967) and *Hearts and Minds* (1975) unwittingly reveal the devices of their intervention.

The anthropomorphism of their titles, for example, signal their mediation. What we see more clearly than on TV is how these directors, Jones and Davis, desired the war to look (as if the war had *looks*, or could ever be an object of sight). And it was to look like TV. For example, *Hearts and Minds*, unlike *In The Year of the Pig* (1969), or Nick MacDonald's *The Liberal War* (1972)[25] contextualizes Vietnam not only within TV's purview, but also within a sentimental understanding of American history. It finds the failures in the brightest and the best, as well as in certain cultural predilections—in our "hearts and minds," as it were. The film never suggests that the best and the brightest are hardly separable from the failures and the predilections. Men make history out of conditions they inherit, and often the conditions are as responsible for the men as the men are for the failures. Hence a simple changing of men's minds or hearts, as the film suggests, does not insure success. This absence of an historical understanding from a film wedded to the lessons of history is troubling, especially when the film ends worrying the question—will the lessons of Vietnam be recalled in the future?

The future has proved that they weren't. As an historical document, an ideological product, not simply an historical documentary, *Hearts and Minds* records some of the reasons why. Witness the film's final minutes. It ends several seconds after the credits roll over a parade, the state triumph where its forces are marshalled and its power flaunted. Children in uniform, police in uniform, Uncle Sam in red, white, and blue all go up the road. Viewers cheer. During this triumph, an incident occurs: some people on the sidelines are demonstrating. The crowd jeers. Paraders flip off the demonstrators. The cops roust the protesters by busting heads. At the film's end, after the credits, we discover that a veterans' group was protesting for jobs. We see the forces of the state win back the war by beating back the losers. Vietnam's countermemory is marginalized (oral narratives like *Nam* and *Bloods* will later recover it) as the state obscures the "voice" of those who fought in the war.

But *Hearts and Minds* is not innocent. It helped legitimize revisionary tactics. It placed the vets *after* the credits and on the *margin* of the screen and film, where few if any will hear what they say. For instance, throughout the film anyone in uniform is portrayed as vulgar, politically naive, or reactionary: ask a grunt during a firefight whether he thinks the war is right or not, then forget that he has his mind on something else; picture two service men in a whorehouse treating women as commodities and ignore the various mutinies and the two brig riots that occurred in country in 1968; [26] never bother to recall those who "found the guts to just call it all off and refuse to ever go out anymore." [27] These omissions mark the uniformed as the uninformed. At best, the soldier in *Hearts and Minds* is seen as a young, ignorant victim, barely able to think for himself, and not the victim of class and economic deprivation. Only upon release or after he had been wounded beyond repair could the vet, according to the film, let his hair down in the manner of the antiwar demonstrators and come to his right mind. But even these moments, with a glimpse of Dewey Canyon III, are all too brief. The film represents the soldier as a mindless tool of the state, as a "grunt"—someone beyond language, whom the horrors of war taught a lesson always known to others. *Hearts and Minds* retains its enlightened perspective, then, because of clichés and at the expense of those who "fought *in* the war," who "learned" the hard way what those who "fought the war" already knew. Hence the lessons learned from war end by justifying this film's perspective. And those soldiers who speak that point of view become eccentric and marginal because they are untypical.

But if *Hearts and Minds* sees Nam this way, *The Face of War* sees it another. In this film, the Marines of Mike Company are well-meaning young heros, curing the old and presiding over births only to get killed or wounded for their pains. In our time of *Rambo*, *A Face of War* stands as a needed corrective, asserting its view of war against Stallone's silly spectacle of glory. But instead of picturing the war with all its tediousness and dirty work, *A Face of War* unwittingly documents nothing less than a documentary's inability to see the war in Vietnam. At a loss to see Vietnam—or even its own inability to see it, as Godard did in *Far From Vietnam* (1967) —it can only record a group of Marines acting like the Corps would have Marines act if they were playing in a classic Hollywood war film. *A Face of War* becomes, then, a real live training film with real live dead.

Its narrative is not unlike World War II films. Each scene is part of a series of ever escalating incidents in which the Marines begin as moving targets and end by destroying the "No-name" ville. In a final scene, Amtracs arrive to evacuate the people. As they plow onto the screen, an old woman scurries out of their way; the might of our technology overtowers the tiny people. The Amtracs nearly swallow the villagers, and when they are taken away, the collective

125

might of our technology destroys their homes. The action that leads to this final conflagration is framed by "the patrol"—a metaphor drawn from World War II films. In the beginning, we see a patrol forming up; at the end we see the same patrol going out. The film closes with the credits rolling over a closeup of each Marine: his name, rank, and hometown listed on the bottom of the screen. All this is coupled with the whistled tune which supplements the credits and helps turn *A Face of War* into the typical Hollywood war film, in which the name of the actor and his character are given as he marches off the screen.

*A Face of War*, then, is hardly the documentary it pretends to be. With its final sequence (flames spewing from the barrel of a flame tank, E-1 Amtracs launching missiles with a quarter-ton of C-4 trailing behind like a kite tail), its focused camera work, and its almost seamless suturing, *A Face of War* becomes a Hollywood film singing the praises of American *techne*. The war never even intrudes on the film. Even when the war's sudden explosions mar the immaculate focus, it does not rupture the film's suturing. These outbursts are neatly folded back into the film. As they are repeated, they become a sign, a transition from peace and quiet to sudden death and maiming. The loss of Vietnam is apparent. And *A Face of War* declares itself to be merely the surface of war which, no doubt, is the only face it has.

Yet it is a surface which audiences seem to crave. Fed a steady diet of TV's illusion of realism, audiences seem unwilling to suspend their belief where Vietnam is concerned. Fictional accounts and devices seem forbidden. The conveniences of fictional representation are not tolerated. Reviewers did not tolerate John Wayne's *Green Berets* (1968) tampering with reality for the sake of production values (e.g., sun setting in the South China Sea) nor did they tolerate the poetic license of Russian roulette in *The Deer Hunter* (1978). "Capturing the reality" of Vietnam on film, as if it were always escaping, is a necessary claim of the Vietnam War film. With the loss of the war, however, the camera lost its object. Unable to recreate the proper aspects that audiences seemed to demand, filmmakers resorted to inserting old news footage. In Nam films, this tradition goes back at least to Fuller's *China Gate* (1957).

The continuing desire to see what we take for the real war, the real Vietnam, obscures any other understanding of Vietnam, as well as any other form of understanding. Our revisions are not rewritings or resightings, merely repetitions that sublate differ-ence. With every repetition of these real TV images from Vietnam, we witness a continued insistence on sublimating an unstable his-torical understanding by means of a violated ideology. Our fidelity to certain pictures and certain modes of picturing underwrite what we know as well as *how* we know. The recurring TV images stablize our understanding and fix the past with known images. They reas-sert a naive epistemology that mystifies technology's role in the production and maintenance. Seeing is still knowing. We leave the films not only assured that we still know what Vietnam was, and what it was all about, but also that our ways of knowing are still intact.

Hence Hollywood did and did not look away from the war in Vietnam. For Hollywood, Vietnam—both the country and the war —seemed to be just off-screen, at the edge and on the frontier, always about to be found. As in most other things, Hollywood helped discover it for the American public. But in the early films, Vietnam is like Morocco in *Casablanca* (1942): exotic and marginal, the end of the earth where criminals and soldiers of fortune retreat, a place without an indigenous population, culture, history, or poli-tics, never a nation, hardly a peninsula, not even a domino, merely a space on a map signifying imperialism's history and its frayed ends. Some twenty years before John Wayne landed with his Green Berets, Alan Ladd met Veronica Lake in *Saigon* (1947). But from all accounts, the film is little more than an extended version of *Terry and the Pirates*. The next year Dick Powell in *Rogues' Regiment* (1948) joined the Foreign Legion to track down a German war criminal. But even a brief battle with guerrilla forces failed to demystify either Vietnam or the enemy.[28]

Like the war, this enemy is not fully discovered until 1952, when Sam Katzman's *A Yank in Indochina* was released. We fought in this war against this enemy for the next twelve years, sometimes *as* the French—in *Jump Into Hell* (1955), sometimes *with* the French—in *China Gate* (1957), and finally alone in *Five Gates To Hell* (1959), *Brushfire* (1962), and *A Yank In Viet-Nam* (1964). As inhabitants of this hell, the enemy is duly depicted. Like the Centaurs of Dante's *Inferno* or Caliban of the Enchanted Isle, they are known by their irrepressible sexual habits. Hence the guerrilla leader, Neville Brand, in *Five Gates to Hell* lets his men rape the five nurses he has captured, even as the enemy leader in *Brushfire* rapes Easter, the wife of an American planter, just as six years later the VC in *The Green Berets* (1968) will rape and torture the young Moi girl.

These dozen years also witnessed Hollywood's initial responses to history's changes, and as it would in the future, Hollywood responded by changing its signs, not its mind. After the Vietnamese liberated themselves from the French, the Yank who had been in "Indochina" in 1952 returned to "Viet-Nam" in 1964; *The Quiet American* of 1957 became the *Ugly American* of 1962, and finally the *Brushfire* of 1961 became a full-scale Hell no longer encompassed in a small place. By 1965, after the French had *Lost Command* (1964), the Yank in Viet-Nam, Marshall Thompson, returned *To the Shores of Hell* (1966) with the Marines. Like the films that had come before (*Brushfire* and *China Gate*) and those that would follow (*The Green Berets, Apocalypse Now, Rambo*), Thompson arrived with a mission and a definite goal in mind: he sets out on a patrol to rescue his brother.

Regardless of the changes, then, Hollywood continued to imagine and still remembers our involvement in Vietnam according to a particular paradigm—the patrol with a definite mission. Hence it imagined the conflict occurring not in a particular place or landscape with a particular population, history, and politics, but in a cinematic frame with a beginning and an end. The patrol mounts up at some safe origin and proceeds through enemy territory until it reaches its goal: sometimes a rescue mission, often a surprise attack on an unsuspecting enemy. Vietnam, for Hollywood and hence for us, became something to walk through.

Samuel Fuller's *China Gate* (1957) has a patrol with a mission and an object: blow up the Commie ammunition dump at China Gate. It also has Communists with barely repressible sexual habits, an international French unit, and a small native child and his puppy seeking refuge with the military. It even has a political endorsement disguised as history lesson. *China Gate* opens with documentary footage of peasants working in rice fields. A voice-over tells us: "This motion picture is dedicated to France. More than three hundred years ago, French missionaries were sent to Indochina to teach love of God and love of fellow man. Gradually French influence took shape in the Vietnamese land. Despite many hardships, they advanced their way of living and the thriving nation became the rice bowl of Asia." Then we are told that this prosperous country is now under attack by Moscow's puppet, Ho

Chi Minh. The rest of the film follows the politics of this opening lesson. Vietnam, like Korea, is a state under siege, where professional soldiers like the Americans Brock (Gene Barry) and Goldie (Nat "King" Cole) go to continue their fight against communism.

*China Gate* also has a woman. Lia, or "Lucky Legs" (Angie Dickinson) as the French call her, is a half-caste hustler with a child, son of the American Brock. Both she and the boy are caught in the struggle. She wants the boy to go to America, because she doesn't want him "killed, carrying a gun at fifteen, or becoming a Communist." In order to assure his safe passage, she agrees to lead a patrol of French Legionaires to China Gate, the hidden ammunition dump. Part Asian, part Occidental, Lucky Legs can "pass," and she does so easily, moving through the two worlds of French occupied towns and Communist fortresses. On the one hand, she is Lia, wife and mother, on the other she is "Lucky Legs," object of desire, signified by particular parts of her body. She is not the dependent she ought to be. Too often she is pictured as resourceful, independent, and intelligent, walking point and leading the patrol. As her American husband Brock had discovered, she looked one way but turned out to be another. Lucky Legs is dangerous. Like the young Vietnamese girl in *Go Tell The Spartans* (1978), she is the monstrous unknown other whose looks tell us nothing more than looks deceive.

Not a complimentary picture of Vietnamese women. "Lucky Legs" is a half-caste whore, with intelligence and a willed independence, but considering the history of women in Vietnam films, Lia is unusual, since she anticipates not our continued misunderstanding of the Vietnamese but the signs of our misunderstanding.[29] On the one hand, she is both the object and the subject of sight; on the other, she is the site of its ambivalence. Lucky Legs undermines epistemology's tropes of sight. Through her we learn not to trust what we see while we learn to look at the seen and our ways of seeing.

She teaches us, then, how to read the film, for what we see is not what we get. In one scene, the patrol must pass a Moi village, friendly to the Communists. Lucky Legs will lead them through. She enters the ville while the patrol waits. In their last ambush the Moi have captured a phonograph along with a record of *La Marseillaise*. She asks the Moi chief if he knows what he is playing; he says he doesn't, but that it makes him feel good. He asks, "What is it?" "The song of the people," she replies. While the patrol passes in the night Lucky Legs, standing on a platform beneath pictures of Mao,

129

Stalin, and Ho, leads the villagers in the song of the people. The pictured three would no doubt be pleased with the ambiguity.

Almost ten years later, John Wayne, with the same politics yet with less assurance and ambiguity, will tell almost the same story in *The Green Berets*. One of the two episodes in the film uses a woman as lure and a VC General as the object of the hunt. The story, an odd coda, is tagged onto an already two-hour long "western." Its authority is, no doubt, Robin Moore's book. Still, it bears a remarkable resemblance to *China Gate*. But the Lin (Irene Tsu) in *The Green Berets* is hardly Fuller's Lia. In short, Lin fufills the role of all the women in *The Green Berets*, as well as in most Vietnam narratives. She is an object of desire, one of the South's "top models" (unlike her counterpart in Moore's book, who is a schoolteacher), and a potental victim. Like his World War I Creel Committee predecessors (e.g., D. W. Griffith *Hearts of the World* [1917]), Wayne gives women a strict role in war. Either the allies protect them or the enemy rapes them. In either case, they signify not only the enemy's unnatural desires and natural inferiority, but also that war is always man's work.

*The Green Berets'* failures are legendary. Renata Adler of the *New York Times* saw it as a "pivotal event" representing "the end of the traditional war picture and a tremendous breakdown of the fantasy-making apparatus in this country."[30] She was wrong. It did not take the glamour out of war, only the romance out of war films. There was no suspension of disbelief. It was, as Herr says, "a film about Santa Monica" or as Joker, Hasford's protagonist in *The Short-Timers*, puts it when he sees the film in DaNang on Freedom Hill, "it is a soap opera about the love of guns." In short, like Hasford's Marines, we saw *The Green Berets* as a movie:

> The audience of Marines roars with laughter. This is the funniest movie we have seen in a long time. . . . At the end of the movie John Wayne walks off into the sunset with a spunky little orphan. The grunts laugh and threaten to pee all over themselves. The sun is setting in the South China Sea—in the East—which makes the end of the movie as accurate as the rest of it.[31]

For, like its sign—the green beret, which the Vietnamese always associated with the French, the film flaunts the marks of its own breakdown. Hence its ultimate success. What in essence failed was the viewer, not the ideological apparatus, for the film itself calls attention to the means of its making.

*The Green Berets* is nothing if not a lecture on the failings of representations and the necessity of "seeing for oneself." From the opening scene at Fort Bragg, when the squad marches on to instruct the audience on the "capabilities of the Green Beret," to the briefing scene that follows, the film insists upon the primacy of sight and authority of experience. Colonel Kirby (John Wayne) tells Beckworth (David Janssen) on at least two occasions that one cannot really understand Vietnam or know the war until one sees it. What the film represents and teaches—for after all it is only a long lecture—is that the war can be seen (although what can be seen is left off the screen) and we can know nothing until we see it for ourselves. Seeing is knowing. What *The Green Berets* claims to tell us, then, is that representations are fraudulent, even as it requires us to look at it *as* a representation. The film sacrifices its own validity for its belief in the primacy of experience, and ends by representing the "failure of the fantasy-making apparatus."

With the failure (or success) of *The Green Berets*, the search for knowledge supplants the earlier films' assured sense of a mission. The earlier films had a direct goal in mind. They knew where they were headed, and what they wanted. The later films do not even know where they are, much less why they are there. After Wayne's folly, the films become epistemological dramas. Each attempts to find a means for knowing and understanding the War. *The Boys In Company C* (1978), *Go Tell The Spartans* (1978), and *Apocalypse Now* (1979) all turn, each in its own way, on the notion of war as an arena of maturation and education, a place where boys become men, and a realm where lessons are learned, surely in contradiction with the first lesson learned in war: that many boys never mature into anything other than dead souls. From the imperative of Ted Post's title *(Go Tell the Spartans)* to the voice-over monologue that begins *The Boys of Company C*, the films seem determined to inform and instruct the audience. But all they tell us, all they can teach is that the tropes of epistemology fail. Seeing is not knowing. The inexplicable grunt tic, "there it is," sums up all that is seen and known. Like the enemy, the War in Vietnam dissipates as an object of sight. It is lost to the eye, even as our films assert the authority of the eyewitness. Even in *Apocalypse Now*, where the War becomes spectacle and the warrior both voyeur and voyager (hence a metonymy for the camera), there is nothing in sight but the end. In grand operatic terms complete with the appropriate apocalyptic tone, we witness the twilight of the idols of sight.

131

Ted Post's *Go Tell the Spartans* (1978) less pretentiously does the same thing. Nothing in this film remains unquestioned, unexamined, or unknown. Everyone asks questions; everyone receives answers. Before the film is over, we know why aging Major Marker (Burt Lancaster) is still a Major, although his old aide is now a General. We find out why the draftee Courcey (Craig Wesson) has, in 1964, volunteered for a tour in Vietnam: like Philip Caputo's protagonist in *A Rumour of War,* he just wanted to know "what a war was like." We even find out where we are.

> Barker asks his Adjunct, "Where are we?"
> The Adjunct answers, "Penang, Vietnam."
> "You sure it's not a loony bin," Barker replies. "Sometimes I think we're in a goddam loony bin."

Nothing remains unknown, except the nature of the enemy and the Vietnamese people. We see them—often. They charge the garrison at Muc Wa in the full light of flares. Courcey even spots a VC scout, who becomes nothing less than his own "secret sharer."[32] We even see the friendly Vietnamese, and we learn that the young female refugee's longing looks are hardly loving. As the interpreter, Cowboy (Evan Kim), tells us "she is VC." But in fact, according to the film, we do not know them at all, even though "the VC know everything we're going to do." According to the Company medic, the Vietnamese don't know why they are fighting. There is no reason why one should fight and die for the south or one should fight and die for the north. They are interchangeable because neither side cares nor knows why they are fighting. This piece of wisdom becomes the film's central lacuna: we know everything including the fact that the enemy knows everything about us but nothing about politics. Hardly the facts, but an extremely telling characterization of ourselves and our understanding. Unlike the Australian film on Vietnam, *The Odd Angry Shot* (1979), Post's film suggests that our cinematic imaginations are incapable of dealing with the politics of the war. In these films, the troops are, at best, tourists, while the VC remain an invisible enemy. They only become visible and political for the American public when our government controls the ideological apparatus as in *Know Your Enemy —The Viet Cong.*[33]

Thus we often leave the films of the war in Vietnam as Willard (Martin Sheen) leaves the besieged bridge in *Apocalyse Now,* refusing to hear or understand. As Willard moves through the trenches, he keeps asking if anyone knows who is in charge. No one answers. But at the end, immediately after Roach, the Black grenadier, knocks out the noisy but unseen VC, Willard asks, "Do you know who is in charge?" "Yes," Roach answers, and sits down.

The answers have always been lucid, but never clear.

At the end of *Go Tell the Spartans,* Courcey looks at the wounded VC, his secret sharer, in the treeline and says "I'm going home, Charlie." He turns his back on his other and drags his wounded leg off the screen. After the defeat of *The Green Berets,* like Courcey, Hollywood returned home. Filmmakers moved the war and relocated it in a more tractable environment. Since the documentary as simulacrum, the usual mode for producing the war, was restrictive at best, the ever-resourceful image-makers found another means of (re)presenting the war to the Americans. As the war continued to escalate, Hollywood discovered the returning vet, and this synecdoche became the major means of reproducing the war. The Vietnam vet came to stand in for the prejudices and contradictions that the home folks had about the war, for after all, the essential quality of the veteran is that he has internalized the war and with a stiff upper lip carries it around with him. Thus Hollywood could take the notion of the returning vet and fill it with the country's sense of Vietnam. In this way it freed itself from making pictures about the war that only reproduced what TV had already shown while it maintained the essential characteristic of both the war film and TV journalism—the eyewitness.

By displacing the war and locating it in the veteran, however, these films eventually took a peculiar turn. For unlike such films as *The Best Years of Our Lives* (1946) or *Till the End of Time* (1946), which imply that violence is merely part of the returning vet's readjustment period, films about returning vets made in the late 60s and early 70s share a dominant structural feature: "In each case, the [vet] is a catalyst for violence if not violent himself."[34] Although films like *I'll Be Seeing You* (1944) and John Huston's suppressed *Let There Be Light* (1945), or Abraham Polonsky's radio play "The Case of David Smith" (1945) (written for *Reunion U.S.A.*), suggest that psychoneurosis was a problem, it is not the World War II vet who is remembered as suffering.[35] (Hollywood would wait until 1985 before making a film about a World War II vet suffering from flashbacks in *Desert Bloom*.) It is the vet from Vietnam whom Hollywood represents essentially as a maladjusted socio-path.

Such film titles as *The Born Losers* (1967), *Angels From Hell* (1968), *Satan's Sadists* (1969), *The Losers* (1970), *Clay Pidgeon* (1972), and *The Stone Killer* (1973) not only convey the country's ambiva-lent attitude toward Vietnam, they also show what others thought of the "Vietnam vet." In the beginning, the vet is associated with outlaw bikers. The position these gangs hold within popular cul-ture explains the relation. Since *The Wild One* (1954), they have come to signify a marginal and irreconcilable counterculture, whose members work within the dominant culture but are hardly part of it. Hence the gang films signify and sublate class differences for sociopathic behavior. In early films like *The Angry Breed* (1968) or *Chrome and Hot Leather* (1971), when the vet opposes the gang, or in *Angels from Hell* (1968) when he rides with them, the vet is merely being placed in a marginal world where he "fights with the gang," as it were. For instance, *The Born Losers* (1967) presents Tom Laughlin as Billy Jack (soon to become a 60s folk hero), a Native American Green Beret veteran who single-handedly takes on and defeats a gang of motorcylists who—*à la The Wild One*—have terrorized a California town and, like their VC counterparts, raped four women. The vet's marginal status is confirmed as he reflects the values of this *other*. Neither for nor against, he is marked as a classless threat to the dominant values. By 1970, *The Losers* erases the illusion of difference. Biker and combat vet are one: "A motorcycle gang [is] recruited to rescue a presidential advisor held prisoner by the Vietcong. The five bikers succeed, but all die vio-lently and in gory slow motion in the process."[36]

By 1972, the veteran is no longer simply marginal; he moves into mainstream culture, where he has become, at best, a passive decoy and target (as in *Clay Pidgeon*) or a professionally trained killer for hire (as in *The Stone Killer*, where a psychologist tells us, after Lipper, one of the killers, is caught: "Vietnam doesn't make heroes—it makes a generation of Lippers").

By now the massacre at My Lai had infected the image. A film like Elia Kazan's *The Visitors* (1972) carries its mark: two vets, Tony Rodriquez (Chic Martinez) and Mike Nickerson (Steve Rails-back), visit Bill Schmidt (James Woods), a former friend and a veteran. The two vets appear to threaten Bill and Martha Wayne (Patricia Joyce), the unwed mother of his baby, because Bill had presented evidence of war crimes against them. While in country, the two had raped a Vietnamese woman. These two visitors enter the white house of Harry Wayne (Patrick McVey), noted writer of westerns, father of an unwed mother, and supposed World War II vet (we never know for sure, since at one time he talks about being in Europe and at another he talks about being in the Pacific). Before the day is over, the two vets have helped Wayne kill a neighbor's dog, beaten the informer, and with a deliberate casualness raped the young woman. Then they drive away.

Kazan called the film a "home movie." No other label could be more exact. It not only describes the style and the economics of this independent production; it also fixes the source of its values. Not since Peckinpah's *Straw Dogs* (1971) has the home and what it signifies been so threatened or so casually wasted. The film establishes its source of values with the opening shot, a picture of a large white house in the snow, and with stunning clarity, Kazan portrays the fears of the viewers. The vet is pictured as an ominous threat to the living room (sign of the home and place of the family). Like their VC counterparts and those other outlaws, the bikers, the vets are rapists, the irrepressibly uncivilized who violently intrude on our peace and quiet. They have returned, crossed over the threshold, and violated the sanctuary of the American dream.

In *Welcome Home, Soldier Boys* (1971) four discharged Green Berets, Danny (Joe Don Baker), Shooter (Paul Koslo), Kid (Alan Vint), and Fatback (Elliot Street), come back to the "world," only to find they don't fit—anywhere. After they buy a second-hand Cadillac and set off for the California Dream, they discover that, although a Cadillac is large enough for the four to live and love in, a white house (Danny's home) is far too small to hold one returning son, much less him and his three partners. Even Texas is too small. When the Cadillac throws a rod, they are confronted with not only the customary dishonest mechanic but a possible barroom brawl with some World War II vets, who insist that these veterans were not fighting a war, "just killing civilians." Finally out of money and gas the four erupt into violence. Working as a whole unit with an inexplicable language of their own, they destroy the town of Hope, New Mexico and massacre its eighty-one citzens with a professional élan that underscores their alienation as it highlights their camaraderie. Their potential for violence grows with their awareness of their alienation, usually the mark in war films of education. In a final shot that obviously alludes to the Kent State

135

massacres, the vets confront the National Guard, gas-masked, weapons at the ready. The four veterans from Vietnam die in black-and-white slow motion, killed on the street of a Western town. John Wayne's and John Ford's Western vision of Nam has come home.

The vet, by 1972, has become the V(i)et Cong. No longer just an ominous threat and rapist, his potential for destruction and mayhem is fully realized. Vietnam's veterans have become indistinguishable from the outlaw bikers of *The Born Losers*. But what the vet has become is hardly of his own making. In *Welcome Home, Soldier Boys*, one "waitress" tells Danny (Joe Don Baker): "You are what you do." This film elaborates, like others, on the spectator's view. For the viewer, the vet *has* become what he has done. (The ambiguity of the pronoun is in order but often goes unnoticed.) According to the viewer, their tour has drawn a line between them and their culture. The Vietnam veteran has become a transient loser, a marginal, who has toured Hell and returned, not wiser or maturer but as a threat to the American dream. Always a killer, the vet is seen as one who is infected spiritually and mentally—never politically—by the senseless genocide in Vietnam, the continuing murder of women and children. In a war of containment, he has failed and is contaminated. He is now part of the problem, a carrier who must be sterilized:

> The stewardess comes through the [airplane] cabin, spraying a mist of invisible sterility into the pressurized, scrubbed, filtered, temperature-controlled air, killing the mosquitoes and unknown diseases, protecting herself and America from Asian evils, cleansing us all forever.[37]

In order to perform this ritual cleansing, Hollywood has had to sublate another vision of the veteran, which an alternative film practice such as California Newsreel has documented. In Newsreel's unfinished *Winter Soldier* (1971) or their completed *DC III* (1971) the veteran is not pictured as the psychotic killer of the country's extravagant imagination, but as organised and politically astute. The former documents the winter soldier investigations in Detroit in which combat vets addressed the issue of war crimes and atrocities; the latter documents the VVAW's 1971 march on Washington, "Dewey Canyon III," where they go so far as to advocate the violent overthrow of the government. "We don't want to fight anymore," says one nameless vet, "but if we do it'll be to take these steps."[38] Both films show vets taking up a politics and directing it, along with their medals, at the nation's Capitol. Not until *The War at Home* (1979) would this suppressed image of the politicized veteran be seen again. In 1980, Hollywood attempted to recuperate this image, but *The Line* (1980), a fictionalized version of the Presdio Mutiny, is seldom seen. By the mid 1980s Hollywood adds a political twist to the ominous threat of the veteran's violence when the heroes of *First Blood, Missing in Action*, and *Rambo* take on not only the Vietnamese but also the American politicians.

Between 1972 and 1978 veterans and Vietnam, it seemed, disappeared from the screen. They made only cameo appearances, as it were (e.g., *American Graffiti* [1973]). In 1978, veterans reappeared, but noticably changed. As Hollywood had reacted to changes in history, it now responded to veteran politics; it changed its signs, not its mind. The vets in *Heroes* (1977), *Who'll Stop The Rain* (1978), and *Coming Home* (1978) bear a likeness to their former incarnations. In *Heroes*, for instance, the motifs of films like *Welcome Home Johnny Bristol* (1972) reemerge, but now the veteran, Jack Dunne (Henry Winkler), is a comic madman, suffering from the hallucinatory effects of Post Traumatic Stress Syndrome. Although he is primarily a comic figure, and to all intents, harmless, there is the obligatory violent confrontation between the vet and the biker. The veteran is still an undecidable figure, capable of disrupting any setting, but seen now through comedy, this potential for excess is diffused. In *Who'll Stop the Rain*, the character of the veteran is split, a technique repeated in other films, like *Cutter's Way* (1979) and *Birdy* (1984). On the one hand, there is Jonathan Converse (Michael Moriarty)—"the asshole"—the sensitive vet and correspondent who has sent home a load of heroin, enough to hook his wife, Madge (Tuesday Weld), anyway; on the other hand, there is Ray (Nick Nolte), the student of Nietzsche, the *Ubermensch:* violent, unpredictable, heroic, and a threat to the order of culture. The latter dies, and the former lives on with the junkie who was once his wife, but now is the sign of his guilt and the burden he must bear. In short, by the late 1970s there are two kinds of veterans: killers and moral killers (as an academic once told me).

In *Coming Home* (1978), the diverse strands of the earlier clichés converge, for this film owes more to the media's production of images and to the history of Vietnam films than it does to the Vietnam War. Hardly the "achingly accurate representation of Vietnam" that Peter Arnett, Michael Arlen,[39] and others would claim, *Coming Home* not only represents the plight of the disabled veteran, as the earlier film *The Men* (1950) did, it also (re)presents the already produced version of Vietnam and its veterans. Just as in *Who'll Stop the Rain*, there are two types of veterans here: the hero Bob Hyde (Bruce Dern), violent and irrepressible, and the wounded, castrated victim, Luke (Jon Voight). Both are potential agents of unrestrained violence who must be arrested, retrained, and removed. *Coming Home* does all three: it represses the potential for violence by re(s)training the wounded vet and drowning the other. Thanks to the insight of a woman, Sally Hyde (Jane Fonda) ("What makes you such a bastard?"), Luke, like most other images of wounded vets, comes to terms with his disability and guilt, while Bruce Dern (who in an earlier version of the screenplay was to have taken his rifle to a nearby hill to snipe at passersby) is put to rest because, no doubt, he refuses Sally's healing Aid.[40] Just as Dern takes off his uniform (the sign of his profession) in order to free himself, Voight confesses before a group of students, professing publicly that he has killed for his country. One veteran confesses; the other drowns. Like the Germans at the end of World War I, Americans have turned "defeat into inner victory by means of confessions of guilt which [are] hysterically elevated to the universally human."[41]

*The Deer Hunter* (1978) was released during the same year as *Coming Home*, and they came up for an Academy Award together. There was an immediate controversy. In his syndicated column, Peter Arnett compared the two, calling the latter "an honest attempt to come to terms with the war in Vietnam," while he called the *Deer Hunter* "Fascist trash," another fraudulent Hollywood view of Vietnam that he feared the public was "interpreting as a deep historical truth."[42] The point of the controversy was clear: one of the two competing films was to be understood as the "proper" view of Vietnam, because it was approved by Vietnam's foremost war correspondent; the other was to be disregarded on account of its apparent politics and propaganda. Like John Wayne, Arnett condemned one point of view and sanctified the other based upon what he had seen "in country." Hence *The Deer Hunter* was dishonest, because neither Vietnam nor the Vietnamese "looked" that way, at least to a liberal reporter.

But what Arnett failed to comment on in his defense of the Vietnamese was that this film was less about Vietnam and more about the American community that fought the war. *The Deer Hunter* was a new twist in the history of Vietnam films. No one prior to

Cimino had bothered to look at the community that fought the war, just as no one had troubled to look at the effects the war had on that community. Admittedly, Cimino's is a vulgar vision, neither idyllic nor middle-class, and founded on a particular reading of American working-class literature. It begins, for instance, like Upton Sinclair's *The Jungle*, with a wedding and a reception. Like Sinclair's butchers or Dalhberg's bottomdogs, Cimino's steelworkers are brutal, often racist, always sexist, and rooted in the myths of America and its past. Like Tressall's ragged philanthropists, who suffer because they cannot see that they are starving because they are giving away their livelihood, Cimino's workers unwittingly bear the contradictions of their class rather than filfilling its potential. They are hardly class-conscious. They come from a particular community fraught with contradictions, at a particular time with a peculiar history, where the desired "unpalatable data relating to the subjective consciousness of the characters and the objective lines of force acting on and within the community [which] would insist on expression" can only be expressed by the viewer, not the viewed.[43] Such an expression from such a community is purely a utopian hope and a middle-class aspiration, hardly congruent with our dedication to a "naturalistic" cinema practice.

In *The Deer Hunter*, the vet is portrayed neither as a psychotic killer nor some secret sharer doubling for someone else's vision of the VC nor some moral killer who needs to confess his crimes. He is not a marginal or a homeless transient, alienated because of some secret initiation rite called "combat" that separates him from others because of a higher plane of knowledge. Mike (Robert DiNiro), Steve (John Savage), and Nick (Chistopher Walken) are members of a community, second-generation Ukrainian steelworkers whose homes and histories mitigate against any form of choice. As the children of Ukrainian immigrants, they are almost destined to fight against communism. They suffer, like the Vietnamese, the effects of the war. Their community is shattered. The film ends with a funeral, where the last suvivor Mike sees his reflection on Nick's coffin (just as other vets would see themselves reflected off black marble), and with a wake, that apocalyptic moment, when the ruined community nostalgically attempts to regain its former intimacy, but must waken to its present conditions and possible futures.

Nothing reigns for them now but alienation. Their day of mourning ends with "God Bless America," a song that many read as just another attempt to recuperate the patriotic myths that led us into the war. Yet it should be understood within its cinematic context: it is not an attempt to reiterate the shoddy values of a hollow patriotism. What we see is a community shattered by Vietnam, trying to express a deeply rooted nationalism, with all its ironies and contradictions, founded on such events as the Homestead Riots. These people, then, are not merely the inheritors of simple freedoms, but the constructors of a history that has both made and unmade them. Like some Vietnamese, they are the ignorant and innocent victims of a war being waged against exploited peoples by exploited people. No doubt this is not the same "honest" and attractive view of the Vietnam War that *Coming Home* was, but it is nonetheless valid.

In *Rolling Thunder* (1977), the POW Charlie Rane (William Devine) comes home. He returns to the states a hero, complete with groupie, and receives his reward: one thousand silver dollars. A gang of thieves looking for the money feeds the obstinate Charlie's hand to the garbage disposal and kills his wife and son. When Charlie recovers, he sets out with his groupie to hunt down the killers. He finds them in a whorehouse south of the border. With another POW, he infiltrates the house and wreaks havoc on house, gang, and hookers. In *First Blood* (1983), John Rambo (Sylvester Stallone), long out of the service, returns to a small town after its sheriff has escorted him out. The sheriff arrests him for vagrancy, and the deputies brutalize him. As Charlie Rane did before him, Rambo flashes back to his wartime experience as a tortured POW. Crazed, he jumps jail and heads for the woods, where he wreaks havoc on the posse. By the end of the film, Rambo has destroyed most of the downtown real estate and returned to the waiting arms of his one-time commander, who just happens to betray him at least twice before the film ends.

By 1984, then, Charlie is no longer the enemy, or just a perfume or even a tuna; like the character in the film *Charly* (1968), he has suffered a sea change. He is now the veteran gone from bone-dumb grunt to super-guerrilla. The Vietnam veteran of the 80s, unlike his earlier incarnations, is a retired, barely re(s)trained, mostly misunderstood, asexual, Green Beret hero occasionally called Charlie. No longer the enemy of *Welcome Home, Soldier Boys* or the ominous rapists of *The Visitors*, the vet has come home and is now recognised for what he is: the long-suffering hero apotheosized into Victor Charlie, complete with politics. The secret sharer of films like *Apocalyse Now* and *Go Tell the Spartans* has emerged, not as an *other* but as an emanation of the combat vet. In good shaman fashion, we have stolen, if not the magic of our enemy, at least his signs.

Take John Rambo. *In First Blood,* after his escape from jail, he runs off to the forest, Indian country, where, almost always unseen, he leads the posse on a merry chase. In the sequel, *Rambo* (1985) he is again sprung from jail and returned to Nam with his bow and arrows. The Indian (like Billy Jack, Rambo is both a Green Beret and part Native American) is returned to "Indian country," the legendary bad bush where Charlie, in all his invisibility once ran free, and where he again, disguised as John Rambo, will rain havoc, only this time on Soviet troops. We will know him by these signs: first, sweat ("no sweat" is the sign of a bygone era). Today the "good guys" sweat, but back in 1957 when Fuller sent Lucky Legs and her patrol upriver, the only people who looked at all as if they were sweating were the crude Commies. Rambo, however, sweats throughout the film. Second, camouflage: as all the major texts admit, Charlie was invisible, couldn't be seen, turned the ground against us. "Forget the Cong, the *trees* would kill you, the elephant grass grew up homicidal, the ground you were walking over possessed malignant intelligence your whole environment was a bath."[44] Who can forget our American poet, Rambo, in the American forest or rising up out of the Vietnamese mud or coming out of the bark of a tree, and not marvel at how literal he has become?

In these recent twists on Vietnam, we imagine the vet as fully (re)covered, re(s)trained, and returned to his rightful place, where he will continue to run through the jungle looking for what America lost. He will continue to fight until he gets it right. The vet of the Vietnam War, now almost ageless, yet well-developed, returns to Nam to retrieve his lost buddies and our lost honor and return them to the United States. What we see in films like *Missing In Action, Rambo,* and *Uncommon Valor* (as well as *Red Dawn* [1983], another Vietnam variation in which only well-schooled American high-school football players are the VC), is not merely the same old marginal vet unable to make it in America, he is exiled and returned to Nam where he is "really" himself. These films dramatize the mechanisms of our cultural repression. What is presented is our cultural obsession with "returning."

In the late 60s we silenced Vietnam, in the 70s we defended ourselves from it, in the mid 80s we return to it (or it returns to us).

141

*Rick Berg*

Like the character in *Cease Fire* (1985), the country is suffering a collective flashback. In films like *Rambo* and *Streamers* (1984), we again prepare for it, (and if Paul Mazursky fulfills his option on *Joyride*, we will, in the future, return to Nam from the West on bicycles). In others, like *The Killing Fields* (1984) and *Search And Destroy*, our past, in the form of Southeast Asians, hunts us up.

By 1984, Hollywood had resurrected the veteran, Vietnam, and the war. Like other systems of representation, it has traced its own process of recovery. *The Stuntman* (1982), one of those Hollywood products compromising Brechtian self-consciousness, represents how the Dream Factory recovered both the war and the veteran. In short, we see a film not merely about filmmaking, but one that displays the fantasy-making apparatus. Vietnam will be revised, hence lost and won, because it will be remade, *The Stuntman* says, in the image of an older war. From the beginning, when Cameron (Steve Riseback—the actor who played the brooding rapist in the *Visitors*) escapes from the cops, until Cameron confesses his crime to his lover in terms of the usual cinematic clichés, we see the already established image of the Viet vet. But this film is a variation, for the vet finds himself in a movie, one about World War I. To hide from the police, he becomes a blond stuntman, someone who not only does other people's dirty work but someone who as another's double is invisible while he is translated into a body of work. The irreality of film will capture the alienated vet and his war, translating him and it into something else, something hardly recognizable, hardly himself, merely a "blond" shadow warrior, standing in not only for an actor but also the image of a warrior. No longer alienated, he will come to stand in for our culture's desires and foibles.

An entire history and counter-memory, however, is lost in such a translation. In 1966 the Puerto Rican artist, Jaime Carrero wrote the play, *Flag Inside*.[45] It is about a Puerto Rican family and the death of a son in Vietnam. In the beginning, the family receives word that the casket will be returned. They prepare a space at home. Around this space marking the family's loss, the drama takes place. For me, this play seems paradigmatic of the discourse I have tried to map, as well as the problems that the discourse as a whole presents. Formally, for example, the play fuels any number of interests, everything from the Heideggerian's notion of the metaphysical presence of absence to deconstructionist's recognition that the breathing in and out of presence and absence is less important than

142

the play it seems to generate, the permutations and changes that take place as the discourse attempts to mute the unavoidable lacuna. But finally the drama's absence from Nam discourse is itself significant, because it represents what has been lost. With rare exceptions, Vietnam has not been presented as an aspect of working-class life. It is seldom seen as an experiential and historical fact of many working-class and ethnic families. Hardly an innocent oversight. The working class gave the most soldiers to the war.

This is not to say that there are no alternative discourses. Far from it. Alternative videos like Dan Reeves' *Smothering Dreams* (1981), and independent film productions, like Michael Uno's *The Silence* (1983),[46] Haile Gerima's *Ashes and Embers* (1982),[47] and Haskell Wexler's *Latino* (1985) have attempted in a variety of ways to picture this counter-memory. Unlike recent Hollywood productions that turn the vet into a sign of our repression and its constant return, these films have inserted Vietnam into an historical continuum. The vet is returned not merely to the history of historians, but to a class history spoken by the oppressed, a counter-memory lost to the dominant discourse.

For instance, *Ashes and Embers* and *Latino* turn on the recognition engendered yet hardly voiced in *The Deer Hunter:* the oppressed have been killing those who were helping to fight against oppression. In each film a character must deal with the fact that he has been used to further imperialism. In *Ashes and Embers*, the black veteran (John Anderson) must, as all black veterans from all American wars, deal with the fact that "the man" has exploited him, and like other Nam vets he suffers from a psychological trauma. Unlike his Hollywood contemporaries, the director has understood that the traumas are as much a product of the state of society, and the vets' place in it, as they are of the war. Hence, while *Ashes and Embers* is an uncompromising psychological drama, it is construed according to a political and historical imagination. The film records not merely the vet's alienation, but his place in history and his return to it. For it is not about a lone, troubled psyche, but about history and its varieties: personal history, cultural history, and ethnic history are the subjects of the film. In a series of dialectical encounters signifying the vet's troubled psyche and unstable relationship to society, it narrates the means of a healthy return.

The major moment in the film occurs when once again the alienated vet feels compelled to tell one more horror story. As usual, when the vet tells the tale, he finds that he has only deepened his

143

alienation. As he authenticates his grief and rage, he also drives a wedge between himself and others. As long as the war is understood as a combat zone where unique events occur, no genuine return for the vet can be achieved. The vet was born elsewhere, as it were, outside history, beyond the world and its culture. Or so the stories say. But in this film, Gerima subverts this understanding. When the vet is through screaming his tale at his lover, Liza Jane (Kathy Flewellen), her young son Kimathi (Uwezo Flewellen) enters the scene and says: "My father was killed in Vietnam." Hardly earthshaking, but the timing is immaculate; it dissipates the tension between speaker and hearer, between the black veteran and his lover, between the viewer and the film, because it suggests that Vietnam is suffered by an entire working class. It is not a singular event in a few select persons' lives; its consequences range throughout a community. With that recognition, he can begin to overcome his alienation.

*Latino*, while not about Vietnam, addresses the same question as *Ashes and Embers*. In this film Captain Eddie Guerrero (Robert Beltran), a Green Beret who fought in Vietnam, has stayed on in the military. As a career soldier he finds he is now part of a Spanish-speaking contingent of American soldiers sent to Honduras to train and work with the Contras. He finds himself leading raids into Nicaragua. Guerrero discovers that he has to come to terms with the fact that the people he is killing look like his own family. The crisis occurs when he confronts his complicity with oppression. Like others, Guerrero must quit or repress his growing recognition that he is fighting for "the man." We witness the moment of repression: when Guerrero expresses his doubts and growing awareness to his partner, Ruben (Tony Plana), he is answered with "Forget that shit," and this refrain is picked up and chanted by the other G.I.'s in the bar. The noise literally drives out his new-found awareness and figuratively drives him back to Nicaragua, where he is captured, humiliated, and led off in disgrace.

Trudeau has written recently, "This just in from Hollywood; we won in Vietnam." But our desire to forget and to win through representation continues to defeat us. *Rambo* and his ilk, with their emphasis on winning, signify nothing more than: "America lost and forgot." They would never have been made without that awareness, and as they attempt to forget and recuperate our loss, they revise our tactics, our politics, and our history. In the process, we lose the element of the war that *Latino* and *Ashes and Embers* displays. What is lost and forgotten with each imagined win are those who fought and suffered. It is all well and good to desire to turn Vietnam vets into heros but not at the expense of their children and their history. As Brecht's *Mother Courage* reminds us, war-profiteering has a long, honorable, and expensive history. I wonder if Stallone and his fellow revisionists are willing to pay the price.

## NOTES

1. This seems as good a place as any to thank the Occidental College students that participated in the two courses that I have taught on Representations of Vietnam. Both the seminar and the "English 30" class helped bring this paper to fruition.

2. See Robert Hilburn, "Pop Breaks Vietnam Silence," *Los Angeles Times*, October 3, 1982, *Calendar*, p. 1. But these, of course, are only the most recent additions to the list of songs about Vietnam. If we return to the 60s, there are the antiwar songs (e.g., Phil Och's "Talking Vietnam," the Fugs, "Kill For Peace," and Country Joe and the Fish, "Fish Chant").

3. "Dancing to the Vietnam Beat," *Newsweek*, May 27, 1985.

4. Bobbie Ann Mason, *In Country* (New York: Harper & Row, 1985).

5. For a sense of this rhetoric, see the various articles in *Time* (e.g., "The Anatomy of a Debacle," *Time*, May 12, 1975; "How Americans Should Feel," *Time*, April 14, 1975; or "Fed Up and Turned Off," *Time*, April 14, 1975.

6. Michael J. Arlen, *The Living Room War* (New York: Penguin Books, 1982), and *The View From Highway 1: Essays on Television* (New York: Farrar, Straus & Giroux, 1976).

7. Charles Montgomery Hammond, Jr., *The Image Decade: Television Documentary: 1965–1975*, (New York: Hasting House: 1981), *passim*.

8. J. Fred McDonald, *Don't Touch That Dial: Radio Programming in American Life, 1920–1960* (Chicago: Nelson-Hall, 1979).

9. See Steve Bognar, "The Omnipresent Eye: Television News and *Special Bulletin*," *Filament*, 4:28–46. Also see J. G. Ballard, "Theatre of War," in *Myths of the Near Future* (London: Jonathan Cape, 1982), pp. 118–40.

10. I should make it clear that what I am calling the *cinema verité* style is a combination of direct cinema and *cinema verité*. Direct cinema is that of the observer-documentarist; it is a form of documentary. The "direct cinema documentarist took his camera to a situation of tension . . . ; he aspired to invisibility and played the role of uninvolved bystander." Direct cinema found its truth in events available to the camera. However, one of the problems hanging over observer-documentarist was the extent to which the presence of the camera influenced events before it. Therefore practioners of *cinema verité* in France "maintained that the presence of the camera made people act in ways truer to their nature than might otherwise be the case." Thus they acknowledge the impact of the camera, but instead of considering it a liability, looked on it as a "valuable catalytic agent, a revealer of inner truth." Erik Barnouw, *Documentary: A History of the Non-Fiction Film* (London: Oxford, 1974), pp. 229–62.

11. "Except for rare instances, what is seen on network news is not the event itself unfolding before the live camera, or even a filmed record, but a story about the event reconstructed on film selected from fragments from it. . . .

Despite the hackneyed maxim that television news 'tells it like it is,' presenting events exactly as they occur does not fit in with the requisites of network news. . . . A former Saigon bureau chief pointed out that 'it is considered standard operating procedure for troops to fire their weapons for the benefit of camera-men. If our cameramen had to wait until a fire fight with the VietCong broke out, we'd have less footage—and perhaps cameramen." Edward Jay Epstein, *News From Nowhere* (New York: Random House, 1973), pp. 152–58.

12. Michael Herr, *Dispatches* (New York: Avon, 1980), p. 21.

13. Michael J. Arlen, "Surprised in Iowa, Surprised in Nam," in *The Camera Age: Essays on Television* (New York: Farrar, Straus & Giroux, 1981), p. 96.

14. Michael J. Arlen, "The Networks Continue to Give us What we Really Want. We Are Immeasurably Grateful & Utter Little Cries of Help," in *The Living Room War* (New York: Penguin Books, 1982), pp. 40–45.

15. Tony Lawrence, "Television Review," *The Daily Variety*, November 18, 1969, p. 29.

16. R. Brewin, "TV's Newest Villian: the Vietnam Veteran," *TV Guide*, July 19, 1975, p. 4; Julian Smith, *Looking Away: Hollywood and Vietnam* (New York: Scribner's, 1975), p. 164.

17. Todd Gitlin, *Inside Prime Time* (New York: Pantheon, 1983), pp. 223–43.

18. Howard Rosenberg, "Merging Comedy With Vietnam," *Los Angeles Times*, January 11, 1980, pt. 4, p. 15.

19. Howard Rosenberg, "Mike Freit: The Saga of a Failed Concept," *Los Angeles Times*, March 3, 1980, pt. 6, p. 1.

20. Marvin Kitman, "*Fly Away Home*, A Story That Won't Quit," *Daily Variety*, September 24, 1981, p. 23.

21. Howard Rosenberg, "Mixing Humor With Vietnam," *Los Angeles Times*, January 11, 1980, pt. 4, p. 27.

22. John J. O'Connor, "These Productions Struggle to Be Provocative," *New York Times*, September 13, 1981, sec. 2, p. 45.

23. "Six O'Clock Follies," *Daily Variety*, April 28, 1980, p. 6.; Jerry Buck, "A Comedy Based on Vietnam?" *Alabama Journal*, April 19, 1980, p. 20.

24. At this point it is worth noting a number of other documentaries; the war it seems was fought not only with bombs and booby traps but documentar-ies as well. In 1954 Roman Karmin filmed *Vietnam;* the NLF did *Hun Tho Speaks to the American People* (1965) and *The Way to the Front* (1969). The North Vietnamese did *Some Evidence* (1969). The Cuban director Santiago Alvarez did *Hanoi, Tuesday the 13th* (1967), *79 Springtimes* (1969), and *Laos: The Forgotten War* (1967). Another Cuban director, Julio Garcia Espinosa, did *Third World Third World War* (1970). Two East German documentaries were *The Job* and *Pilots in Pyjamas*. Others were Joris Iven's *17th Parallel* (1967), Poland's *Fire* (1968) directed by Andrzej Brzozowski, Canada's *Sad Song of Yellow Skin* (1970), and the Syrian film *Napalm* (1970). For a more complete discussion of these films see Barnouw, *Documentary*, pp. 268–81.

25. See David James, "Discourse of Presence/Presence of Discourse: The Vietnam Documentary," *Wide Angle* (4):41–51. For a complete historical per-spective, see David James, *Allegories of Cinema: American Film in the Sixties*, forthcoming.

26. See David Cortright, *Soldiers in Revolt: The American Military Today* (New York: Doubleday, 1975), pp. 29–49.

27. Herr, *Dispatches*, p. 69.

28. See Julian Smith, *Looking Away: Hollywood and Vietnam* (New York: Scribner's, 1975) and Gilbert Adair, *Vietnam on Film* (New York: Proteus, 1981).

29. See Susan Jeffords, "Friendly Civilians: Images of Woman and the Fem-inization of the Audience in Vietnam Films," *Wide Angle* 7(4):13–22. As for

women in Vietnam, although there are two recent films—*Don't Cry, It's Only Thunder* (1980), and *Purple Hearts* (1984)—little has been published, besides Kathryn Marshall's *In the Combat Zone* (New York: Little, Brown, 1987).

30. Quoted in Smith, *Looking Away*, p. 136.

31. Gustav Hasford, *The Short-Timers* (New York: Bantam Books, 1980), p. 38.

32. William J. Palmer, *"Go Tell the Spartans:* The Forgotten Vietnam Film," unpublished paper.

33. See Guy Hennebelle, "Le Cinéma Viétnamien," *Ecran* 73; and Peter Gessner, "Films from the Vietcong," *The Nation* (January 24, 1966), 202(4):110–11.

34. Smith, *Looking Away*, p. 143.

35. Abraham Polonsky, *"The Case of David Smith:* A Script by Abraham Polonsky," *Hollywood Quarterly* (1945–1946), 1:185–95.

36. See Franklin Fearing, "Warriors Return: Normal or Neurotic?," *Hollywood Quarterly* (1946–1946), 1:97–109.

37. Tim O'Brien, *If I Die in A Combat Zone Box Me Up and Ship Me Home* (New York: Dell, 1979), p. 203.

38. See John Kerry et al., *The New Soldier* (New York: Macmillan, 1971).

39. Arlen, *The Camera Age*, p. 101.

40. See Leonard Quart and Albert Auster, "The Wounded Vet in Postwar Film," *Social Policy* (Fall 1982), pp. 25–31.

41. Walter Benjamin, "Theories of German Fascism," trans. by Jerolf Wikoff, *New German Critique* (Spring 1979), 17:122.

42. Peter Arnett, "Vietnam's Last Atrocity," *Los Angeles Times*, April 4, 1979, sec. 6, p. 1.

43. Andrew Britten, "Sideshows: Hollywood in Vietnam," *Movie* (Winter 1980/Spring 1981), 27/28:2–23.

44. Herr, *Dispatches*, p. 69.

45. Jaime Carrero, *Flag Inside*, in *Teatro: Flag Inside, Capitan F4C, El Caballo, Pipo Subway No Sabe Reir* (Rio Piedras: Ediciones Puerto, 1973), pp. 7–55.

46. "A dramatic story set in the period of the Vietnam War. An American soldier is stranded in the jungle with a Vietnamese woman who buries the dead." *Program Notes 1983 Asian American International Film Festival.*

47. Haile Gerima, *Ashes and Embers*, A Mypheduh Films, Inc. Release, 1982.

# Eyewitness: Documentary Styles in the American Representations of Vietnam

## JOHN CARLOS ROWE

*And, above all, I wanted to write about what I saw. I might not have been the best war correspondent that ever lived, but one thing would be sure, I would write it the way it was, and I would tell the people the plain and unvarnished truth.*
— *Flavio Bisignano,* Vietnam—Why? An American Citizen Looks at the War (1968)

My epigraph is from one of the hundreds of books about Vietnam that very few will ever read: those nonfictional, often autobiographical, and usually privately published accounts that express a desperate need to understand a war that remains inexplicable to the American public. Such narratives traditionally do not figure in even the broadest categories of "popular" literature and culture; their extremely limited audiences and minimal distribution disqualify them from consideration as "exemplary" or "typical." These works often remind us of Americans' extraordinary historical and political ignorance regarding Vietnam and Southeast Asia. As such, they are excluded from most accounts of the continuing effects of the war in our culture. In terms of traditional forms of literary or political history, these personal accounts of war seem to have no value in explaining events or evaluating general cultural effects of the war. I want to argue, however, that these eccentric works give explicit expression to a tendency in the writing about Vietnam that has a much more general cultural significance. Although every war has produced fiction and nonfiction that attempts loosely to "personalize" the experience of war and thus make it possible to experience vicariously the region and psychology of war, Vietnam is unique among other American wars for the volume and variety of subjective accounts it has generated. "The Vietnam experience" is now a popular phrase that refers not merely to the actual accounts of combat soldiers and other personnel in Vietnam, but also suggests a genuine *alternative* to official documents, media reports, and scholarly and popular histories. These subjective accounts clearly *compete* with these other modes of interpreting the war, and this unusual competition has produced a certain generic confusion as popular media have tried to employ the rhetoric, tone, and technical devices of the personal account. Such works remind us of how tempting it is to substitute personal experience for historical and political knowledge, especially in an American culture that has tended to mythologize the special value of direct experience, even when its impressions are uninformed or unconsciously biased.

Our attitudes toward Vietnam over the past fifteen years have been shaped significantly by a "revisionary" desire that aims to redeem the war and thus absolve us of responsibility. One of the strategies of this revisionary desire is to employ the presumably cathartic value of personal confession, anecdote, and relived experience. Ostensibly "realistic," each of these modes of dealing with the war presumes that the contact it offers is the equivalent of knowledge and understanding, even when such direct contact yields only clichés or baffled incomprehension. Certainly the best antidote for this tendency to confuse personal accounts and direct impressions with understanding and scholarly knowledge is careful study of the historical and political forces informing any particular impression or experience. Certainly we need better histories of Southeast Asia, America's involvement there, and the veterans' and Southeast Asian immigrants' postwar lives. Several of the essays in this collection address just these historical and political issues; Noam Chomsky and Stephen Vlastos challenge us to substitute such knowledge for the political mystification that continues to govern our foreign policies and shape our cultural consciousness of Vietnam.

We also need, however, better understanding of how this confusion of personal account and historical knowledge works in the American representations of Vietnam, especially those representations offered under the guise of a certain strategic "realism." Students of the novel know well enough that "realism" is merely a literary mode whose devices give what Henry James termed the "air of reality" to generalized situations and abstract psychological types that often have only tenuous connections with everyday life. By the same token, modern historical writers—indeed, our western historical consciousness itself—have often taken their tricks from the novel.[1] The confusion of historical and fictional accounts of the past is an unavoidable characteristic of modern writing, and deconstructive critics have insisted that no history, not even any "event," can be distinguished from the complex will-to-meaning through which history is staged.

The enormous volume of conflicting accounts of Vietnam has given special significance to the irreducible *textuality* of history. In fact, the general tendency to confuse unwittingly or combine deliberately history and personal account in the American representations of Vietnam is an especially good way to test some of the historical and political claims of deconstruction. From the perspective of those deconstructive critics who have remained content merely to demonstrate the "literary" character of otherwise realistic or informational discourses, the personal and subjective narratives about Vietnam would be of relatively little interest.[2] I want to follow what I consider a stronger, *political* deconstruction, which begins by interpreting the relationship between stylized and "factual" discourses as one measure of an historical period and thus of its cultural values. To be sure, when "deconstruction" addresses that relationship in terms of those texts that ordinarily are not understood as "literary" or "philosophical" (or even serious "history"), then it perhaps becomes something other than deconstruction. This is the moment in which deconstruction becomes cultural criticism. It is also the moment in which the politics of interpretation is no longer governed by irony, but directed by the need for specific reforms, often because the generic boundaries between "history" and "personal account" are so undecidable.

American society over the last quarter of a century certainly has operated with a certain popular conception of the "textual" situation; we refer to it generally as our postmodern condition. What was once the "New Journalism" of Norman Mailer, Tom Wolfe, and Truman Capote now is encompassed by such neologisms as "faction." The media are full of daily stories that tell of our constant drift between televised representations and ordinary experience. Early moderns like James and Wilde loved to point out how "life imitates art," but in our postmodern culture we are accustomed to the common and obvious ways in which our experiences imitate television. Given this situation, we can no longer maintain simple distinctions between information and fiction, or between "stylized" art and historical account. On the other hand, we can begin to understand how certain conceptions of realism are maintained by stylized means and how such "realism" continues to hold a certain epistemological status in our culture. It should not surprise us that "personal experience" is a crucial element in contemporary American discourses that also claim knowledge and truth as their objects. This personalist epistemology has a venerable history in America, but it has assumed a particular popularity in our recent representations of Vietnam. Indeed, the complexity and anomalous character of the war may well have served to expose a fundamental confusion, if not contradiction, in the "realism" and "pragmatism" observers as diverse as Alexis de Tocqueville and Henry Adams have associated with the "American Character."

For all of these reasons, then, I want to begin with Bisignano's curious book, because it expresses dramatically and in an exaggerated way some of the assumptions governing our recent confusion of personal and documentary accounts of the Vietnam War. The need to give documentary credibility to the war belongs to a more general rhetoric of realism—a *naive* realism, I would add—that has assumed particular ideological power in American culture in the fifteen years following the fall of Saigon. By the same token, the documentary often draws upon the personal account and subjective impressions of the war in ways intended clearly to legitimate the historical and informational claims of documentary.

Bisignano, a former Merchant Marine, closed his small southern California business, withdrew his savings, and hitched a ride on a merchant ship to Saigon in 1967, in the middle of that critical period, 1966–1968, now considered to be the apogee of American involvement and the prelude to the 1968 Tet Offensive, which for many continues to mark the beginning of the end of our military presence in the war. With little difficulty, Bisignano obtained proper credentials as a freelance war correspondent and photographer, sufficiently authoritative to entitle him to attend the Five O'Clock Follies in Saigon and receive precisely the same sort of briefing as any other professional war correspondent. Not only that, Bisignano's credentials qualified him to accompany combat troops on various missions: before returning to California, he obtained firsthand experiences in a search-and-destroy patrol, an airstrike on Vietcong jungle sanctuaries, and naval operations in the Gulf of Tonkin. What is most extraordinary about his "direct" experience of the war during his brief visit is the degree to which it resembles the sort of tourist accounts of foreign countries in which: a) the insecurity of the traveler is expressed as a certain distrust of the native population; b) the individuality of the traveller assumes defensively an especially strong identification with the home country; and c) an extraordinary reliance on popular clichés regarding the native population (the special ethnocentrism of tourism, we might say). The psychology of such tourism is instructive, because it tells us just what sorts of rhetorical appeals will work in more sophisticated documentaries, designed to move an audience in emotional ways as it offers apparently analytical explanations of historical causes and effects. The most important characteristic of this psychology is its reliance on some functional analogy between the individual and the state. "No man worthy of the name (nor nation worthy of respect) turns tail and runs away from his problems," Bisignano writes at the end of this little book.[3] The initial cliché, "Be a man," just barely disguises another, more pervasive American assumption: in a democracy designed to foster individual freedoms, the "individual" must be a microcosm of the state.

The bathos of Bisignano's tourism is certainly obvious, but has certain affinities with rhetorical strategies employed by the revisionary historians of the war. Stanely Karnow's *Vietnam: A History* begins with his account of his 1981 return to Vietnam. Unlike Bisignano, Karnow knows a good deal about Southeast Asian political, social, and cultural history; his history is subtitled, "The First Complete Account of Vietnam at War," and serves as the historical companion to the PBS television series, *Vietnam: A Television History*. In his personal, "new journalistic" account of this return visit in 1981, Karnow details the immense social and economic problems of postwar Vietnam: "America's postwar troubles pale in comparison to conditions in Vietnam, which I revisited in early 1981. I rediscovered a land not only ravaged by a generation of almost uninterrupted conflict, but governed by an inept and repressive regime incompetent to cope with the challenge of recovery."[4] In a history that Karnow himself bills as "unpolemical," the rhetorical frame is constituted by a profoundly critical view of postwar Vietnam that is based on the emotionally powerful claims of a recent visitor to that country. Leaving aside for a moment the "accuracy" of Karnow's observations, we may conclude that his selection of these personal observations to introduce his study has a very polemical purpose indeed. Above all, that literary decision involves Karnow's understanding of how important such observational realism is for contemporary American readers. It establishes *credibility*, even if it does so largely by means of a well-established literary convention.

The tourist's tendency to transform particular incidents into exemplary events, to transform individual experience into cultural fact, is all that much stronger in cultures which assume some organic relation between individuality and social form. Bisignano observes that his Saigon hotel is unsabotaged, and he concludes that the hotel must be paying off local officials of the National Liberation Front, who "were in this thing for the plunder they could extract from it." Yet his special concern with economic corruption in Saigon is shaped initially by his tour of the black market. Rather than conclude (as most did) that the enormous influx of American aid and personnel in an extremely short time and in such an economically undeveloped country would result in corruption of this sort, Bisignano first attributes such corruption to the Vietnamese people (as an inherent trait of the Oriental), then to the "greed" of the rebellious NLF. It goes without saying, I hope, that Bisignano is not a very good observer, but the reasons for that failing are instructive. First, he hasn't taken into account his own cultural assumptions in the observational process. Second, he has failed to realize that one's ignorance of a foreign culture prior to its "observation" will very often result in the activation of particular psychic defenses; such defenses may well transform any particular "perception" into a representation of *that defense mechanism*, rather than into some "fresh" or "spontaneous" image of the observed culture. Finally, Bisignano hasn't addressed his own authorial claim, his own justification for addressing an "American" audience, except on the basis of his initial assumption that "everyman" will recognize the same truths when those truths are made available in "direct" experience.

Documentary accounts of the Vietnam War played an especially important role in "explaining" and legitimating the war in the early 1980s. The important documentaries in this period all appeared on television; the two most popular television documentaries were Peter Arnett's and Michael Maclear's *The Ten Thousand Day War: Vietnam: 1945–1975* (1982) and *Vietnam: A Television History* (1983; filmmaker Richard Ellison and journalist Stanley Karnow). Both claim to be "liberal" critiques of American conduct in Vietnam; yet both succumb, often unwittingly, to meanings that their images convey but their writers and directors did not intend. These conscious rhetorical devices as well as the unintended, unconscious side effects of the documentary are the objects of my concern in this essay. In particular, the *unconscious* of the docu-

153

mentary very often betrays the personalist epistemology employed in many autobiographical accounts and impressions of the war. We have been encouraged by the popular media to make sharp distinctions between such personal accounts (a number of which the media have produced and directed) and the informational accounts of the war intended to educate the American viewer to help put Vietnam "behind us." The less obvious—but still very operative—complicity of these two modes helps explain the ideological rhetoric whereby genuine understanding of Vietnam has been displaced by story lines reaffirming the cognitive and political values of a very traditional American individualism. In fact, it is just such individualism and its peculiar claims to know the world by way of experience that the Vietnam War destroyed. The war could neither be conducted nor resisted by individuals; the "corporate" character of this war forced the populace to recognize that the old Emersonian dream of American self-reliance was dead. Yet, the outmoded myths are often the very ones that a society facing an historical crisis tries defensively to revive.

Documentary has become an enormously complicated subject since John Grierson first used the word "to describe Robert Flaherty's *Moana* (1926)."[5] What Grierson considered "a creative treatment of actuality," and which was assumed to be visual and cinematic has come to include several different media—still photography, motion pictures, a certain kind of nonfiction narrative, and forms of journalism lying somewhere between "New Journalism" and mere reportage. In short, documentary is now a transgeneric mode, rather than a cinematic genre, even if its particular identity derives from film. Rather than throw myself into the ongoing debates concerning the definition of "documentary" and the classification of various works under that heading, I shall borrow an instructive definition from the American filmmaker, Philip Dunne—a definition that might be considered an expanded version of Grierson's early but still provocative formulation of a "creative treatment of actuality." "Most documentaries," Dunne writes, "have one thing in common: each springs from a definite need, each is conceived as an idea-weapon to strike a blow for whatever cause the originator has in mind. In the broadest sense, the documentary is almost always, therefore, an instrument of propaganda."[6] This definition of documentary's commitment to political persuasion, however, leads many scholars to conclude that the *form* of the representation is still relatively backgrounded, relatively subordinate to the *content* of the material represented. The assumption is, I suppose, that the principal device of documentary form is selection (or "editing") and that such selection so overdetermines the form of the work as to direct our attention to the "content" in its relatively transparent arrangement according to the polemical aims of the filmmaker.

In practice, I think that just this sort of effect—content overdetermining the relatively simple formal devices—is often what is achieved by documentaries: the *effect* of an anthology of images organized by a narration following the principle of selection (or editing) that has the appearance of an analytical essay, in which the images merely support a clearly developed narrative thesis. Indeed, it is the substitution of narrative analysis for any notion of narrative action or development that seems to distinguish the documentary from other forms of cinematic or novelistic representation. It is an *effect*, however, that is achieved by means of complicated style and by formal manipulation that goes well beyond mere selection of materials for the delivery of a simple message (propaganda is, too often, judged to be "simple" in its very didactic nature). As a designed and consciously manipulated effect, the *illusion of realism* that governs the documentary is part of a larger and ultimately *uncontrolled cultural desire* ("uncontrolled," that is, in terms of the directors, writers, and producers of the film, even as they wish to manipulate such a desire on the part of their viewers) to explain, justify, and rationalize unacceptable sociopolitical events, such as our failure in Vietnam.

In short, even when documentary functions in its original *political* sense to offer an alternative history, generally at odds with the "official story," it is *received* in ways that threaten to normalize its arguments. Antiwar documentaries made during the War often went to considerable lengths to remind their audiences that the mass media tend to substitute vapid patriotism for more informed reporting. Peter Davis, in *Hearts and Minds* (1974; 1975 U.S./Columbia distribution), not only criticizes news coverage of the war, but also suggests that his own filmmaking is potentially complicit with such media mystification. In one scene, two Vietnamese men are picking their way through the rubble left by an American air strike, and turns toward the camera as a voice-over translates: "First they bomb us, then they film us." Repeatedly, the shadow of the camera is shown crossing the cinematic image, and interviewers talk in stage whispers regarding sound levels and technical quality. Although Davis based *Hearts and Minds* on a good deal of footage edited from network television news, he clearly means for us to question his own filmmaking, as if to remind his audience that *any* representation of Vietnam is bound to be shaped by the assumptions and politics of its authors.

Yet even such metacinematic commentary may be insufficient to prevent viewers from turning "documentary" into comfortable "realism." Eugene Jones' early documentary of the war, *A Face of War* (1968), repeatedly reminds the viewer of the camera's presence, as shots wobble and camera angles veer crazily as the film crew follows a platoon through jungle terrain and into fire. Jones preferred the look of a "rough-cut," in hopes of capturing the intensity and unpredictability of the soldier's experience in Vietnam. The politics of Davis' *Hearts and Minds* and Jones' *A Face of War* are, of course, immediately distinguishable; Jones treats the United States as struggling to make the best of a "difficult" foreign policy situation. Like the postwar liberal documentaries on television, Jones' film documentary subscribes to most of our myths of American innocence, self-reliance, and commitment to duty and family.

Only Emilio de Antonio's *In the Year of the Pig* (1969) manages to overcome the tendency of viewers to transform the documentary's politics into such mythic propaganda. *In the Year of the Pig* does this by covering Vietnamese history from the perspective of the North Vietnamese and the NLF. More radically than Davis, de Antonio pursues an explicitly Marxist analysis of the war, setting the solidarity of the Vietnamese revolutionaries against the decadence of the puppet governments in the south and the corporate interests pursued by the U.S. military. Even so, de Antonio must work hard to "fill in" that history of anti-imperialist struggle in Vietnam from the Vietminh to the North Vietnamese Army and the Vietcong. Both Davis and de Antonio knew well enough that a certain "shock-value" was necessary in order to prevent their documentaries from being understood primarily as "informational" and thus "realistic." But de Antonio relies on U.S. censorship of news footage taken by the North Vietnamese (or in some cases the East Germans), and this footage edited into his documentary thus appears as utterly new to his American audience. It is a documentary that tries to make the American audience "see" with the eyes of the North Vietnamese, and it is thus far more effective in terms of questioning not only our myths about ourselves but also many of our Orientalist myths about the Vietnamese. The risk of such documentary filmmaking is obvious. Before *In the Year of the Pig* was screened in one Texas theater during the war, the screen was splashed with red paint, and demonstrations at many other theaters protested such "communist propaganda."

Erik Barnouw has argued that part of the problem in the popular reception of "documentary" goes back to the "docudramas" of the late 1930s and early 1940s. Such docudramas, unlike our highly fictionalized television docudramas, were collages of news, thematically organized to provide a reading that generally celebrated patriotic values. They are the precursors to the World War II propaganda films discussed by Claudia Springer in another essay in this collection.[7] Henry Luce and *Time* produced *The March of Time* in 1937 and *This Is America* in 1942, and they are typical of this sort of docudrama.[8] These news docudramas built upon the techniques of some of the most radical documentary filmmakers of the 1930s, and yet they turned such technique to the service of mass news and mainstream politics. Thus, well before antiwar activists employed documentary forms for purposes of political protest, American viewers had come to associate its form with an unproblematic "informational" mode distinctly different from the original purposes of documentary. It is, of course, this dimension of documentary, as well as its relatively rapid transformation into *docudramas* about Vietnam in the later 1980s, that is of special interest to me in this essay.[9] Important as Davis' *Hearts and Minds* and de Antonio's *In the Year of the Pig* were, they were not followed by postwar documentaries willing to address the real sources of our failure in Vietnam: those unexamined myths of national and personal identity that are still very much central to our domestic and international conduct. So-called "liberal" documentaries took their place, and this liberalism found a happy home in the familiar mythologies of American culture.

Documentary films are often distinguished from "theatrical films," also called "story films." One of the popular assumptions about documentary is that it substitutes analysis for narrative or story. Chronology, thematic groupings of accounts, clusters of images— such devices of narrative organization appear to be as simple and value-free as possible, so that the "contents" and the analysis made possible by the selection of such contents will receive our central attention. Yet, it is remarkable how often the filmmakers and writers of postwar documentaries concerning Vietnam set their own projects up as *alternatives* to the conduct of the war; the very *form* of the work itself, with its claim to coherence and understanding, is set against either the *mystifications* of Press and Government or the misconduct of the Pentagon. This is not just a liberal phenomenon; it is characteristic of those "revisionary" histories of the war that have appeared with some frequency in the past decade and which are often distinguished by their conservative politics. In the oral histories that attempt to capture the veteran's actual experience in the war and those revisionary histories that try to analyze where we made our "mistakes" (and thus how we might have *won* an essentially immoral war), special privilege is claimed for the author-function. In both kinds of writing, the author's credibility is generally established both by his direct experience of the war *and* his criticism of American conduct in the war. These credentials are generally supported by the popular American mythology of the "author" as a "free agent," who assumes full responsibility for his statements and intentions. Such a pose is utterly at odds with that of de Antonio in *In the Year of the Pig*, in which the filmmaker claims his authority as a consequence of his solidarity with Marxist revolution, or Davis in *Hearts and Minds*, who repeatedly reminds us that the authority for the documentary comes from the antiwar movement.

The oral histories of veterans' experiences of the war are excellent illustrations of the ways that such formal elements and narrative devices help determine our reception of documentary accounts often billed as alternatives to "stylized" representations, whether those of Francis Ford Coppola, Walter Cronkite, or Lyndon Johnson. In Mark Baker's *Nam: The Vietnam War in the Words of the Men and Women Who Fought There* (1981), the realism of the oral history is associated initially with the personalities of those who fought a war designed to use them as martial objects (extensions of military technology), and whose conduct was an effective means of stripping them of any psychological complexity (a process of dehumanization that followed such practices as frequent duty-rotations, the customary hierarchies of the military class-structure and its disciplinary order, and the schizophrenia of everyday military life occasioned by this guerrilla war as well as the frequently equivocal commands of MACV). Interestingly, however, Baker does not identify his veterans; selections are grouped thematically and merely separated by asterisks. An extraordinary effect of reading results from these different "voices" drifting into a single narrational voice, which is Mark Baker's own and which "organizes" the selections made from Baker's interviews by means of interpolated, italicized "prefaces" to each of the major sections of the book and their appropriate subsections. Baker claims in his introduction, like so many historians and journalists who have written about Vietnam: "I just wanted to record what they could remember about the intersection of their lives with the Vietnam war and the consequences of that experience."[10] Baker's desire to communicate the emotional and personal experience of Vietnam is certainly genuine, but in the course of this depersonalized "oral history" he himself assumes the authority of a controlling voice. When he writes: "Something is missing from their story, something personal and palpable. . . . No one has bothered to talk of the men and women who went to Vietnam and fought the war," he unquestionably addresses our real need to understand the war. As someone who did not fight in Vietnam and admits it at the outset, Baker enables most of his noncombatant readers to identify with him. It is a narrative perspective designed to bring us into a more personal relation with the veteran, but one that presumes the foreign quality of such an experience. There are two interesting consequences of such narration. Framed as they are by Baker's narrative prologues, the individual stories told by veterans are overtaken by the explanatory, controlling voice of Baker; we identify with that voice and look to it for explanations of what all too often are, inevitably, discrete and unintegratable stories, mere anecdotes of the war. Once again, the veteran, who is claimed to be the one who justifiably would be able to *teach us* about war and its devastations (physical and psychological), is depersonalized for the sake of an author-reader relation that increasingly turns the "veteran" into a "character" in a narrative that has left the domain of documentary and entered the region of the novel. The narrative logic of Baker's *Nam* follows precisely the recognizable features of what literary critics term the *Bildungsroman*, or "novel of education."

Baker's contents are organized under the following large headings: INITIATION, OPERATIONS, WAR STORIES, THE WORLD. Baker's paradigm is that of mythic heroism, in which the hero undergoes a process of "initiation" by means of a struggle and heroic contest, and returns from this spiritual and physical ordeal to "the world" having achieved his identity as hero and subsequently *realizing* that identity more fully in the deeds he performs back in the world: lifting the plague, solving the riddle, restoring social order. "The world" is, of course, the term soldiers in Vietnam used to describe the United States, but the "return" becomes possible in Baker's oral history only as a consequence of *Baker's* integration, his "explanation" of the significance of the veteran's various stories. The actual return to the world by these and other veterans hardly meets the requirements for the epic hero or protagonist of the "novel of education." Yet, in following the rhetoric of such literary "education," Baker has attempted to redeem the traumatic experience of war and tried to make it serve some "useful" purpose. The use to which Baker puts these veterans' stories, however, ultimately serves the American myth that an individual's experience must be significant. Veterans themselves often discuss the psychic defenses they employ to avoid admitting that what they did in the war was useless and futile; the more complicated and insidious defenses are those deployed by American society to maintain the very cultural myths that drove us into the war and that ought to be the central subjects in our *critical* understanding of the War's consequences. As John Hellmann has argued in *American Myth and the Legacy of Vietnam:* "Even in the realistic accounts of veterans the search for the meaning of Vietnam demands that American consciousness reexplore the experience in the same psycho-symbolic dimensions in which it originally—if unconsciously —went there."[11]

Let me illustrate this notion with a familiar scene from *Coming Home*, a movie that legitimates its own fictional representation of the war by means of a prologue that is an *imitation documentary.* In the original script for *Coming Home*, Bob Hyde (Bruce Dern) and Sally (Jane Fonda) race along the ocean highway in Bob's El Camino, with Janis Joplin blasting from the radio. On their way to a military funeral, they have to stop while Bob repairs the fanbelt on the El Camino and Sally buys a six-pack (it's a scene that will be echoed in a much later scene in the actual movie, when Sally goes to the market while Bob prepares to commit suicide).[12]

This bit of ironic realism is transformed in the final version of the film into the now-familiar bit of docudrama, in which actual disabled veterans of the war are filmed discussing the ways in which they and their fellows rationalize the war's effects on them. Gathered about the pool table in a "recreation room" of the VA Hospital, the veterans establish an authentic context for the introduction of Jon Voigt, who will become their cinematic representative in the subsequent drama. Voigt is seen immediately, and a black veteran, moving around the table to line up a shot, brings him into the realm of the docudrama by saying, "You're going to have to move out of there, man" and "we don't want no cheap feeders [parasites] hanging around the table." The black veteran establishes camaraderie with Voigt by ironically recalling the treatment disabled veterans receive in the "world" outside the hospital. Voigt is not so much in the way of the veteran's pool shot as he will be in the way of normal American social life. Indeed, everyone in the room is a "cheap feeder" in the eyes not only of the VA, but also of the culture that refuses to welcome them home. Voigt fades out of the camera's field, and the veterans talk among themselves about their different views of the sacrifices they've made. But Voigt returns to the visual field just as actor and veteran, Lou Corello says, "I have to justify killing people, so I have to say it's okay." At that moment, there is a close-up on Voigt, with head down, which serves as an objective correlative for Corello's speech, as if his character now stands for all the anguish represented by the tableau of genuine emotions expressed by these authentic veterans. Voigt's head then fades to Bruce Dern's running feet, with the Stones singing "Out of Time," and Dern's face coming into the picture to replace Voigt's lowered head. The docudrama of veterans with its cinematic fade to Bruce Dern's entrance, together with the veterans' conversation fading into the Rolling Stones, constitute the prologue to *Coming Home*. It is, in effect, the subtext or meta-cinematic frame for the formal strategies of the movie: the substitution of theatrical personalities (Voigt, Fonda, Dern) for the veterans and the war they represent. When we recall that the plot of *Coming Home* generally retraces the melodrama of *A Star Is Born*, we should realize that the veterans are made to serve a much more complicated purpose than that of mere "realistic detail." The introduction of the fictional form of the movie is achieved by means of the veterans' mediation; they are the means by which we suspend our disbelief and accept the film's "drama." And they become the foils by which the theatrical personalities of Jon Voigt and Bruce Dern are introduced, not entirely unlike the way in which Baker's voice in *Nam* controls and gives shape to the voices of the unnamed veterans whose discrete anecdotes are organized by *his* oral history.

In *Everything We Had: An Oral History of the Vietnam War by Thirty-Three American Soldiers Who Fought It* (1981), there is a deliberate effort to avoid Baker's authorial domination of his materials—his transposition of the apparently anecdotal into his narrative of ironic or unrecognized heroism. Al Santoli barely acknowledges his special role in collecting and editing the stories: "The American people have never heard in depth from the *soldiers themselves* the complicated psychic and physical realities of what they went through in Vietnam. To encompass those realities in a book, one veteran traveled around the country and spent countless hours, talking, crying and laughing with other veterans and their families. I was that veteran, and we present our story."[13] And although Santoli gathers the stories under different headings—Gathering Clouds, Sand Castles, Peaks and Valleys, etc.—the order of the stories is chronological, according to the time each veteran spent in Vietnam, and each of the accounts carries a title, name of the author, and some specific details about the author: name, rank/role, group or division, location, and dates of service. The consequence is that the book serves as a true "anthology" of documentary responses—that is, recollections with specific polemical or narrative purposes of their own. Further, such an organization prevents the editor as author from transforming these accounts—particularly "real" in their combination of psychological and historical details—into "images," that is, "figures" for some mythic appropriation of the war by existing cultural forces, as we have seen *Nam* and *Coming Home* doing.

Even so, *Everything We Had* hardly employs a value-free rhetoric in its overall organization and aims. Santoli's idea for a "communal book" is a marvelous response to the overdetermined forms of *Nam* or *Coming Home*, and it contributes to the Vietnam Veterans of America's commitment to political, social, and human solidarity as their only means of achieving some redress for such demonstrable crimes committed against them as: use and denial of the side effects of Agent Orange and other herbicides and defoliants in the chemical warfare we waged in Southeast Asia; the lack of adequate psychological counseling, medical treatment, and educational programs for returning veterans; and the general embarrassment of the population about its Vietnam veterans. In that last category, I would suggest that what we have done to dissipate such embarrassment, to avoid our discomfort, is to engage in the sorts of stereotyping—exploitation by means of the image—that we now recognize as the concerted labor of network television, commercial cinema, and the publishing industry. Certainly the communal aims of the veterans who wrote *Everything We Had* are part of a deliberate political strategy that belies somewhat the claims for "fidelity" to experience that govern Santoli's preface.

Indeed, the claim that documentary narratives will help us understand the war by bringing it *personally* home to us is at once an attractive and yet still potentially dangerous characteristic of documentary's claims on our attention. The documentary has the capacity to slip in and out of its "factual" mode at will, substituting personal interviews and the personality of the one interviewed with a discretion and design often lost on us. Living as we do in a culture in which "personality," "role," and "identity" are often difficult to untangle, we are more than ready to be *used* as viewers. This is especially true in those visual media that are so difficult for us to study in terms of their formal devices and rhetorical effects. The "speed" with which the image is deployed in such media poses considerable problems for the casual analyst, even if scholars now have adequate means for detailed studies.

The oral history evolved in the 1980s beyond mere anthologies of personal accounts to include the "letter" or "testament" as a particular artistic and political form. Bernard Edelman's collection for the New York Vietnam Veteran Memorial Commission, *Dear America: Letters Home from Vietnam* (1985), was part of the Commission's activities to honor America's veterans of the Vietnam War.[14] Published on May 7, 1985 (to coincide with "the tenth anniversary of the official end of the war . . . and the dedication of the New York Vietnam Veterans Memorial"), *Dear America* is part of a larger, avowedly communal enterprise to use the honest, direct impressions recorded in letters by soldiers and their friends and families to correct government lies and media mystifications (*Dear America*, p. 23). A national advertisement for the paperback issued by Pocket Books announces: "The Vietnam correspondents who got the story right."

The designers of the New York Memorial—"a translucent glass-block structure 66 feet long and 16 feet high, etched with excerpts of letters sent to and from servicemen during" the war, conceived it as "both an object and event" that incorporates both letters and "news dispatches and public documents" (*Dear America*, p. 16, back cover). What Peter Wormser, William Fellows, and Joseph Ferrandino call the "apparent contradictions" of the Memorial are designed to "symbolize . . . the Vietnam Years" (*Dear America*, back cover). In both the form of *Dear America* and the architecture of the

163

Memorial, the personal letter represents the interpersonal emotions and values deliberately suppressed in the government's conduct of the war.

Yet, the presumed grass-roots character of the personal account of Vietnam inevitably claims some explanatory authority that is belied by the contents of most of the letters in *Dear America*, as in so many of the other such collections from over the past twenty-five years. All of these collections are dominated by letters testifying to the soldiers' inability to comprehend the aims and purposes of the war. When explanations are offered, they are generally transparent reflections of general cultural attitudes contemporary at the time the collection was published. One of the earliest collections, *Letters from Vietnam* (1966), represents the same despair and bewilderment one finds in *Dear America*, but the efforts to explain the war more commonly appeal to the responsibility Americans have to combat international communism. Although some of these sentiments are expressed in the letters in *Dear America*, the political activism of the Vietnam veteran of the 1980s seems to be foregrounded.[15] Rather than offering genuinely alternative explanations of the war, such collections more often reflect the dominant attitudes (and thus the illusions) of the times in which they were produced.

As we have seen in the cases of *Nam* and *Everything We Had*, the rhetorical effects of these anthologies are determined significantly by their editorial arrangements. Edelman claims that *Dear America* is arranged "in a sequence that would relate a year's tour in Vietnam," but the narrative organization from chapter 1, " 'Cherries': First Impressions" through "Humping the Boonies" and "Base Camp: War at the Rear" to the final chapters, " 'We Gotta Get Out of this Place' " and "Last Letters" (*Dear America*, p. 24). As these contents suggest, *Dear America* transforms "one year's tour" into a panoptic view of many different soldiers' jobs and experiences. The collective aim of the book remains governed by the desire to make these different experiences coalesce in a "representative" picture of the American soldier's experience in Vietnam. From the naive first impressions of arriving soldiers to the despair and pathos of the last letters written by soldiers killed in action, the narrative of *Dear America* follows the pattern of disillusionment and defeat so often experienced by the antihero of modern literature.

The collective political solidarity announced by the general project of the New York Vietnam Memorial Commission (of which *Dear*

*America* is only one part) seems contradicted by effort to individualize a *representative* experience of the war. The individual and his personal attachments to family and friends become those types with whom we may identify, but such identification actually discourages the kind of political activism suggested by the overall project. *Dear America* fashions a *representative grunt* from the fragmentary impressions that speak of the incomprehension and terror of combat. Insofar as the letter and anecdote are intended to *personalize* and *individualize* the experience of war for the sake of understanding, these *souvenirs* serve the same function as those monuments that realistically represent the combat soldier in sculpture (such as the sculpture added to the Vietnam Veterans Memorial in Washington or the sculpture of a soldier reading a letter from home in the Sacramento memorial). Sentimentalizing the war and thus remystifying the political questions posed by it, these personal mementos serve as chimerical forms of "understanding," always framed already by familiar myths of American individuality and the family as *alternatives* to the interrogation of those American sociopolitical attitudes (including the individual and the bourgeois family) that contributed to our involvement in Vietnam.

I want to turn now to a set of related illustrations from *The Ten Thousand Day War*, a documentary with a very specific thesis (i.e., our indecision and internal divisions were no match for the nationalism and historical solidarity of the North Vietnamese). *The Ten Thousand Day War* does not avoid entirely the suggestion of other "revisionary" histories that our "military mistakes" are what "cost" us the embarrassment of Vietnam and that the "lessons" to be learned are technical ones for future reference (i.e., how to fight a *successful* jungle or guerilla war). If there is some element of such revisionary history in *The Ten Thousand Day War*—for example, General Westmoreland is revealed as unequipped to conduct such a war—there is also a substantial effort to explain our lack of cultural understanding, our American ignorance of the Vietnamese people, their history, and their relations with their neighbors. By and large, *The Ten Thousand Day War* is a liberal documentary, whose length (thirteen hours) and political sentiments kept it off the major networks, which countered in the Fall of 1983 with the WGBH production of *Vietnam: A Television History*.

The *Washington Post* called Michael Maclear's book based on *The Ten Thousand Day War*, "a living history," which has been used from time-to-time as a term for the documentary. But there is a real rhetorical reason for this term's appropriateness here, because one of the devices of the visual version of *The Ten Thousand Day War* is to intersperse the factual footage with interviews (many conducted by Peter Arnett) that would provide a sort of "running commentary" on the footage. Actually, the reverse happens; the footage of battle scenes and Vietnamese countryside and cities assumes the tone of a sort of "local color" for the personalities, whose explanations are offered in ways that seem to make the war increasingly "understandable," "accessible" to those who were not there (and perhaps to many who *were*, as well). There are frequent suggestions that the "narrative" of the factual footage is far more designed than we might have thought on first viewing. The overall structure of this documentary depends on a preview in the special first hour of the twenty-six part television series. One of the consequences of this is that the abbreviated summary of the entire series, concentrating as it does largely on events and dates, tends to be confusing and serves as a simulation of the experience of war itself.

The one-minute prologue to that first-hour preview (a prologue repeated at the beginning of every part in the rest of the series) seems at first merely to convey the confusion and fragmentation experienced in combat. From the air, we watch a rocket descend lazily into the jungle, where its red exhaust explodes into a fireball that then fills the screen. The voice-over begins as Richard Basehart calmly and carefully says: "America at war. The Vietnam conflict is America's largest, costliest, and most mysterious war." A pilot's helmeted head is shown in profile as he receives an audible but incomprehensible command. The camera offers a close shot of bombs being released from a wing. A helicopter gunship flies low over rice paddies dotted with explosions; combat soldiers are barely visible as dark shapes inside the helicopter's open door. A helicopter door-gunner is shown in close-up, firing a machine gun, but his features are hardly distinguishable behind the helmet and from the sharp camera angle. A bareheaded officer is shown in close-up and frontally, talking on a radiophone: "Be careful, though, uh, there're thirty of them [stutter] out there, and if you make contact, you'll have a fight on your hands. Over." A patrol leader turns directly to the television audience and says in a whisper, "Drop back five meters [holds up five fingers], *five meters.*" A grunt swings suddenly into the visual field, crouches into the jungle, and the camera (and viewer) follows his back. Documentary footage of the Vietminh is shown in black-and-white; numerous Vietminh rush across an open field, in the manner of a World War I charge. The leader for the title rises up onto the screen: VIETNAM.

In the course of the series, virtually every one of these images will be repeated in different contexts; each "image" will have its own story associated with it. This is hardly unusual in terms of the customary function of such prologues in cinema and television as an anticipation (foreshadowing) and summary (recollection). But the images here, unrecognized as yet in terms of any sort of narrative significance, are extremely important in shaping our own expectations and determining our own sympathies. I will provide only a brief and incomplete analysis. The dehumanized figures of the jet pilot calling in inaudible information about the target, the indistinguishable forms of American troops in the helicopter, the barely visible face of the door-gunner—all call attention to what the war did to the individuals who fought it. Only as the reasonable, theatrical, and well-paced voice of the narrator (Richard Basehart) begins to assert its authority in the midst of a chaos of conflicting visual images—only then does the narrative *personalize* the combat soldier, who appears to be warning his comrades of a dangerous situation. His face is visible, the technology of war minimized, his look not entirely toward us, as if caught in a bit of candid camera. And he stutters vulnerably, realistically. The platoon leader then warns *us* in turn, directly substituting *us* for the soldier he addresses in the actual situation: "Five meters, drop back five meters," in a direct address to the screen. Then the soldier he was really addressing comes into view as he is turning into the jungle, as if turning from the space beyond the camera into the jungle scene itself ("reality" in this rhetoric?). Alienated from the violence and technology of the war, finding such violence and technology to be associated with the faceless figures of the American combat troops, the viewer is reprieved from this desolate vision by the documentary itself, which turns us toward identifiable and sympathetically drawn soldiers. It is an elaborate form of the narrative "hook" used to catch the reader's interest in any sort of dramatic narrative, from "story" film to just plain story.

Richard Basehart's narrative voice maintains its distance from the action by means of a certain equanimity that is in marked contrast with the confusion on the screen; his introduction of characters for interviews has the authority of an attorney introducing evidence. There is a curious similarity between Basehart's narrative tone and that of Willard's (Martin Sheen) voice-over narration in *Apocalypse Now* (1979). Both serve the function of some Conradian Marlow redivivus, who enables us to mediate between our own circumstances and the alien action of the war. In one particular scene, Willard seems to prefigure perversely the tone and role of those narrators of Vietnam documentaries who would become so familiar to television audiences in the early 1980s. In the darkened hold of the river patrol boat, Willard uses a flashlight to read the classified file on Kurtz. As the camera switches from Willard's face floating in the darkness (anticipating Kurtz's disembodied head later) to newspaper clippings, diplomas, photographs, and letters, the scene establishes one of those conventional scenes of discovery in the detective narrative. In fact, we see only fragments of information: parts of pictures, letters out of focus, reports half-covered by other documents. Only Willard's voice, with its atonal calm, makes any sense of the pieces that confuse us. In documentaries like *The Ten Thousand Day War*, the voice-over is intended to provide a rational and historical distance on the confusion of the war. In *Apocalypse Now*, Willard's voice makes sense of Kurtz only by personalizing him and then identifying with his individualism: "The more I read and began to understand, the more I admired him. . . . A tough motherfucker."

Willard tries to control those documents by personal identification, but in the very next scene the cook on board the patrol boat is shown writing a letter home, whose subject is the unpredictability of the jungle: "Dear Eva, Today was really a new one. Almost got eaten alive by a fuckin' tiger." The comic relief of this scene interrupts the melodrama of Willard's scene of identification, and it helps remind us that Willard's identification with Kurtz is part of his preparation for his successful *termination* of Kurtz. In many ways, then, the documentary's effort to show the chaos of the war only to "order" the events of its history in the voice-over narration shares something of Willard's will to mastery. One of the mechanisms of such mastery is the capacity of *personalize* and identify with actors in the war in order to dispel the chaos of what Basehart terms our "most mysterious war."

The opening scenes in *The Ten Thousand Day War*, especially this little narrative of the jungle patrol, will recur several more times in the complete series. Like a literary repetition, each further repetition of this bit of narrative *develops* the story of the patrol just a little more, actually expanding the narrative action until the "event" (the patrol itself) begins to make "sense." The "event," of course, makes no more sense than it did originally for the soldiers forced to trek through that jungle. What the event has been made to do, however, is counterpoint a particular argument, establish principal views with governmental officials or with representatives of veterans' groups.

Following a description by General Depew of search-and-destroy methods (a description intended to answer his critics), Basehart's voice notes: "The Vietcong executed an estimated 37,000 villagers and officials." An incident in the documentary is shown in which an American slowly smothers a VC suspect in an effort to extract information. Up to this point, the narrative is working in an equitable manner (although we should point out that this argument concerning "equal atrocities on both sides" is a stock one for the more conservative revisionary historians). In keeping with the liberal aims of the documentary, however, the balance is tipped in favor of the suffering of the American combat troops. Ivan Delbyk, former Special Forces, acknowledges the hatred the Vietnamese felt for American troops. It's a classic moment of *self-conscious recognition*, which gives Delbyk a personality that attracts our sympathies. Jim Webb, Delbyk again, then Tim O'Brien—famous veterans, two of them well-known writers—discuss Vietnam, then O'Brien describes the terror of the Bouncing Betty mine. The camera cuts to an American soldier wounded by this vicious mine, and a close-up shows another soldier holding the wounded soldier's hand in an expression of compassion. Suddenly, the voice of a marine says: "Damn sniper out there." The platoon leader from the one-minute prologue to the series reappears, warning us again, "Drop back five meters, *five meters*." Events are beginning to make sense for us, or so it would seem. The "sense" being made is more emotional at this point than intellectual, even though there has been a great deal of intellectual weight put behind the "images" of camaraderie and human suffering. Given this narrative of images and voice-over, we are well-prepared to accept the actions of the patrol as normal responses to aggression.

The conclusion I would draw from this reading of the narration of the "event" of this single jungle patrol is that every form of "realism" in the representation of complicated cultural and political events like Vietnam will have its purposes, will be working out certain polemical aims and satisfying certain basic (psychic) needs on the part of its viewers. I will speculate here that Peter Arnett and Michael Maclear did not intend the sort of narrative coherence that we have observed in the "story" of the jungle patrol. Their design in repeating characters and scenes that culminate in this patrol to flush a sniper was most likely a gesture toward coherence in the midst of a virtual chaos of documentary footage. The fact that they did not "mean" what I have read into the images does not disqualify the reading, because I think there is a good deal of wish-fulfillment and of the basic psychology of compensation at work in the "viewing" and the "making" of works representing our longest and least-understood war. In fact, the very effort to organize documentary materials inevitably brings with it those cultural mythologies that always already shape our concepts of order. The order Americans continue to bring to the "things" of the Vietnam War remains profoundly ethnocentric. We shall never be able to address adequately the effects of the Vietnam War on American culture and the Vietnamese people until we have understood the rhetoric and style of such ideas of order as America continues to impose on its historical materials.

I think that the realism of these documentaries—in both the form of oral histories and of television/cinematic histories—needs to be subjected to the closest scrutiny by historians as well as by literary and cinema critics/scholars. We must learn how to read the rhetoric of these representations—that is, the forms by which they make their claims to be "realistic" representations. And as we learn how to read the ways of such representation, we ought to recognize that some of the apparently attractive liberalism of a documentary like *The Ten Thousand Day War* may work unwittingly to support the very cultural blindnesses and prejudices it would criticize. In each of the works I have discussed in this paper, I have had recourse to the tendency of their realistic accounts to employ "character" for the sake of some reaction to the dehumanizing effects of modern warfare. Our abilities to sympathize with a real human being, whose actual experience of Vietnam has much to teach us, may be our best means of healing the wounds that continue to be inflicted by that war. On the other hand, there is a point at which such "sympathy" becomes a way of diverting attention, transforming the real suffering of the veteran into the "device" of some explanatory account, some realistic rendering of the war (some rendering of the war's realism). In addition to this sort of danger, we must also be aware of the old delusion popular still among many literary critics: that a "real" account may be patched together from varied perspectives, from the "anthology" of anecdotes assembled from those "who were there," from those exemplary "witnesses" whose varied accounts might assume a certain and ultimate form.

In yet another and even more pervasively acceptable cultural sense, the *resistance* registered by documentary realism to the regimenting, dehumanizing forces of the military and government conducting the war is a resistance that assumes the form of a certain *radical individualism*. I have suggested that there are two conflicting impulses in the oral histories of the war: Baker's desire to give a "voice" to the veterans' various responses to their experience in Vietnam; Santoli's desire to let the "voices" tell their own stories. Both oral histories, however, assume that the spontaneous, personal story will have some effect in *counteracting* what was done by the military and the government. Baker's individualism belongs to a long tradition in letters of the artist as ideal individual, capable of giving self-expression some archetypal, even universal, dimension. Santoli's perspectivism, his multiauthored project, escapes the mythologies of such an "authorship" of the Self; nevertheless, that perspectivism relies on the integrity and variety of the different "points of view" represented. Truer perhaps to our theatrical age, *Coming Home* uses the veteran to give "reality" to John Voight and the subsequent "story" film; the actor is quickly and effectively individualized by his prefatory association with "real" disabled veterans. The examples I have drawn from the television documentary, *The Ten Thousand Day War*, combine some of *Coming Home*'s theatricality with the "realistic" assumptions of Santoli's perspectivism in *Everything We Had*.

In the second half of the 1980s, the documentary of the Vietnam War would virtually disappear, to be replaced by *docudramas* that overdetermine a story line and rely on all the conventions of the fictional narrative. Most often, these docudramas assume that knowledge comes from experience and that the individual can resist and even reform his or her society. Certainly the box-office successes of Oliver Stone's two Vietnam films, *Platoon* (1987) and *Born on the Fourth of July* (1989), rely on this slide from documentary to docudrama. The liberal sentiments of these films are obvious enough, and it is just the quality of such liberalism to attempt to redeem from this war a "wisdom" or "knowledge" that will render such painful experience meaningful. There is, of course, nothing wrong with such an aim, but there is powerful evidence that documentary accounts of the Vietnam War in both print and on film have helped give new credibility to fictionalized versions of the war. The high-art films of the late 1970s—*Apocalypse Now, Coming Home,* and *The Deer Hunter*—tried to question the ideological assumptions of filmmaking as part of the problem in our conduct of the war. But in the intervening decade, fiction and fiction film have renewed their claims to *historical* credibility, in part by adapting the techniques of documentary and giving special authority to docudrama, which more than ever assumes a central place in the American family room.

The personalities, the strong narrative voice-over, and the splicing of interviews with combat footage in *The Ten Thousand Day War* seem to link "understanding" of the war with some individual act of judgment, knowledge, and reason. Yet, the cult of "individualism" may itself be the last and most desperate gesture of the social ideology, of the set of cultural assumptions and values that led us to Vietnam in the first place. Writing of late nineteenth-century realism in the novel and of the advent of literary Modernism, Fredric Jameson concludes: "The fiction of the individual subject—so-called bourgeois individualism—had, of course, always been a key functional element in the bourgeois cultural revolution, the reprogramming of individuals to the 'freedom' and equality of sheer market equivalence. As this fiction becomes ever more difficult to sustain . . . , more desperate myths of the self are generated, many of which are still with us today."[16] It may be that the dominance of the documentary forms of representing the "Vietnam Experience" (to use the title phrase from the Time/Life Books series) during the 1980s was part of some unconscious effort by the American people to identify more fully with a war whose "reality" in the late 1970s seemed utterly elusive, better left unspoken or subject of "high-art" adaptation. It may be that this same documentary impulse is yet another version of a "realism" invented by modern, bourgeois man as a confirmation of his Reason, a legitimation of his individuality, and a naturalization of his contradictions in the form of that ongoing narrative we term social reality. The subtlest and most powerful arts are not to be found solely in literary classics, but rather in the rhetorical devices by which a powerful ideology maintains its rule, even by employing those specific works that would hope to escape its authority. America's pyrrhic victory in Vietnam may well be accomplished in the ways by which such hegemonic practices determine what only seem to be our freely chosen, our individual interpretations of Vietnam. We thought in 1975 that there could be no return to the nationalism and militarism that led us into such a tragic war; in those years, Rambo seemed unthinkable. Yet, it is not just the success of Sylvester Stallone's three Rambo films that we should investigate as we try to understand our cultural reception of the Vietnam War. Rambo's radical individualism, his nearly *Emersonian* bid for a renewal of American idealism, is just the other side of the cultural work of liberal documentaries and the more recent liberalism of our docudramas and story-films, like Stone's *Platoon* and *Born on the Fourth of July*.[17]

"Realism," whether it is characterized by the techniques of realistic description (local color, anecdote, direct impression) or archival legitimacy, is a mode of representation of very recent invention. I am troubled by the *need* for a realistic account of the war, which is an utterly modern need that somehow speaks to us regarding our occasional distrust concerning the "governance" of social reality. It goes without saying that we must interrogate the *form* and *purpose* of every sort of literary realism. The same procedures ought to be applied to those accounts of Vietnam that claim some direct, some personal, some authentic, and finally "true" account of a war whose truth belongs to the entire complex of cultural forces that contribute to the shaping of an "event." Yet, it is equally true that the "realistic" accounts of the Vietnam War have become by the 1990s hopelessly entangled in the fantastic work of American ideology, so that no discrete category, such as "realism" or "documentary," may be said to distinguish any longer certain works from others. This is not to say that "Vietnam" is undecidable or unrepresentable. Quite the contrary, "Vietnam" has in many ways already been decided in this culture and is endlessly represented in very familiar and recognizable ways and in a host of different forms and styles. What is needed, however, is a better understanding of the social arts by which these versions of Vietnam are designed and then accepted by Americans anxious to substitute myth for knowledge, understanding for responsibility.

NOTES

1. In particular, I am thinking of the recent work of Homer Obed Brown and Michael McKeon on the dialectical relation of the rise of the modern novel and the development of modern theories of history. See Homer Obed Brown, "Of the Title to Things Real: Conflicting Stories," *ELH* (Spring 1989), pp. 917–

54; Michael McKeon, *The Origins of the English Novel, 1600–1740* (Baltimore: Johns Hopkins University Press, 1987).

2. The "aestheticizing" of deconstruction is often identified most closely with Geoffrey Hartman, as Michael Sprinker has argued in "Aesthetic Criticism: Geoffrey Hartman," in Jonathan Arac, Wlad Godzich, and Wallace Martin, eds., *The Yale Critics: Deconstruction in America* (Minneapolis: University of Minnesota Press, 1983), pp. 43–65.

3. Flavio Bisignano, *Vietnam—Why? An American Citizen Looks at the War* (Torrance, Calif.: Frank, 1968), p. 132.

4. Stanley Karnow, *Vietnam: A History* (New York: Viking Press, 1983), p. 27.

5. Richard Barsam, *Nonfiction Film: A Critical History*, as quoted in Gerald Mast and Marshall Cohen, eds., *Film Theory and Criticism: Introductory Readings* (New York: Oxford University Press, 1974), p. 367.

6. Philip Dunne, as quoted in Barsam, *Nonfiction Film*, p. 367.

7. See Claudia Springer, "Military Propaganda: Defense Department Films from World War II and Vietnam," in this volume.

8. Erik Barnouw, *Documentary: A History of the Non-Fiction Film* (New York: Oxford University Press, 1976), pp. 121–22.

9. I treat the development of docudramas about Vietnam, as well as their dependence on documentary techniques, in "From Documentary to Docudrama: Vietnam on American Television in the 1980s," *Genre* (special issue on "The Vietnam War and Postmodern Memory," edited by Gordon O. Taylor) (Winter 1988), 31:451–77.

10. Mark Baker, *Nam: The Vietnam War in the Words of the Men and Women Who Fought There* (New York: William Morrow, 1981), p. 13.

11. John Hellmann, *American Myth and the Legacy of Vietnam* (New York: Columbia University Press, 1986), p. 119.

12. Waldo Salt and Bob Jones, *Coming Home*, unpublished screenplay (author's possession), 1978, p. 1.

13. Al Santoli, *Everything We Had: An Oral History of the Vietnam War by Thirty-Three American Soldiers Who Fought It* (New York: Random House, 1981), p. xvi.

14. Bernard Edelman, ed., *Dear America: Letters Home from Vietnam* (New York: Simon and Schuster, 1985).

15. Glenn Munson, ed., *Letters from Vietnam* (New York: Parallax Publishing, 1966). My claim that these collections reflect rather dramatically their different historical periods can be demonstrated by comparing the titles of the final three chapters of this 1966 collection—"A Different Kind of War," "Why Are We Here," and "The Face of War"—with the final three sections of *Dear America*—"What Am I Doing Here?" "We Gotta Get Out of This Place," and "Last Letters."

16. Fredric Jameson, *The Political Unconscious: Narrative as Socially Symbolic Act* (Ithaca, N.Y.: Cornell University Press, 1981), p. 221.

17. I offer a fuller account of Stallone's *Rambo* films in " 'Bringing It All Back Home': American Recyclings of the Vietnam War," in Nancy Armstrong and Leonard Tennenhouse, eds., *The Violence of Representation: Literature and the History of Violence* (London: Routledge, 1989), pp. 197–218.

# PART THREE

## The Vietnam War and Popular Media

# Remembering Vietnam
## MICHAEL CLARK

*Only that historian will have the gift of fanning the spark of hope in the past who is firmly convinced that even the dead will not be safe from the enemy if he wins. And this enemy has not ceased to be victorious.*
— Walter Benjamin, "Theses on the Philosophy of History"

Since the final withdrawal of American troops from Vietnam in 1975, the media in the United States have worked doggedly to represent that war and its veterans in a form compatible with the traditional norms of popular culture, and the various events surrounding the tenth anniversary of the fall of Saigon testified to the complete success of that program. New memorials were dedicated, complaints about Agent Orange paid off, and lingering problems with unemployment, crime, and the emotional complexities of Post-Vietnam Syndrome dismissed as the adolescent whining of chronic malcontents by upwardly mobile veterans whose happy families and fine jobs proved that the Vietnam vet was really OK. POWs and MIAs could not make the ceremonies, but CBS News did its best to put that issue to rest when ex-POW John McCain returned to the site of his imprisonment at the side of Walter Cronkite, an avuncular Rambo who ushered McCain out of his cell to meet the smiling faces and soft giggles of the friendly villagers. Completing this image of the Vietnamese as a willing if bemused host, Le Duc Tho asked *Nightline*'s Ted Koppel to thank the American people "for their support and contribution to our present victory," and the entire town of Ho Chi Minh City changed their plans for a gala celebration of their independence day (September 2) to put on a huge parade in honor of their city when they discovered that American television wanted to broadcast such an event. "There was no doubt they played up to us," said David Burke, an executive vice president for ABC News. "They're no different from anybody else."[1]

And most impressively, the tortured outrage of forgotten soldiers, which had forced this country to confront its hypocrisy in the early 1980s, was drowned out by the cheerful cadences of prodigal sons on parade as 25,000 middle-aged men marched through the streets of New York in faded fatigues and waved to the cheering crowd. Beaming veterans left the street to hug tearful spectators, and the air was filled with streaming ticker tape, fluttering paper, and joyful chants of "U.S.A.! U.S.A.!" and "Welcome Home!" "Westy! Westy!" the troops cheered back as they passed the reviewing stand where Westmoreland stood, taking a break from his ultimately futile attempt to prove that he had not lied continuously to the American people and to his men during the last years of the war. Such incongruities clearly had no place on a day like this, and Westmoreland climbed down from the stand, telling his aide, "I'm going out there. I'm going to march with these guys." Greater sins than his dissolved into the communal will of the crowd, whose happy mood of reconciliation was best expressed by John Behan after his legless body had been wheeled down the street by Mayor Koch. "It was a lousy war," Behan said, "but a helluva parade." [2]

Everyone loves a parade, and few seemed willing to deny a homecoming to those who still wanted it and who, after all, were so grateful as Jim Casanova, who said at the end of the march "Before we felt forgotten. And now it's time for us to say thank you." [3] The curiously perverse occasion of a decade-old defeat lent the festivities an air of historical surrealism, however, that was compounded by the oblique focus of many events. What *was* Walter Cronkite doing in that Vietnamese prison, anyway, and why were the firsthand accounts of experienced veterans so often supplemented or even supplanted by the spectacle of famous newscasters recounting their own war stories and retracing the steps of earlier campaigns? And perhaps the most puzzling question of all, who *were* those guys waving flags and choking back grateful tears in response to the cheering crowd in New York? Could they be the same men whose rage and frustration found such an eloquent expression at the time the first memorial was dedicated? If so, what had transformed them? And if not, where were they then, and where are the others now?

An indirect answer to some of these questions had already appeared improbably enough in an episode of *Murder She Wrote*, a lighthearted television mystery series starring Angela Lansbury as a kindly if somewhat frumpy mystery writer who is weekly called upon to solve cases much like the ones she writes about. The episode for March 10, 1985, began with a literary awards banquet that is attended by an aging, burnt-out novelist who was promoting his comeback book, which he describes as "the definitive novel about the Vietnam War." The first time we see the manuscript, it is lying on the bed of his hotel room, where he is bragging about it in hopes of impressing a Sweet Young Thing who has appeared at his door. Unlike her elder sisters of the 1950s, however, this SYT is not hopelessly smitten by the more mature celebrity but is instead a young editor on the make, hoping to peddle her considerable charms for a chance to handle the book. The novelist appears to be making progress when his ex-wife abruptly strides through the door and heads toward the bar. She casts a bored look at the SYT, who becomes flustered and leaves, and then she excoriates her former husband for playing a game he can't win because, as she tells us later, "writing isn't the only thing that he's burnt out at." The plot thickens when the novelist is murdered, and we discover that he only spent two weeks in Vietnam as a correspondent for *Playboy*. The novel actually turns out to be the work of a young vet, who had spent years getting his story down on paper while working at a loading dock in Brooklyn, and who had given it to the novelist for a critical reading. The vet is arrested for the murder, but as it happens it was his sister who killed the old man, so he is freed and we are assured that she will get off with a light sentence for self-defense against the lecherous advances for which the novelist was so infamous.

The lurid sensationalism and tenuous credibility of this plot are commonplaces of the genre, but the stake of the conflict is not. The resolution of the plot hinges on the rights of ownership to the story of Vietnam, and the complications that suspend that resolution over the course of the hour all turn upon the extent to which the memory of that war is implicated in the cynical union of manipulative sex and literary vanity that serves as the cultural apparatus charged with its preservation. Television mysteries seldom aspire to sociopolitical comment, of course. But it is difficult to imagine such obvious implications escaping network executives like David Burke and his colleagues, and the events of May 1985 extended this plot beyond the disingenuous ideological modesty of prime-time programming and made it the script for the documentary realism of network news. Bored with Reagan's hesitancy to invade anything larger than a tiny island, or perhaps just losing interest in

Central America, many news commentators seized the story of Vietnam that week and made it their own. It was not the war that was the object of those reports, but rather the memory of the war that emerged as their object, and as one anchorman after another returned to the scene of his story, it became equally clear that it was not the veteran who was remembering, either. Instead, Vietnam was recollected by the cultural apparatus that had constituted our memory of the war all along, the intricate web of technology, political efficacy, cultural paradigms, and institutional supports that makes up the ideological framework of our society and assigns each of us a seat as it traces its own image on the screen of the past. With an audacity far surpassing the redemptive fantasies of President Reagan and his ersatz adviser Sylvester Stallone, this apparatus reversed time and revised space, transporting the figures of its own authority into the setting of the war and projecting its own need for narrative consistency onto the convenient characters of the ex-POW, the aging veteran, and the former enemy. It summoned a cast of thousands to the streets of New York, and edited out information that was out of step. It healed over the wounds that had refused to close for ten years with a balm of nostalgia, and transformed guilt and doubt into duty and pride. And with a triumphant flourish it offered us the spectacle of its most successful creation, the veteran who will fight the next war.

André Breton once said that "the work of art is valuable only in so far as it is vibrated by the reflexes of the future." If that is true, then in terms of our cultural continuity with the past, the most valuable art engendered by the Vietnam War will probably turn out to be not the more ambiguous works such as *Dispatches* or *Apocalypse Now* but the cultural flotsam of television characters and B-movie heroes that were the earliest avatars of the Veteran of Future Wars who emerged last spring. Paradoxically, this heroic figure first began appearing in mass media of the late 1960s as a crazed psychopath who threatened at every moment to bring the war home with him in the form of flashbacks that turned firecrackers into artillery and passersby into the enemy. This image bore little resemblance to the vast majority of veterans, who had simply walked off their planes and picked up their lives at the point where they had been interrupted. It did, however, serve an important ideological function. While it titillated the viewer with promises of sensational violence and furnished an instant psychological profile of the character, using Vietnam as the signature of this stereotype also thoroughly laundered the violence of that war by relegating it to some "other" place: Southeast Asia and the psychotic unconscious.

This character thus absolved the veteran for the violence associated with him because "he" didn't do it—it was an unconscious impulse—and he didn't do it "here"—Vietnam is a long way from home. Ironically, the psychotic killer thus became one of the few avenues through which the veteran could be readmitted to the social order in the 1970s without denying his past altogether. The instability inherent in this psychic split prevented the veteran's full assimilation into the cultural forms of normalcy, however, until the tenuous protection offered by the individual ego against this reservoir of irrational aggression was replaced by a temporal distinction between past and present. No longer a primal scene that had to be integrated into the psychic structure of an autonomous consciousness, Vietnam became a sign of the veteran's connection to a past we all shared, and the imminent psychosis of the earlier stereotype was replaced by the problem of personal memory and its relation to the individual's sense of his place in the present social order. And as that individual was assimilated into the community, his personal memory came to represent a popular form of history that could reconcile the violence of war with the placid stability of the status quo.

One of the earliest examples of this fundamentally conservative evolution in representative types of the veteran can be found in the film *Born Losers* (1967), where the hero Billy Jack is a social misfit whose Green Beret skills have earned him little respect and less income since he returned from the war. They do come in handy, though, when his girlfriend is captured by an evil motorcycle gang, and they enable him to overcome tremendous odds, an inept police force, and public indifference to free the girl and set things right. The character of Billy Jack is an obvious compromise between the psychopathic killer and a fully integrated member of society, and it has its roots in the righteous loner who was so popular in the westerns produced after World War II. Rather than the mysterious aura of self-sufficiency and pop metaphysics that lent these characters their power, however, Billy Jack's triumph derives from his ability to transform a form of violence specifically associated with Vietnam—his Green Beret training—into a force for social justice. The political and moral contradictions of that war never impinge on this transformation despite the film's moralistic obsession with political corruption and human depravity, and while the film stops short of portraying war as the source of Billy Jack's ethical superiority to the townspeople that scorn him, it clearly represents the veteran's "memory" of the Vietnam war—represented in this case by the skills he has retained—as a purifying influence and potential source of communal harmony.

This tendency to treat the veteran's recollection of his war experience as a source for social purification has since been reflected in many other films that portray the alienated veteran as a paradigm of moral order. In *Rolling Thunder* (1977), ex-POW Major Charles Rane uses his memory of surviving torture by the NVA to make it through the sadistic punishment inflicted by some thieves who eventually murder his wife and child and leave him for dead. Rane recovers, and after the police lose interest in the case, he tracks down the murderers to a Mexican whorehouse where he executes them (destroying the whorehouse in the process). Although they are set mostly in Vietnam, the lengthening series of back-to-Nam films by major stars such as Gene Hackman, Chuck Norris, and Sylvester Stallone also draw upon this impulse in their treatment of heroes who return POWs home in the face of official indifference or overt interference. Even Travis Bickle, of Martin Scorsese's *Taxi Driver* (1976), draws upon this stereotype as he befriends a fourteen-year-old prostitute and then, after his plan to assassinate a presidential candidate fails, dons his old fatigue jacket, kills her pimp, and so frees the young girl to return to her family.

Scorsese's treatment of this narrative paradigm is, of course, heavily ironic, since Travis's heroic deed occurs only as an alternative to his plans for a heinous murder and seems inspired more by a deranged sexual frustration than by the altruistic motives for which the girl's parents are so grateful. This irony returns the figure of the redemptive avenger to its original twin, the psychotic killer, and coupling these types in the same character suggests that the absolute moral distinction society draws between them may in fact hide a more profound connection between the violence that purifies society and the violence that threatens to tear it apart. In each of these cases, that connection is the veteran's memory of Vietnam.

The ambiguous status of violence in these films reflects the ambiguous status of the veteran's relation to the social order and the equally problematic relation of that society to its past. Just as it is the memory of Vietnam that isolates these characters from their community, it is the historical link to Vietnam that threatens the moral and political complacency sustained by ordinary forms of everyday life. A potential contradiction therefore exists between representations of individual continuity and of social coherence that resists the easy solution of the alienated hero offered by films such as these. In one of Joseph Wambaugh's more popular novels, *The Choirboys*, this conflict between forms of personal and social continuity is dramatized in the character Roscoe Rules, an undisciplined cop who is also a Vietnam veteran. Rules carries a photograph of himself leering into the camera and holding the severed head of a Vietcong, and he likes to use the picture to illustrate the war stories he shares with other veterans on the police force. One day Rules is assigned to patrol the scene of an accident in which a young woman has been decapitated. He quietly rages at the public's fascination with the gore of these roadside crashes until he suddenly remembers his photograph. After diverting the flow of traffic through a nearby gas station, Rules calmly walks up to a car that has slowed to pass the scene of the accident and smiles down at the woman in the passenger seat. "Anyone hurt bad?" she asks him, and in response he steps up to the window, raises the bloody head he has pulled from the wreck, and replies, "Yeah, this one got banged up a bit."[4]

Roscoe Rules is recognized as a borderline psychopath even by his friends, but the parallel he draws between the scene around him and his memory of the war is reinforced by Wambaugh's less outrageous associations between the personal conflicts of more central and representative characters and the siege of Khe Sanh, which is described in the novel's prologue. In the light of those more general associations, Rules' grotesque prank appears as something more than the idiosyncratic aberration of a veteran unable to put the past behind him. It radically transforms this hackneyed theme by suggesting a profound continuity between Rules' obsessive attraction to the lurid excesses of wartime violence and the fascination with accidents that we recognize as an ordinary aspect of our everyday experience. The radical implications of this parallel are blunted, however, by the fact that Roscoe's stunt earns him a place in police folklore as a "Legend in His Own Time," and Wambaugh's sympathy for the more commonplace forms of working-class machismo and tough-guy cynicism that hold this group of cops together suggests that Rules' absorption with violence may even be an effective if perverse avenue of his socialization.

The cynical overtones of this suggestion are limited to some extent by Wambaugh's portrayal of the cops in *The Choirboys* as an idiosyncratic and self-destructive subculture within the police force. The image of the veteran as cop persisted, however, and as the American society grew more and more conservative, it came to represent the ideal reconciliation between the isolated loner with a violent past and an orderly community in the need of forceful direction. As the hero of *Blue Thunder*, for example, Frank Murphy uses the skills he learned as a helicopter pilot in Vietnam to protect the public from corrupt officials who plan to use a powerful new police helicopter for their own ends. Similarly, Lieutenant Stanley White of Michael Cimino's *Year of the Dragon* (1985) turns his racist hatred of an old enemy into righteous indignation at the Asian greed that has infected the streets of New York's Chinatown, and sets out to clean up the city. To be sure, neither character is a completely unambiguous hero: Murphy is a cynical voyeur not above using surveillance technology for his own illicit thrills, and White's useful racism is still racism. But unlike the righteous loners who preceded them, the crusades they wage are for social, not just personal, redemption, and when they are opposed by villains in positions of power, that opposition is portrayed as a corruption of an essentially good and necessary institution. The conservative thrust of this character thus overcomes its more complex heritage, and on television it usually dominates the narrative entirely. So while the SWAT-team commander Howard on *Hill Street Blues* is characterized by a rabid xenophobia and an obsession with militaristic rhetoric left over from his time in Vietnam, his racism and aggression are principal sources of order on the hill and are deflated ironically when they are not needed. The violent past of the veteran heroes in even newer shows such as *Magnum P.I.*, *Matt Houston*, and *Miami Vice* is seldom mentioned at all and so presents even less of a problem to their community service as incorruptible cops or private investigators who work closely with their local police. Their identity as veterans serves no consistent thematic or narrative function, and in the few episodes where their connection with the Vietnam War does emerge, it is usually represented as merely a personal conflict that must be worked out while the hero solves more immediate and pressing threats to the public good.

The banal stereotypes of such television shows assimilate the veteran into society in much the same way that other stereotypes have socialized characters who "happen to be" black or female. They relegate the specific, concrete contradictions involved in being a veteran at a particular moment in history to the realm of private experience and personal memory, and they divorce that realm entirely from the forms of social interaction that are represented as permanent and universal. This solution remains problematic, however, because the separation between personal memory and public order on which it depends sets individual continuity and identity against the need for social coherence. Consequently, in *all* of the preceding examples, those men whose public function is the enforcement of communal norms are either unwilling or unable to establish ordinary family ties in their personal lives. This separation thus marks a formidable limit to the assimilative power of the character of the veteran as cop because the image of the family is an even more powerful mechanism of socialization in popular culture than the police.

Vietnam veterans have not fared well as family men in mass media. As our primary means of representing individual recollection and aspiration as a vision of communal harmony, the image of the family cannot accommodate a character such as the veteran described above, whose personal past appears so alien to present social forms and yet threatens them with an immanent intimacy. Consequently, most portrayals of the veteran in a family have insisted on his incompatibility with its normal function, quite apart from whatever basis that image might have in the family relations of actual veterans.

That incompatibility, and its basis in the assimilative mechanisms of mass culture, formed the central theme of an early and extremely bitter treatment of the returning veteran. David Rabe's *Sticks and Bones* (1972) represents the family in the anachronistic and idealizing terms of television sitcoms from the early 1960s, and the deliberately clichéd nature of the characters' response to the son home from the war dramatizes both the role those clichés play in the process of socialization and the tragic inability of the veteran to share the vision of a community of happy consumers that sustains that process. The family is obviously modeled on the Nelsons of *The Adventures of Ozzie and Harriet,* and David is the son who went to war and who has been sent home blind and bitter. Ozzie refuses to recognize him at first, but then the family tentatively accepts him back until David's fantasies of violence and sex with a Vietnamese whore take on substance and disrupt the household. Finally, Ozzie, Harriet, and Ricky convince David to commit suicide, and Ricky helpfully stands by his side, ready to record the death with his Instamatic and reassuring David that once he is dead, "You can shower and put on clean clothes. I've got a deodorant you can borrow" (p. 223).

Banished to the Nielsen wasteland of public television, *Sticks and Bones* had little impact on the general public and cannot be taken as a "popular" image of the veteran in any sense. But more recently (November 27, 1984), CBS broadcast the made-for-TV movie *Memorial Day,* which starred Mike Farrell as Matt Walks, a father haunted by the accidental death of some Vietnamese children who stumbled into an ambush he set one night while on patrol near Ben Moi. *Memorial Day* thus conflated the disruptive threat of the veteran's memory with the ideal of paternal responsibility that normally joins the individual to the family unit and the social order. The film opens with a reunion party for four veterans who were on patrol the night the children were killed. One of the men, "Gibby," complains obsessively about not being able to forget the sight of the wounded children and about his inability to hold a job after returning from the war. Matt claims to have put the war behind him and advises Gibby to do the same, but a few days later Gibby shoots himself in the head and dies with the same expression on his face that he described seeing on the face of friends killed in Vietnam. Just before he dies, Gibby writes a letter to Matt asking him to explain Ben Moi to his son, and Matt does that as well as he can, with uncertain success. Through a series of flashbacks, however, we see that Matt himself is still tortured by memories of the ambush after he returns from his talk with Gibby's son, and at a barbecue in his backyard a little later, that anguish erupts. Listening to his self-satisfied neighbors condemn veterans who cannot forget about the war and get on with their lives, Matt suddenly interrupts, and over the protestations of his wife and friends, he insists on telling them the story of Ben Moi, which he concludes with what must be one of the most astonishing lines ever uttered on prime-time TV: "You were all part of it," he screams at his neighbors, "we killed those kids for you."

*Memorial Day* backs off from this radical assertion of continuity between the community represented by the barbecue and the atrocities of the war represented in the flashbacks that constitute Matt's memory of his experience in Vietnam. The film recasts the conflict between memory and community as Matt's own moral dilemma, and then resolves that dilemma by having Matt resign from the big corporate law firm where he works, deflating the social thrust of his outburst at the barbecue into some moral clichés about his personal responsibility to Do The Right Thing. *Memorial Day* thus falls back on the same assimilative strategy used by works that center on the veteran as cop, even though it problematizes the separation of private and public by portraying the veteran-father's conflict within the intermediate, and so more vulnerable, domain of the family. The full integration of the veteran into the communal norms of everyday life required a quite different representation of the relation between the individual and the past, one in which memory would reinforce those norms rather than mark their limits, and so would naturalize their hegemonic function and render invisible the exclusionary violence that sustains them.

This requirement was met by a television movie broadcast during the spring of 1985, *The Lady from Yesterday*. It starred Wayne Rogers as Craig Weston, a Vietnam veteran who is a happy family man and a successful executive in his father-in-law's construction firm. Suddenly one day he is contacted by a Vietnamese woman who had been his lover during the war, and he is torn between guilt over the affair and a desire to resume their relationship. The dilemma is compounded when he discovers that their affair had resulted in a son, and further complicated when the woman tells him that she has only a short time to live and that she wants him to take care of the child after she is gone. At first, he agrees only to pay for the boy's education at a boarding school, but after meeting him Weston decides to bring the child into his own family. When he confides in his father-in-law for advice, the old man's first response is that of a comrade-in-arms who understands such wartime indiscretions: he advises Weston to support the woman and boy on the sly. After he finds out that Weston plans to bring the boy home, however, he rages at the thought of his daughter and neighbors having to live around a "chink" kid and threatens to disown his son-in-law if he carries out this plan. When Weston finally tells his wife, she objects on the more reasonable grounds that she should not be responsible for taking on the child of her husband's affair, especially since he has to this point shown little interest in helping her care for their own children. The wife's resistance brings to light deeper problems with their marriage, and she decides to divorce her husband and takes their children back to Daddy's ranch. Eventually, though, she softens and agrees to take the boy in, and the film concludes with husband and wife agreeing that they should leave the house that Daddy bought them anyway and carve out a new life on their own.

The maudlin sentiment of this plot and its entirely predictable conclusion are typical of most television melodrama, and the film's treatment of the veteran's personal memory as a threat to traditional forms of the social order reflects a central theme in most of the Vietnam films that preceded it. Representing that memory as a mother and child rather than combat horrors distinguishes *The Lady from Yesterday* from those other films narratively, however, and ideologically as well since it allows for an easy resolution of the contradictions that memory usually poses within the conventional paradigms of the family romance. As Weston's Vietnamese lover, the Lady from Yesterday creates an obvious contradiction within his social role as a devoted husband; and as a representation of his relation to the past, she poses an equally formidable threat to the reconciliation of his personal memory of the war and his current position in the community. Had this original impact of the woman's presence been developed narratively, it would have functioned just like the bloody flashbacks or obsessive guilt that many previous works have treated as a persistent obstacle to the veteran's full assimilation into the social order. So her death not only restores a penitent husband to his long-suffering wife, it also allows the film to transcribe the broader historical dilemma her presence evokes into a more tractable complication by representing the veteran's relation to his past in a form that is more easily integrated into the status quo: his little son. He's lovable, he's cuddly, he's cute, he's the Boy from Yesterday, and what mother could turn him away? Certainly not one worthy of the name, and as the film focuses on the wife's struggle to accept this literal embodiment of her husband's past, the specific historical dimension of the original conflict disappears entirely into a murky cloud of sentimental cliché. The veteran's acceptance of responsibility for the boy translates his memory of Vietnam into the comfortable—and timeless—obligations of the dutiful father, and the difficulties that role poses for his wife are already resolved in the corollary role of mother that she initially resists but finally accepts as her own. The story of their reunification thus takes on a narrative inevitability within the genre of domestic fiction that reinforces while at the same time disguising its ideological necessity as a vision of historical reconciliation, and this conjunction between the conventions of domestic fiction and the idealized paradigms of social harmony makes this character of the family vet one of the most ingratiating and convincing images of socialization that has yet appeared in the mass media.

The reactionary thrust of such character types has gone largely unchallenged in recent years, and the popularity of films such as *Uncommon Valor, Missing in Action,* and, of course, *Rambo: First Blood, Part Two* indicates a tolerance for witless illusions of American omnipotence and historical revision that continues to draw popular tastes even further to the right. The dominance of this rightward drift in mass fantasies undoubtedly reflects political fashion to some extent, but it also testifies to the inability of the political left in the United States to establish viable forms of ideological or aesthetic resistance. The dwindling number of works that do attempt a more critical perspective on our memory of the Vietnam War have been content to relegate that memory to the private domain of individual recollection and then to try to evaluate the veteran's struggle for personal redemption in terms of a quest for historical truth. Consequently, they tend simply to rehearse the tired image of the tortured vet while stripping that character of its vestigial social implications in favor of a pompous rhetoric of existential vision.

The most widely-known of the critical works that take the memory of Vietnam as their central thematic focus are Robert Stone's *A Flag for Sunrise* (1981) and Phillip Caputo's *Horn of Africa* (1980) and *DelCorso's Gallery* (1983).[5] All three of these novels isolate the veteran geographically by setting his quest in the exotic locales of Central America, an African desert, or the streets of Beirut, and then constituting the veterans as a community among themselves through what Stone calls the "dread nostalgia" that links them everywhere they go "in excuses and evasions, in lost dreams and death" (p. 117). These veterans self-consciously avoid social contact, and when forced to deal with more normal human relations, they treat the ordinary forms of everyday life with a condescending affection that barely disguises their bravura contempt for such "illusions" in the face of the darker truth they have learned at war.

189

In Caputo's novel, for example, the photographer DelCorso compulsively flees the domestic comfort of his wife and children to augment the "gallery" of atrocity photos he has taken in an effort "to make the indictment he had failed to make in Rach Giang," where his unit had massacred some Vietnamese villagers (p. 225). One day while working on his collection he glances up at a portrait he had taken of his wife, Maggie, and he is comforted to realize that "photographing wars has not destroyed my faith in beauty." His eyes shift to another photograph of a "flock of sheep flooding over a barren Irish hill," and he observes:

> Maggie had turned out as he had wanted, her looks and innocence intact. Her innocence: she wore it like a suit of armor and DelCorso kept the metal bright. He saw in that mirror a reflection of his own innocence, an image of himself untarnished by the guilt of his filthy little secret; and if that image was merely an illusion, well, he'd dealt with enough gritty realities to know that illusions were sometimes necessary to get through the day without cracking up.
> *Village.*
> DelCorso stood and paced the room. (p. 222)

DelCorso's taste for these gritty realities finally gets him killed trying to "get close" to the truth of a street skirmish in Beirut, and he dies in the arms of a colleague with the word "shit" on his lips. The novel then quickly concludes with a brief reminiscence about DelCorso's exploits in Vietnam as two of his friends are returning his body to the United States, and when one of them reports DelCorso's last word, his eyes gleam with "the twinkle of a cynicism so deep it delighted in itself" (p. 352).

Such postures pass for historical vision in these novels, which flaunt the characters' hackneyed generalizations as the expression of cyclical recurrence. So, in *Flag for Sunrise*, the narrator tells us that "once again Holliwell caught the saffron taste of Vietnam [while in Central America]. The green places of the world were swarming with strongarm philosophers and armed prophets. It was nothing new" (p. 271); and the book ends with Holliwell's bitter but comforting thought, "A man has nothing to fear . . . who understands history" (p. 440). Perhaps not, but readers have little to learn from him, either, since such softheaded philosophizing is little better than a parody of the revelation mimicked by its rhetoric. The veterans in these novels seem suspended in a curious time warp that simply replays the Vietnam War over and over again in locales that are so remote as to offer no resistance to the characters' projection of their pasts onto the present scene, and as a result that projection can masquerade as the Truth of History seen by a time-less eye. Problems of individual continuity and social coherence are irrelevant to that vision and the myth of personal insight that sustains it, and the level of philosophical abstraction at which these novels operate has little to do with the specific circumstances and concrete contradictions faced by veterans in more modest do-mestic settings. Consequently, whatever critical intent and intel-lectual seriousness may be behind these works, they are vitiated by an archaic tone of combat aestheticism that has been borrowed from Ernest Hemingway and Stephen Crane and that pointedly marks the time lag that separates these philosophically ambitious novels from their more commercial—and conservative—counter-parts in television and film.

The differences between these works of "serious" fiction and the hackwork of mass media are more than a matter of intellectual fashion. As we have seen, most recent representations of Vietnam veterans take as their central theme a conflict between personal memory and social coherence that insists on a dialectical tension between the individual's private and public identities. The autono-mous realm of individual experience that constitutes a privileged point of view for Caputo and Stone, however, ignores the mundane particularities of everyday life and reduces the constitutive forms of social normalcy (such as the family or business) to meaningless illusions. That perspective does substitute a kind of memory for the naive faith in eyewitness authenticity which justifies more tradi-tional war stories, but the simplistic distinctions between public and private and between truth and illusion on which the perspec-tive is based belie the subtlety with which ideology stitches those categories together. These novels render invisible the ideological function of such distinctions, whereas the dialectical nature of more popular works, rudimentary as it usually is, actually thema-tizes the constructed character of positions occupied by the veteran outside as well as inside the social order. Having seen *Memorial Day*, for example, it is difficult not to understand the veteran's position in the family as a product of various conflicts that have been systematically resolved by a hierarchy of values and the cul-tural forms that support them, such as paternal responsibility and the nuclear family unit in which that responsibility is typically expressed in Western societies. To be sure, the ideological basis of that systematic resolution is naturalized and so disguised by the sense of narrative inevitability endemic to the generic assumptions that govern the film's reception as a television melodrama, and that mystification discourages a critical view of the process. But the very fact that the veteran's position in society depends on that process in such works allows for the possibility of a deconstructive reading that is foreclosed entirely by the transcendental character of the position that the veteran comes to occupy in these novels by Caputo and Stone.

That possibility is realized in Jayne Anne Phillips' *Machine Dreams* (1984).[6] As subtle and uncertain as these other novels are direct and assured, *Machine Dreams* traces the impact of three wars on the sense of community that evolves from the photographs and letters which make up the collective memory of a family living in a small American town. Cast in the form of a series of recollections and correspondence by various members of the family, Phillips' novel begins with a simple statement that comes to signify the principle informing each of the chapters and the book as a whole: "It's strange what you don't forget" (p. 3). Unlike the naive faith in the truth of history that holds *Flag for Sunrise* and *Horn of Africa* on their steady and predictable course, *Machine Dreams* portrays recollection as a serendipitous collection of details from the most ordinary forms of experience—the telephone number of a childhood friend, old photographs from a worn album, the flying horse on a Mobil gas sign at the garage where Father serviced his cars— and it treats the sense of identity that emerges from this memory as an accidental effect of chance encounters among the congeries of impressions that make up the characters' lives. Letters home from Vietnam take a place beside a quotation from Hesiod, an SVNLF propaganda pamphlet, a passage from Laurie Anderson's "O Superman," and the soft sounds of WLS playing late at night in a darkened house, and that bunch of discourses mixes with a jumble of bright yellow cement trucks, the smell of new leather, and the slick oilcloth on a kitchen table that never finds a privileged point of order in either time or space. The consciousness behind the eye that passes over the old pictures or the ear that strains to hear "The Lion Sleeps Tonight"—or the body that burns in an exploded helicopter—is no more secure for Phillips than the procession of I's that record those impressions in various sections of the novel. Neither perception nor narration ever coalesces into the coherent history and unified family that the characters all desire, and by the end of the book even the realm of desire and dream disintegrates into the random clatter and repetitive drone of an impersonal machine.

The title of the novel focuses Phillips' interest in the depersonalized character of individual subjectivity. Throughout the book, literal machine dreams make up much of what might ordinarily pass as the personal unconscious of the people she describes. Little Billy, the son and brother who eventually is reported missing in action in Vietnam and never found, is obsessed with the trucks and cars that play such a large part of his father's fantasies of success, and as a young child Billy's dreams are filled with visions of cement mixers and big Chevrolets that "were just sitting in his dreams, big and vacant as abandoned houses. There was almost a kind of music near them, like a humming of motors or heat" (p. 147). Once he is in Vietnam, he realizes that his life and the entire firepower of the American army exists to "protect the machine" at least as much as to save the men who fly it, and near the end of the novel he disappears in a burning helicopter, never to be seen again. Similarly, the adolescent sexuality of his sister, Danner, surfaces in her own machine dream, which lifts her unrecognized desire into the realm of myth on the back of the Mobil gas horse:

> Danner sinks deep, completely, finally, into a dream she will know all her life. . . . In the cloudy air, winged animals struggle and stand up. . . . The horses are dark like blood and gleam with a black sheen; the animals swim hard in the air to get higher and Danner aches to stay with them. She touches herself because that is where the pain is; she holds on, rigid, not breathing, and in the dream it is the horse pressed against her, the rhythmic pumping of the forelegs as the animal climbs, the lather and the smell; the smell that comes in waves and pounds inside her like a pulse. (p. 132)

In the last section of the novel, which is the only one without a specific character named as its point of view and which is simply titled "Machine Dream," this conflation of subconscious processes with the inhuman apparatus of commercial icons and the machine emerges as the discourse of memory itself, and it translates the story of Danner and her brother into an oneiric scene of hidden longings and suspended despair.

> Danner and Billy are walking in the deep dark forest. Billy makes airplane sounds. Danner, oblivious to her brother's play, is stalk-

ing the magic horse. . . . Billy pays no attention and seems to
have followed his sister here almost accidentally. They walk on,
and finally it is so dark that Danner can't see Billy at all. She can
only hear him, farther and farther behind her, imitating with a
careful and private energy the engine sounds of a plane that is
going down. War-movie sounds, *Eeee-yoww, ach-ack-ack.* So gentle
it sounds like a song, and the song goes on softly as the plane
falls, year after year, to earth. (p. 331)

The memory of Vietnam that is embodied in the song of this
falling plane, like the rest of the "reminiscences" scattered through
the novel, differs significantly from the kinds of memory represented by Caputo and Stone and by most of the more popular
works on television. Associating that memory with a woman who
never left the United States internalizes Vietnam within American
society as a dislocation in the usual mechanisms of order and
significance rather than as a threat from the outside, and representing those ideological mechanisms as a literal machinery of personal desire and family continuity dramatizes the constructed nature of both memory and history. Rather than serving as a point of
reference to the past or as a geographical and ethical limit of social
coherence, Vietnam is situated by Phillips within a network of
images and recollections that is arranged by accident and that
accords a general equality to all the sources of those images. The
pattern they eventually assume across the different sections of the
novel constitutes the "continuity" of the family and Danner's place
in it, and so comes to make up her identity; and it has a place for
Vietnam as well. But that place, and the order that determines it,
are not the product of an underlying truth of history or even a
personal memory understood as an individual's point of view. What
order is there is purely discursive, constituted within the "strange"
persistence of recollections whose relations are determined by the
chance encounters of ordinary life and by a narrative will to meaning that comes to define what certainty there is in looking back at
the past. "Later you look back and see one thing foretold by another," Danner's mother tells her in "Reminiscence to a Daughter,"
the first section of the novel; "but when you're young, those connections are secrets; everything you know is secret from yourself"
(p. 4). By the end of the novel, however, Danner realizes that her
mother's faith in the significance of this retrospective vision is
sustained only by her obsessive repetition of stories about Billy's
childhood and the illusion of permanence those recollections con-

vey, and Danner remains suspended between those tales and her place in a history she cannot comprehend. "My mother can't talk about Billy in the present," she says. "Her stories about the past seem to comfort her, but they sadden me. After all, I'm in the stories. I'm here, relating the stories to the present and to the future, and I'm always looking for hints" (pp. 305–6).

In *Machine Dreams*, the various paraphernalia of private recollection such as tattered photographs, letters, and the old stories told by Danner's mother compete on equal terms with the most banal emblems of commercial fantasy, and none of these devices serves Danner as a master narrative that will link past to future through a secure sense of personal identity and historical continuity. The memories that result from any arrangement of this heterogeneous collection of impressions can only be "strange," never coherent or fully significant, because Phillips refuses to grant individual subjectivity a transcendent perspective that can tell the story of history and so make sense out of an alcoholic father or a foreign war. Without this coherent sense of history, concepts such as personal identity or normative social forms such as the family lose their inevitability as "natural" forms of human experience, and even the existence of the Vietnam War as a significant "event" comes to depend on the random conjunction of meaningless details. Phillips does mark this lack of organic continuity with a sentimental pathos that represents it as a loss rather than pure absence, and as a result the critical thrust of her book is vitiated by a nostalgic tone of regret and longing. But her refusal to treat Vietnam (or war in general) as the external cause of that loss, like her refusal to offer personal recollection or family unity as ways of overcoming it, makes *Machine Dreams* the most radical of all recent books about Vietnam because it represents the memory of that war as symptomatic of profound dislocations in the fundamental categories by which our society is organized rather than portraying it as a threat to an otherwise stable and functional social order.

Danner's effort to restore her link with the past through a collocation of private memory and public fantasy is reflected in Bobbie Ann Mason's *In Country* (1985), which traces a young girl's obsession with the war that killed her father before she was even born.[7] Searching her father's letters, boring history books, and old reruns of *M\*A\*S\*H* for some hint of what Vietnam was really like, Mason's Samantha gradually pieces together an image of Southeast Asia that serves her as a setting for the odd scraps for firsthand information she can badger out of the other veterans she meets through her Uncle Emmet. (Emmet helps Samantha take care of the small house her mother left her when she remarried, and he suffers from vague illnesses that Sam attributes to Agent Orange.) Eventually, Sam begins to impose her confused picture of Vietnam onto every detail of her life, and one day when she returns home to find that Emmet has set off a flea bomb in their living room, she decides to live that illusion:

> She imagined that the smell was Agent Orange. Her lungs were soaking up dioxin, and molecules of it were embedding themselves in the tissues, and someday it would come back to haunt her, like the foods that gave Emmet gas.
>
> Probably dioxin wasn't in flea bombs. But for all anyone knew, they could have a chemical just as deadly. Those chemical companies didn't care. (p. 208)

She then packs a cooler with Pepsi and cheese, crams a space blanket, some potted meat, and Doritos into her pack, and sets out for the local swamp.

> That rotting corpse her dad had found invaded her mind—those banana leaves, reeking sweetly. She knew that whenever she had tried to imagine Vietnam she had had her facts all wrong. She couldn't get hickory trees and maples and oaks and other familiar trees, like these cypresses at Cawood's Pond, out of her head. They probably didn't have these trees over there. Rice paddies weren't real to her. She thought of tanks knocking down the jungle and tigers sitting under bushes. Her notions came from the movies. Some vets blamed what they did on the horror of the jungle. What did the jungle do to them? Humping the boonies. Here I am, she thought. In country. (p. 210)

The next day, Emmett comes to the swamp and finds Samantha crouched behind a tree, wielding an open tin of smoked oysters in ambush. He persuades her to return home, and soon afterward they pick up Sam's grandmother and all three of them head to Washington to see the Vietnam Memorial. When they arrive, they find her father's name on the wall, and Sam goes to look for it in the alphabetical directory.

> She wants to see her father's name there too. She runs down the row of Hughes names. There were so many Hughes boys killed, names she doesn't know. His name is there, and she gazes at it for a moment. Then suddenly her own name leaps out at her.

> SAM ALAN HUGHES PFC AR 02 MAR
> 49 02 FEB 67 HOUSTON TX 14E 104
> Her heart pounding, she rushes to panel 14E, and after racing
> her eyes over the string of names for a moment, she locates her
> own name.
> SAM A HUGHES. It is the first on a line. It is down low enough
> to touch. She touches her own name. How odd it feels, as though
> all the names in America have been used to decorate this wall.
> (pp. 144–45)

While Sam is staring at her name, her grandmother comes up and
asks if they have lost Emmett, and the novel concludes with the
following paragraph: "Silently, Sam points to the place where
Emmett is studying the names low on a panel. He is sitting there
cross-legged in front of the wall, and slowly his face bursts into a
smile like flames" (p. 145).

Sam's stubborn effort to transform herself into a Vietnam veteran is saved from being ridiculous by the self-consciousness with
which she critiques her schemes, but her ironic detachment from
these fantasies cannot disguise her very real need to establish a
connection with her father that can offer her some sense of personal
identity and give meaning and direction to her life. Deserted by her
mother and impatient with the nostalgic reminiscences of her
grandparents, Sam does try to construct an ad hoc family history
out of the few mementoes she can find, but even when she discovers
a journal and some letters her father had written in Vietnam, they
offer few clues to the secret of her past or the experience of the war:

> Sam dropped a Dorito fragment on the letter and she picked it
> up with a moistened finger. Atoms from the letter mixed with
> atoms of her saliva, across time. . . . She was disappointed that
> her father didn't say what Vietnam was like. His mind was on
> the fish in Kentucky Lake, not on the birds and fish over there.
> . . . The dead took their secrets with them. She wondered how
> far to go in honoring the dead if the dead offer you nothing except
> a little mindless protection, by keeping their secrets from you.
> This picture was there in the mirror frame, his eyes on her as she
> munched Doritos and read the old letters, and it almost seemed
> that he was playing a joke on her, a guessing game, as if he were
> saying, "Know me if you can." (pp. 180–83)

The next-to-last letter Sam reads finally does reveal the origin of
her name, which her father says may be in Chronicles, but when
she looks it up in the Bible she finds that "there was no Samantha

in either the first or the second book of Chronicles. Sam finished the Doritos. All the ice in her Pepsi had melted" (p. 183). Thus as the parallel between this scene and the end of the novel makes clear, her discovery at the memorial offers the connection to the past and sense of identity that these more traditional forms of historical continuity cannot. The wall replaces the Bible; the war replaces the family; and "SAM ALAN HUGHES" replaces history.[8]

Mason's careful record of the trivial details of everyday life echoes Phillip's attention to the domestic motifs of her characters' memories, but unlike Phillips' nostalgic yearning for something better, Mason's interest in the sentimental twists of *M*A*S*H*'s final episode, the number of holes a young girl can pierce in her ears and still be found acceptable, or the numbing repetition of rock videos on MTV suggests that this is the material which Sam and the other citizens of Hopewell, Kentucky, must use to make sense out of their lives. And while Mason clearly recognizes the ludicrous discrepancy between the arcana of pop culture and the needs they address, she refuses to ridicule the people who use them or to dismiss their efforts as misdirected or futile. So while *In Country* may be, as its dust jacket proclaims, a "finally devastating account of the moral fallout of Vietnam," it is also a survivalist's tale of making do with what is left, and the modest apocalypse of its conclusion is earned through the realization that Vietnam, like history, is what you make of it.

The combination of personal continuity with the past and communal unity in the present that Sam imagines in the names on the surface of the wall is the proper function of all public monuments, but like the random associations that constitute Danner's tenuous sense of her self and her family, Sam's discovery merely parodies the traditional narrative order of monumental history, with its emphasis on great men, heroic acts, and eternal truths. The failure of any monumental form of historical representation to deal with the experience of Vietnam was, of course, a persistent theme in most works about that war during the late 1970s and early 1980s. This theme found perhaps its most succinct expression in the words of Jan Scruggs, who supervised the selection of the Vietnam Veterans Memorial in Washington D.C. and who defended the choice of Maya Lin's stark black wall by observing at its dedication, "Too bad it wasn't a simple war. Then we could put up a heroic statue of a couple of Marines and leave it at that."[9]

Since then, however, the place of Vietnam in the nation's past has been considerably revised, and the place of the wall on the grounds of Constitution Gardens significantly altered by the erection of a representational group of three soldiers that is, as its sculptor Frederick Hart said, "consistent with history." The trite realism of these updated doughboys clashes aesthetically with the austere lines of the original monument, but the clichéd vision of dogged endurance and determined comradery behind Hart's statue is certainly more consistent with the history that was being rewritten in 1985 than the silent mirror of the original memorial. For unlike the polished surface of Lin's wall, which returns the viewer's own gaze across an imaginary space carved out by the names of the dead, Hart's realistic figures offer a comforting illusion of referential meaning to those names that promises to transform personal loss into a shared grief and common past, and that in fact happens as viewers walk from the wall to the statue. People scatter personal notes, old medals, and faded pieces of torn uniforms in front of the wall, and they touch it; but they file past Hart's sculpture, take a snapshot, and remark on the lifelike textures of the painted web-belts and polished boots. Like the veterans' parade, Hart's romance of realism assures the spectators of an orderly correspondence between our separate recollections of the past and the representational forms with which we give them meaning, and the recognition of that correspondence establishes a continuity between private experience and public expression that functions as a modest and more democratic counterpart to the transcendental humanism that inspired the superhuman dimensions and classical motifs of the traditional monumental sculpture in our capital. Instead of assimilating the Vietnam War and its veterans into some eternal form of historical truth, Hart's statue actually portrays the individual *as* history, and it elevates the particularities of the war (including the racial mix of its combat patrols) into touchstones of our contact with the past and our commitment to the future of our present community.

This tendency to transform individual experience into an icon of communal redemption is even more apparent in the Vietnam memorials erected in New York and California. Both of these memorials represent the most private form of communication, the personal letter, as a universal discourse of social unity, and as Mayor Koch said of the New York memorial, they are both clearly intended to serve as "an extraordinary example of how a community can begin to heal the wounds inflicted by the Vietnam War and to pay back the debt it owes to those who have suffered and sacrificed in its service."[10] A communal dimension of personal communication is actually built into the New York memorial, a translucent glass wall on which are carved excerpts from diaries and poems written by soldiers in Vietnam and letters they sent to family and friends back home: "Just as the Memorial invites reflection," an accompanying pamphlet says, "so, too are visitors invited to leave their own thoughts and mementos on the granite shelf which runs along both sides of the wall." Such a gesture would be appropriate, the pamphlet suggests, because the Memorial is "intended to evoke reconciliation and an awareness of the enduring human values which are reflected in the conflicting experiences of the Vietnam War. . . . It embodies the contradictory yet universally shared experiences of war and peace, danger and relief, weakness and strength, isolation and comradeship."

The universalizing thrust of the Memorial is even more evident in the collection of letters published by the New York Vietnam Veterans Memorial Commission, *Dear America* (1985).[11] Made up from a selection of letters submitted for the memorial, *Dear America* presents the texts as part of an intimate yet universal discursive community between the nation as a whole and each soldier as Everyman. This point is obvious from the title of the book and from its organization, which groups letters from various writers into sections arranged to represent a typical tour of duty: "Cherries: First Impressions," "Humping the Boonies," and so on through the final section, "Last Letters," written by soldiers killed soon after the letters were written. It is also evident in the editor's choice to edit out personal idiosyncrasies in spelling and grammar, as if the vagaries inherent in private discourse were too unseemly to embody the communal ideals expressed here in the prestigious dialect of Standard Written English. In addition, the book is introduced with a detailed account of reading and writing in Vietnam that makes explicit the ritualistic significance of these acts for the individual's sense of self and community:

> With the possible exception of his rifle, nothing was more important to an American in Vietnam than his mail. . . . Usually we wrote our letters late in the afternoon. . . . When I came in from the mountains to work in division headquarters I was able to type my letters neatly; in the mountains I scrawled on paper so damp from humidity and sweat that the pen went right through the paper. Sometimes paper was not available: I remember writ-

ing letters on C-ration cartons. . . . The important thing was to write. In my platoon, for example, most of the men were still teenagers, unformed and vulnerable, away from home for the first time. Letters were the bridge between Vietnam and America, between what the war had made them and what they had been before. (pp. 9–10)

The unifying effect of the memorial extends the personal contacts sustained by the letters to the whole community as it rewrites them in monumental form. Rather than just bridging the geographical gap that separated the bush from home, though, the letters now span the temporal gap between past and present and so have come to represent a collective memory of Vietnam that can resolve the "conflicting experiences" and contradictions of a nation changed by war in a timeless vision of national unity and historical inevitability. "These letters are so powerful in part because we know what the author does not," William Broyles, Jr., explains in the Foreword; "we know what Fate has in store. . . . But these simple dreams have a fresh power, even some twenty years later. The honest, fundamental human emotions of men at war is one of them. . . . Most of the men in my platoon had volunteered. They didn't believe in the war, the way policy-makers might have. They were simply patriotic young Americans; there was a war going on, and they decided to do their part" (pp. 11, 13).

The memorial in California visualizes the identification between the individual and History that is implied by the New York Memorial. Located in Capitol Park in Sacramento, the California memorial consists of two concentric walls surrounding a statue of a GI standing by himself, reading a letter. The outer wall serves as a border for the monument and separates it from the viewing area around the edge. The inner wall will be eleven feet high. Its inner surface is covered with brass reliefs depicting scenes from the war, and on its outer surface is a list of names of people killed in the war. Envisioned by one of its designers as a reaction to the "abstract monument" in Washington D.C., this sculptural group nevertheless bears an obvious resemblance to the national memorial, with its uneasy conjunction of representational figures and stark black cenotaph.[12] The California memorial, however, exploits the stylistic discrepancy and ideological contradictions between these two kinds of monuments to suggest a more secure relation between the personal loss signified by the names and the collective memory associated with the statues. For unlike the imaginary space that captures the gaze of the viewer in the polished surface of the memorial in Washington—along with that of the bronze figures who also stand staring at the wall—the California memorial centers the individual losses signified by the names on a figure of private communion with distant relations that promises at least a momentary respite from separation and despair. The referential function of those names is reinforced by the community idealized in the exchange of the letter the soldier holds in his hand, and it implies the presence of dead sons from the past just as surely as the letter recalls the comforts of home. Spectators search the list with the same intensity that the soldier directs at the page. And the brass frieze that surrounds that scene of reading translates the soft lawn and young cherry trees around the memorial into timeless images of duty and courage.

Rather than bringing the war home, which was the intent of earlier, more radical representations of the memory of Vietnam, these memorials represent our presence in Vietnam as a memory of home and family that rewrites history in the form of a private fantasy of communal redemption.[13] This strategy inverts the more traditional aim of monumental art, which generally portrays the private individual in his most public role and transforms personal experience into a heroic act. But the Vietnam War destroyed the possibility of such monumental histories, in part because the war itself lacked the images of collective engagement, mass landings, and huge crowds of returning troops that constitute the media memory of World War II. Even the medium in which Vietnam was brought to America had no room for social relations, since the tiny intimacy of the television screen replaced the collective viewing of huge images from the cinematic newsreels of the 1940s and 50s. The police action in Vietnam simply did not fit the forms in which war is usually represented as part of a society's past, and the way most of our society perceived the war at the time—literally as well as ideologically—has equally resisted the traditional forms of personal continuity and communal bonds. It was inevitable, then, that the earliest attempts to represent the memory of the Vietnam War would portray that memory as a disruptive, alienating force that isolates the veteran from the community, and even when that popular perception was replaced by more serious attempts to represent veterans as a heterogeneous group with quite different experiences and responses to the war, the primary format would be collections of oral accounts that explicitly rejected the possibility of a single point of view that could unify the separate accounts in a single coherent narrative.

Nevertheless, the desire for that unifying perspective persisted, and as the image of the veteran remained incompatible with ordinary forms of social relations, it was those forms themselves that came under attack. A new image of the veteran came to dominate popular culture, that of an idealistic avenger whose mission was to set society back on the right track. Although the war itself lost none of its controversial political effect, the memory of the war yielded to a nostalgia for all those "honest, fundamental human emotions" that had disappeared from our everyday lives. That is why Rambo rejects the offer of a medal after bringing a chopper-load of POWs back home and claims instead that all veterans want is for their country to "love them as much as they loved it." The motive underlying *Rambo: First Blood, Part II* and all of the other back-to-Nam films is not just a desire for vengeance and a chance to do it right this time. Rather, it is a desperate wish to restore the community broken apart by that war, and despite the adolescent machismo that inspires the costuming and dialogue of their characters, these films possess an undercurrent of bitterness and indignation at the betrayal of innocence that reflects the more profound and overt utopian longing behind the poignant conclusion of *The Deerhunter,* the sappy optimism of *Lady from Yesterday,* and the sentimental ritualization of personal correspondence embodied in the most recent memorials. The utopian impulse behind all of these works has come to dominate popular representations of the memory of Vietnam despite the lingering political animosities stemming from that war, and the only uncertainty that remains now seems to be whether that impulse will find expression in the xenophobic vengeance of a chromed steel jungle knife, or the sentimental family ideal of a letter home.

The dream of a reunified society that these two stereotypes share has become as important to contemporary representations of the Vietnam veteran as the motif of tortured recollections was to earlier images of the vet. To some extent, this change simply meets the insatiable need for novelty that motivates most innovations in commercial media, but the evolution of the character of the veteran that I have sketched here suggests a more profound continuity between the dream and the memory than is apparent in the shifting winds of public taste and political doctrine. As the veteran's participation in the Vietnam War ceased being represented as an obstacle to his assimilation and started to appear as a moral corrective and strategic support for the social order, the historical contradictions that the war raised within the traditional forms of social coherence were transformed into psychological conflicts in the veteran's sense of continuity between his present position in society and his past actions in the war. And just as the violent skills that the veteran acquired in Vietnam represented solutions to social problems in the figure of the veteran as cop, traditional forms of social coherence such as the family came to represent solutions to the psychological conflicts of the individual. The reciprocity between these imaginary solutions did, of course, suggest a disturbing parallel between the violence of the war and the ordinary forms of social interaction, and works such as *Cutter's Way* and *Sticks and Bones* turned the memory of Vietnam into an image of historical disruption and social disintegration. In the most recent memorials, however, the critical implications of that parallel have been supplanted by a vision of historical continuity that represents the veteran's presence in Vietnam as a memory of home; our collective relation to the past as a family reunion; and the restoration of the prodigal son as our national destiny.

It is ironic that the letter home has come to stand for our reconciliation with the memory of Vietnam, for in one of the earliest and most powerful accounts of the war's impact on American society, *Friendly Fire* (1976), it is Peg Mullen's response to letters about her son's death in Vietnam that destroys her faith in the ideals of American patriotism and begins the dramatic process of her radicalization.[14] Constantly frustrated in her effort to find out who was really responsible for Michael's death, Peg quickly comes to realize that the official responses to her inquiries are designed to represent her son's experience in a form that is compatible with military procedure, as well as with more abstract ideals of courage and duty. And when Michael is finally returned to her at the funeral, carefully preserved and made up to resemble himself, Peg's rage at that design finally breaks out in a desperate fantasy of her son's dismemberment:

> "When ... I ... saw ... Michael ... whole. ... When I saw Michael without a mark on him, I wanted—I don't know what I wanted, but I don't think ... I don't think [....] I don't think I wanted to see him ... *whole*, you know? I got so angry ... so furious because he ... Mikey doesn't look as if he ... as if he...."
> Peg shook her head and took a deep breath. She faced Patricia,

and for a moment, her voice became very matter-of-fact. "I don't think I wanted him whole, see?" Because I've got to believe that he died in a war—and I can't. I can't believe it. [. . .] I do think I wanted him to have been blown to bits . . . I do! . . . I know I did," she said, and anguish flooded her face as she wept. "He was *all whole! All whole!* . . . Oh-h-h, why? . . . Why couldn't he have been blown to bits? So I could believe he . . . died . . . in . . . a . . . *war?"* (pp. 92–93; elipses in original text except where bracketed)

Peg's willingness to sacrifice the comforting illusion of her son's peace in order to lay bare the violence of his death is eventually dismissed by the author of the story as the hysterical obsession of a middle-aged farm-wife, but it prefigured a more general resistance to the ideological apparatus supporting the war that characterized most images of the veteran during the late 1970s. The veterans who suddenly appeared in 1985 on the streets of New York and on our television screens, however, bore much more resemblance to Michael's embalmed corpse than they did to the people who fought the Vietnam War. Decked out in tiger stripes and business suits and propped up for the parade, this new veteran embodies an ideal of historical continuity that turns Vietnam into just one more chapter in the epic narrative of the American dream, and the eagerness with which that character has been welcomed home by all those who feed off that dream has reaffirmed what Walter Benjamin told us about the power of Fascist culture fifty years ago. *"Even the dead* will not be safe from the enemy if he wins," Benjamin said, "And this enemy has not ceased to be victorious." [15]

The threat of cultural hegemony posed by the reactionary tastes of audiences in the United States today lacks the terrible immediacy of military aggression that Benjamin faced, of course, although our continuing disregard for international law, the Geneva accords, and the national sovereignty of elected governments differs from Mussolini's foreign policy less in kind than in degree. But Benjamin himself realized that the issue drawing the world toward war in the 1930s was not one of geographical boundaries or political doctrine so much as a vision of history and the future to which it led; and that vision had less to do with "Truth" than a will to cultural domination and ideological coherence. That is why he claims that "there is no document of civilization which is not at the same time a document of barbarism" (p. 256), and why he insists that "to articulate the past historically does not mean to recognize it 'the way it really was' (Ranke). It means to seize hold of a memory as it flashes up at the moment of danger" (p. 255). Benjamin adds that the job of the historian is therefore not the construction of coherent narratives but the reconstruction of the conflict and struggle that those narratives have suppressed: our task, he says, is to "bring about a real state of emergency" (p. 257). We would do well to remember that today, when the self-righteous indignation of the American left simply masks its utter failure to compete with the smug complacency left over from the Reagan presidency, and when the memory of Vietnam has ceased to be a point of resistance to imperialist ambition and is now invoked as a vivid warning to do it right next time.

## NOTES

1. Burke's comment reported in *Time*, May 13, 1985, p. 57.

2. Behan's comment reported in the *Los Angeles Times*, May 8, 1985, sec. I, p. 26.

3. Ibid.

4. Joseph Wambaugh, *The Choirboys* (New York: Dell, 1979), p. 58.

5. Robert Stone, *A Flag for Sunrise* (New York: Ballantine Books, 1982); portions of this novel appeared for the first time in 1977 in *American Review #26*. Phillip Caputo, *Horn of Africa* (New York: 1981) and *DelCorso's Gallery* (New York: Holt, Rinehart, and Winston, 1983).

6. Jayne Anne Phillips, *Machine Dreams* (New York: Dutton, 1984).

7. Bobbie Ann Mason, *In Country* (New York: Harper & Row, 1985).

8. While reading the letter that describes how she was named, Sam also discovers that her father's favorite name was really Samuel, and Samantha had only been a contingency plan if the baby was not a boy. Her identification with the man's name at the end of the novel therefore also focuses a number of tensions in Sam's sexual identity that remain implicit throughout the book.

9. Reported in *Time*, November 22, 1982, p. 45.

10. Quoted in *Dear America*, p. 76. See note 11.

11. Bernard Edelman, ed., *Dear America: Letters Home from Vietnam* (New York: Norton, 1985). In describing this collection of letters as a fundamentally conservative ideological gesture, I do not mean to imply that all of the letters express conservative political doctrines. Many do, but some don't. It is the form itself that is conservative because it relies on an image of dutiful correspondence between friends and family that assumes stable social relations and traditional norms of behavior and sentiment.

12. *Los Angeles Times*, May 18, 1985, sec. I, p. 29.

13. The importance of such memories to the war effort itself was emphasized much earlier in a television film produced in 1972, *Welcome Home, Johnny Bristol*. Johnny Bristol is a soldier in Vietnam who tries to protect himself from the chaos of the war by remembering his happy childhood in Charles, Vermont. When he finally gets back to the United States, he is shocked to discover that Charles, Vermont, does not exist, and he eventually finds out that he was really born in a Philadelphia slum at the corner of two streets named Charles and Vermont. The point of the film is, of course, exactly opposite to that of the

memorials, which disguise the specific ideological needs they meet as universal desires, and the solutions they offer as fundamental truths of human nature.

14. C. D. B. Bryan, *Friendly Fire* (New York: Putnam, 1976; rpt. New York: Bantam Books, 1977). *Friendly Fire* was later made into a television movie for ABC starring Carol Burnett and Ned Beatty.

15. All of the quotations from Benjamin, including the epigraph above, are from "Theses on the Philosophy of History," translated by Harry Zohn, in Hannah Arendt, ed., *Illuminations* (New York: Schocken Paperbacks, 1969, rpt. 1973), pp. 255–57. The "Theses" was complete in spring 1940, and first published in *Neue Rundschau* (1950), 61:3.

# Tattoos, Scars, Diaries, and Writing Masculinity

## SUSAN JEFFORDS

When Paco tells Ernest Monroe that he was "wounded in the war,"[1] Monroe replies quickly, "Me too," and lifts his T-shirt to point to a "crescent-shaped scar on his right chest," an emblem of a battle he fought as a Marine on Iwo Jima. But Paco's scars, which mark him as the sole survivor of Fire Base Harriette, are neither so easily hidden nor so benignly identifiable. Tattooed by the war, Paco's body is covered by "dozens and dozens of swirled-up and curled-round, purple scars, looking like so many sleeping snakes and piles of ruined coins" (p. 174). Speaking without indexical marking, these nondescript scars are for Larry Heinemann, author of *Paco's Story*, the multiple voices of the ninety-two men who did not survive Fire Base Harriette, or, more generally, all of the men who did not survive the war in Vietnam. A walking memorial, Paco's monumentality is audible in the movement of his surgical bolts and pegs that squeak, grind, and snap, proclaiming him *the* survivor of the war, now homeless, taciturn, and rejected by those for whom he fought.

But Paco's is also the anonymous body of masculinity, remembering itself across America by impressing its scars on the bodies of women through a strategy of desexualizing/metaphorizing rape and displacing its violence as sexualized inscription. More clearly, Paco's "story" is a narration of the operations of the gender system that defines contemporary American dominant culture and is currently reconstituting, through Vietnam representation, a revived masculinity.

I want to begin by "reading" Paco's body next to that of a woman equally scarred by battle, yet whose scars yield different significations. In Maxine Hong Kingston's *Woman Warrior* (1975), Fa Mu Lan has etched into her back the names of all those who suffered at the hands of bandits and barons and of the ruthless emperor they represented, of those who have died and the atrocities that were committed. "We will carve revenge on your back,"[2] her father tells her. Only at certain moments during her successful battle does Fa Mu Lan reveal the scars on her back, as to the baron who declares "I've done nothing to you" (p. 43) before she beheads him. When the war is over, a new emperor is installed, the palaces are washed clean, and those who have done wrong are punished. Fa Mu Lan's scars are both marks of suffering and of victory, for herself and for the people whose names are carved on her back and whose revenge she achieves as prelude to a new society.

But Paco's scars are anonymous, and none of the men whose scars he bears "ever bothered to ask" (p. 5) why they were in Vietnam or what they were fighting for. The ghosts that haunt Paco's dreams remain unnamed, and even Paco is nameless to those who rescued him: "He wasn't wearing his dogtags like he was supposed to, so God only knew who he was" (p. 24), and the medics who worked on him would ask, "Who *are* you, Jack? What's your name? What *happened* there?" (p. 46), and get no answer. We know him only as Paco because the narrative voice—the voices of Paco's dead companions—tell us so.

As if his scars were a map for his life, they dictate only a confused and circular movement, self-centered and going nowhere. Where Fa Mu Lan's markings are motivated by history and for revenge, Paco's "sleeping snakes" are purposeless, the result of an unsuccessful battle whose goal is never known, Heinemann's metaphor for the war itself. Because Paco's signs cannot be read as can Fa Mu Lan's, even in the event of her death, his narrative seems to live and die only with him. Paco arrives in Boone only because this is as far as his bus fare would take him. His past begins at Fire Base Harriette, and his future takes him no farther.

Heinemann writes of Paco as a scar on the body of the Vietnam War. Paco's character, identity, and appearance are consequences of that war, as if his very existence were spawned by it, his life a painful and unconscious memorial to it. But unlike the scars on Fa Mu Lan, Paco as a scar is voiceless, telling only "I was wounded in the war" (p. 103) and no more, knowing no more than the other scars, unconnected to them except as wounds of the same body. For Heinemann, Paco *is* the emblem of the war—unknown, suffering, halted in time, alone. Walking in Paco's body are all of the ghosts of the war, for, as the medic who finds Paco remarks, *"everybody's* pulled time at Harriette, you understand" (p. 23). Like Fa Mu Lan,

Paco carries the stories of others, but unlike the Woman Warrior, no one can read them, not even Paco.

The ghosts begin their narration with one "clean fact": "This ain't no war story" (p. 3). On its surface, this comment might mean nothing more than that Paco's story begins when he gets out of the war, and that the novel takes place in a small New England town far from Vietnam, and that Paco's encounter with Cathy, his land-lord's niece, has nothing to do with war stories. Or that, as Paco's ghosts tell us, people claim that war stories put them to sleep, or that they're a "geek-monster species of evil-ugly rumor" (p. 3), and that "the people with the purse strings and apron strings[3] gripped in their hot and soft little hands denounce war stories" (p. 3). But I take it to mean that the story told here is not a war story because it tells more than that, in fact, narrates the social relations of masculinity and femininity that underlie war but "ain't no war story." In such a context, Paco becomes emblem of more than those who died in the war and instead takes on the position of the "Man Warrior," one whose body tells the memory of masculinity and is intent on installing its story as *the* story. It is a story that is anony-mous, unreadable, and (because it presents its own bodies as "ghosts") enforceable only through and upon lived bodies—specif-ically the bodies of women. "Paco's story" narrates how the text of masculinity writes itself, makes its "mark" through a system of gender that positions itself as neutral and is therefore not involved in "war stories."

One possibility also remains—that Paco's story is not the "war story" he can or does tell but the one story he is trying to repress: the story of his platoon's rape of a fourteen-year-old Vietnamese girl who ambushed a night patrol. The recollection is prompted by Paco overhearing Cathy making love to her boyfriend, Marty: Paco "winces and squirms; his whole body jerks, but he cannot choose but remember" (p. 174). The story he recalls is of how his friend Gallagher dragged the girl by her hair into a bombed-out building, strung her arms over a ceiling beam with wire, forced her to lay forward on a table, and raped her. After Gallagher, every man in the platoon rapes her, some more than once. Gallagher then takes her outside, places a gun to her head, and kills her.

On its most obvious level, this story is important to the plot in terms of Paco's relation to Cathy, the landlord's niece who "per-forms" for him in her window as he takes his break every night from his job at the Texas Lunch diner. Though there is a suppressed violence in their attraction to each other—she is fascinated by his wounds; he imagines that he will "ambush" Marty, "yank him off" of Cathy, and take his place, only "by this time Paco's cock is iron hard and feels as big as a Coke bottle" (p. 173)—Paco's fantasy figures Cathy as a mediator between himself and another man, revealing how clearly the economy of masculinity is the focal exchange of the novel. It is in turn this vision of Cathy that prompts Paco's recollection of the rape, eliding his feelings about Cathy with the act of raping the Vietnamese girl. Because Paco's fantasy about Cathy is prelude to the rape recollection, it is equally clear that this remembrance is not a "war story" about the Vietnamese girl but a vehicle for Paco's exchange with the ghosts, masculinity itself. The professed link between the two scenes—sex with Cathy/sex with the Vietnamese girl—is only a spectacle to defer the real relation being made here, in which violence between men—Paco's attack on Marty—is defused through its reorientation as violence against women—Alpha Company's rape of the Vietnamese girl. Consequently, the narrative functions to solidify connections between men by displaced violence upon women.[4]

Though I will return to the parallel between Cathy and the Vietnamese girl later, I want here to examine a more subtle and yet more important parallel that Heinemann puts forward in order to further his arguments about treatments of veterans, and that is the parallel made between *Paco* and the Vietnamese girl, a connection made exclusively through Paco's scars, a parallel made exclusively through signification. This is the room in which she is raped:

> We took her into a side room, and there wasn't much of a roof left, but there were chunks of tiles and scraps of air-burst howitzer shrapnel. . . . You walked on the stone parquet floor and the crumbs of terra-cotta roofing tile, and it crunched—like glass would grind and snap and squeak underfoot. (p. 178)

And during the rape,

> The line of dudes crowded the low and narrow doorway . . . watching one another while they ground the girl into the rubble. Her eyes got bigger than a deer's, and the chunks and slivers of tile got ground into her scalp and face, her breasts and stomach. . . . (p. 180)

Raped by each anonymous man, her body pressed deeper and deeper into the rubble of the building, the Vietnamese girl's body becomes covered with the same minute and undecipherable marks that make Paco's scars. Her body, *if she had survived*, would have looked much like his.

More than this, Paco's memory of the rape is prefaced by the same vision he attributes to her—the close sight of Gallagher's dragon tattoo. After thinking of Cathy, Paco "abruptly . . . remembers Gallagher's Bangkok R & R tattoo, the red-and-black dragon that covered his forearm from his wrist to his elbow. . . . He sees the tattoo, then suddenly remembers the rape of the VC girl" (p. 174). In the only moment when he imagines what she sees, Paco tells us that "the whole time the girl looked at that red-and-black tatto out of the corners of her eyes. . . . She could see only the slick-sweated tail, curled and twisted and twined around itself, and the stumpy, lizardlike legs; the long, reddish tongue curled around the snout and head and the long, curving neck and forelegs, but she could not see that much because of the way Gallagher had her by the hair" (pp. 175–76). Paco's memory of the rape and the rape itself are iconographically fixed by Gallagher's phallic tattoo, an image, the ghosts tell us, for which "all of us" had a fascination (p. 136).

Heinemann constructs then a deliberate parallel between the experience of the Vietnamese girl and Paco, both "raped" by the war and scarred by its tiny, relentless injuries. To enhance this analogy, Heinemann has Paco see the dragon as she sees it, narrating from her point of view. But this strategy is not limited to Paco seeing the dragon; it occurs several times in the novel, establishing imperialism as a pattern of a narrative position that inhabits the viewpoints of those it narrates. It happens most clearly when Paco adopts Cathy's viewpoint of himself.

When Paco sneaks into Cathy's room one night—he was "the company booby-trap man" (p. 190) and expert at moving quietly into enemy territory—he stops briefly at her door to repeat a game they play with each other in which she watches him from the door to her room as he enters the hotel each night. Their unspoken rule is that if he can reach her room before she closes the door, he can enter. He never does, until this night, when he rewrites the "rules" by entering the room when she is gone. Stopping at her door,

> he glances sidelong behind him, down through the railing rungs, from the vantage point where Cathy usually stands in the doorway, staring at him, teasing, when he comes into the hotel from work. He tries to imagine himself standing at the foot of the

stairs next to the phone booth, sweaty-filthy, stinking from work, leaning on his black hickory cane—half drunk some nights, his back always killing him, tired as hell. (p. 189)

For Paco to narrate himself, Cathy, like the Vietnamese girl who does not survive her rape, must be absented from the "field of battle."

It might be objected that Paco's vision of himself from Cathy's viewpoint is none too flattering, and therefore not appropriative but disruptive. But Heinemann's language makes it clear that Cathy's manipulative "teasing" is in stark contrast to Paco's authentic pain. Earlier in the novel, in an example of the "ghosts" narrating a woman's viewpoint, Heinemann offers a version of Cathy's "teasing" vision of Paco in the eyes of Betsy Sherburne, a wealthy young woman who sees Paco at the Texas Lunch when he first enters town:

> She sits clammy and chilly on that first stool, thinking how nice it would be to sleep with Paco, getting him drunk and taking him home, where they would fuck on that sofa bed in the side den (her folks on one of their annual world cruises). . . . She imagines the swirled-around scars up and down his back, and how they disappear over his shoulder and up into his hairline; how she would lay her head on his shoulder and stroke the scars of his belly (watching his cock rise . . .), the pink and purple scars going every which way—Paco's belly strong and hard, the scars not smooth. (pp. 100–1)

As preface to Cathy's erotic performance for Paco in her bedroom window, and her subsequent "teasing," Betsy Sherburne's fantasy-image of Paco marks these erotic appraisals as self-generated by a feminine imagination and completely separated from "who Paco really is." Perhaps more to the point, if Cathy saw Paco as he describes himself here, there is little likelihood that she would find him attractive enough to "tease," certainly not attractive in the same way. Consequently, Paco's assumption of Cathy's point of view is not one in which he "sees as she would see," but instead one in which he shapes her vision to show a part of himself that he might prefer her to see—a real person, tired, in pain, in need of sympathy and understanding, not schoolgirl "teasing."

This too could seem starkly interventionist, Heinemann insisting that Paco's viewers see him—and the veterans he represents—realistically, as Paco portrays himself, not as part of viewers' own fantasies, whether erotic or patriotic. In this context, assuming a feminine point of view would be not an act of appropriation, but an act of demystifying the image of the veteran and the war that produced him.

But when Heinemann later presents Cathy's all-too-realistic vision of Paco as she records it in her diary, it does not elicit the sympathy Paco's vision of himself would seem to command.

> He gives me the creeps. He has such a dogged way of working. He gets up in the morning, dresses. Clean, dirty, it's all the same to him. . . .
>
> How could I have ever thought it might be fun to sleep with him?
>
> And he's all pasty. And crippled. And honest to God, ugly. Curled up on his bed like death warmed over. Like he was someone back from the dead. . . . I hear him stretching his back, cracking the vertebrae. Then he draws his foot onto his lap and massages it. Cracking more joints. By then it's 3 o'clock in the morning and what this guy is doing to his body is obscene. (pp. 206–7)

Rather than the "tired" man that Paco sees from Cathy's room, she finds someone "obscene." And rather than deriving pleasure from her "realistic" vision, as he did from his own version of Cathy's sight, Paco, frightened by what he has read, decides to leave town that night, "thinking, Whatever it is I want, it ain't in this town; thinking, Man, you ain't just a brick in the fucking wall, you're just a piece of meat on the slab" (p. 209). The novel quickly ends with Paco getting back on the bus that drove him to town, and he is "soon gone" (p. 210), apparently a "victim" of a feminine narration distinct from that which Paco has offered.

Heinemann's portrayal of these disparate visions—Paco's and Cathy's "realistic" view of his condition—combined with Paco's own frightened retreat from Cathy's description, suggests a dual critique of both Cathy's early flirtation and Paco's self-image, a critique in which the masculine appropriation of the feminine point of view is only a stage in the self-critique of the constructions of masculinity. In this context, Heinemann's novel would seem to be a remarkably "feminist" vision, one in which the experiences of the war brought men to reevaluate their investments in stereotypical images of masculinity. While *Paco's Story* is clearly more questioningly self-conscious about its portrayals of gender than most Vietnam narratives, there are several reasons why I think this is not the case: first, because the second appropriative position of the ghost-narrators subsumes both Paco's *and* Cathy's point of view and thereby reinscribes a comprehensive masculinity that can sustain self-critique; second, because the parallel of the Vietnamese girl's rape with the veteran's treatment both in the war and at home elides a clearly *sexual* violence that depends upon distinctions between men and women with one that does not, finally displacing this violence as inscription; and third, because the "feminism" portrayed in *Paco's Story* is not one generated by the conditions and treatment of women in U.S. society, but by recently constructed versions of "male victimization," in which it is men and not women who are the key focus of an analysis of oppression. Let me take each of these points in order.

It is clear from the outset of the novel that the ghosts are narrating the story of Alpha Company through "our man Paco" (p. 18). He is the funnel through which the collective scream of the decimated Alpha Company is to be heard:

> Oh, we dissolved all right, everybody but Paco, but our screams burst through the ozone; burst through the rags and tatters and cafe-curtain-looking aurora borealis . . . un-fucked-with and frequency-perfect out into God's Everlasting Cosmos. . . . That blood-curdling scream is rattling all over God's ever-loving Creation like a BB in a boxcar, only louder. (p. 17)

The ghosts speak from Paco's mind, dictate his dreams, and shape his pain. Their only point of separation from Paco is that they seem far more at ease with their position than he, able to appreciate the satiric quality of their deaths without the pain Paco suffers.

But if these ghosts were simply extensions of Paco, as Heinemann would have us accept Paco as representative of veterans' conditions—they would be aligned only with him and with his point of view. But this is not the case. These ghosts narrate from the minds of other characters as well—Betsy Sherburne, Cathy, the bus driver, an old shopkeeper, and others whom Paco encounters in Boone, as they see Paco and react to him. When Paco is in Cathy's room, he looks out her window into his room as she would: "He stands at the foot of her bed with the grainy burlap diary under his arm, and can easily see out her window into his own room" (p. 198). What prevents this from being another instance of

Paco assuming Cathy's viewpoint is that we then learn her thoughts about looking out that window, not from Paco, but from the ghosts (clued by the ghosts' narrative use of "James" as auditor):

> Some nights Cathy would sit slouched in the dark, James, across the foot of her bed, and watch Paco in his room with that diary on her knee—Paco's eyes shining in the moonlight dark (the ache of his wounds at such times stirring him deeply; his craving for medication urgent and everlasting). Cathy would ponder the tight, dark bulge in his crotch and the endless mosaic, the wonder, of all those scars, while she scribbled notes and strummed her 14k gold anklet. (pp. 198–99)

The ghosts here echo Paco's own separation of visions, validating his over Cathy's as they show Paco's fatigue and Cathy's fantasy, confirming Paco's sense that she is simply unable to see him as he really is. Offering not only Cathy's view—"Paco's eyes shining in the moonlight dark"—but Paco's as well—"his craving for medication urgent"—the ghosts are clearly more than Paco's voice and can inhabit any viewpoint in the novel, though their range of attention is consistently focused around Paco and those who look at him.

Narrating both Paco and Cathy, the ghosts would seem to be a neutral voice, adapting neither gender position. But because they are the ghosts of Alpha Company, and because Paco is their vehicle, their voice is clearly masculine, though not affiliated with any individual man. Their voice is that of a collective masculinity, of all the members of Alpha Company, of all those who fought in the war[5] ("*everybody's* pulled time at Harriette"). Speaking for and to a masculine community—the ghost's audience is exclusively addressed as "James"—their voice is necessarily not neutral, but engendered as masculine. Because they narrate Paco, the bus driver, and other male characters, as well as the numerous anonymous voices of Alpha Company, they represent the voice of "men" and not individual men, what I have elsewhere called the masculine point of view,[6] a position that subsumes individual men and their differences into the larger category of masculinity as a representational construct. This masculine point of view erases differences between men and projects them as collectively interconnected.

But this voice narrates women as well, marking its other significant distinction from individual men as points of narration, and creating the masculine point of view as comprehensive of a feminine voice. Far from neutral, this voice subsumes the position of women *and* men[7] through a masculine voice—though as the rape makes clear, men continue to inhabit a hierarchically superior position within this paradigm—cloaking its appropriation in anonymity, speaking for and from a position of power essential to the operation and enactment of a gendered structure of relations.

One of the most effective features of this strategy and one most often at work in contemporary projections of masculinity is the capacity for self-critique implied in Paco's ability to "see himself." Because Paco's portrait of himself is not a flattering one, it seems that he is able to recognize his own shortcomings—"sweaty-filthy, stinking from work . . . half drunk . . . tired as hell" (p. 189). More than this, the ghosts recognize him as dirty, scarred, even eerie, suggesting that they too are able to "see" him for what he is. This is a masculinity aware of itself, able to acknowledge its own inabilities to realize ideal images of manhood. Having faced itself during a war that demystified traditional notions of manhood in and as war, this masculinity can confront, accept, and possibly change itself.

While there are some positive aspects of this kind of a position, much of what is constructive in it is deferred by the ghosts as masculine point of view. While they oversee Paco's self-image, they are not interested in altering it or themselves. The self-critique placed within the novel is recuperated by the acceptance the ghosts offer Paco and those he represents. In these terms, the masculine point of view separates itself from masculinity proper, viewing its failures and shortcomings, at the same time that it maintains its own stability, anchored in a gender system. Thus the appearance of self-examination is in fact a mechanism for a more general confirmation of the structures and operations of the masculine point of view that underlies U.S. gender systems.

The postulate of neutrality is at work in my second point as well in the analogy between the Vietnamese girl's rape and Paco's and the veterans' treatment in U.S. society. Here, a necessarily sexual crime that depends for its enactment and effectiveness upon recognized differences between women and men is translated into a nonsexual frame—veterans have been metaphorically "raped" by U.S. society—so that sexual difference is again elided as neutrality. That the parallel made between Paco and the Vietnamese girl is on the level of signification—their scars and their vision of the tattoo —reinforces the extent to which such connections can be made only by abstracting sexual difference.[8]

More to the point, the Vietnamese girl, unlike Paco, does not survive her rape. More than simply an element of "realism," her death is crucial to the enactment of the metaphorization of rape. If she had survived, the position of rape victim would have remained active through her survival; through her death, that position is vacated and open to habitation by the veteran. Her death is a necessary prelude to desexualizing and metaphorizing rape. In turn, the desexualization of rape is a necessary prelude to the *sexualization* of inscription, whereby the gendered violence of men against women as rape is deferred through signification to seem not to be gendered.

The problems with this logic are made clearest in the numerous feminist critiques of Michel Foucault's efforts to "desexualize" rape as a crime.[9] In summarizing these critiques, Teresa de Lauretis concludes, "to speak against sexual penalization and repression, in our society, is to uphold the sexual oppression of women, or, better, to uphold the practices and institutions that produce 'woman' in terms of the sexual, and then oppression in terms of gender."[10] Further, "Even when it is located, as it very often is, *in* the woman's body, sexuality is an attribute or property of the male" (p. 37). Similarly, to suggest Paco/veterans as "women," as "rape" victims, is to elude the historical and social conditions of women's oppression as women and collapse it into the general situation of men. By becoming a social treatment specific to a certain historical moment (i.e. the Vietnam War), such oppression is stripped of its systematic and systemic operations over centuries of patriarchal culture and instead made to appear as the product of a localized and rectifiable set of circumstances.

In addition to illuminating novels like *Paco's Story*, an examination of Foucault's arguments marks as well the extent to which much contemporary theoretical discourse is allied with the narrative strategies of the masculine point of view. Foucault's concept of discursive power as a totalizing social operation, as well as the ways in which that power exercises itself through translating other discourses into its own terms and producing modes of social control, such as sexuality, is remarkably similar to the enactment of a masculine point of view in Vietnam representation. But rather than being simply an instance of Foucault's general theory, the masculine point of view, as a factor unacknowledged in Foucauldian discourse, reveals itself as underlying rather than being examined by Foucault's scheme.

Finally, *Paco's Story* dovetails with a larger movement at work in contemporary U.S. dominant culture to portray men as victims, principally of a social structure revised and altered in response to feminism. In such a framework, it is suggested that men are discriminated against—in jobs, domestic relations, divorce and custody battles, as well as other cultural arenas where traditional masculine roles are being questioned. As I have suggested before,[11] Vietnam veterans are one of the principle focuses of such arguments, in which they are presented as victims—of the war, an unsympathetic government, an embarrassed society, as well as the traditional images of manhood that shaped their own expectations for self-evaluation.

Such proposals of victimization are produced by what Anthony Wilden calls "symmetrizing" hierarchically related terms, collapsing their levels of distinction so that they appear to share the same plane. Importantly, Wilden recognizes that such leveling "neutralizes" terms so that "the levels of contradiction are made to appear as the 'two sides' of an imaginary equation."[12] The purpose behind such an operation is not simply to make hierarchically related elements seem equivalent but then to invert actual positions of domination with an appearance of reversed power relations: "Symmetrization is an imaginary operation that by neutralizing a real hierarchy prepares the way to turn it upside down" (p. 33).[13] In the terms of this essay, the hierarchically enacted oppression of women is "neutralized" in its represented equivalence to the treatment of Vietnam veterans and soldiers. The mechanism for this equation, in *Paco's Story* and elsewhere, is the metaphorization of rape.[14] Neutralization through representations of rape then makes possible the proposal not only of the oppression of men but of their victimization by women.

*Paco's Story* makes such a maneuver clear, not only in Paco's rejection by the people of Boone—"victimization of the veteran"— but in the consistent representation of that victimization through an opposition of veterans and women, made most explicit in a veteran's fantasy revenge upon a coed:

> Been waiting for one of those mouthy, snappy-looking little girlies from some rinky-dink college to waltz up and say ... "You

219

> one of them *vet'rans*, ain'cha? Killed all them mothers and ba-
> bies. Raped all them women, di'n'cha". . . . "I ain't putting out
> for you, *buster*. . . ." Okay by me, girlie . . . 'cause I got seventeen
> different kinds of social diseases. . . . And when this happens—
> this conversation with this here girlie—I'm gonna grab her up
> by the collar of her sailor suit . . . , slap her around a couple
> times, flip her a goddamned dime . . . and say, "Here, Sweet
> Chips, give me a ring in a couple of years when you grow up."
> (p. 156)

In addition to generalizing the rejection of veterans and their characterization as "baby-killers" as the voice of women, this fantasy
reintroduces the sexual level of distinction that the rape analogy
eliminates, again as a form of antagonism and violence, but this
time largely on the part of women. In this way, the coed's presumed reaction to veterans is linked to Betsy Sherburne's and
Cathy's eroticization of Paco so that all three contribute to a portrayal of women as relating to men only in sexual terms, whether
positive or negative. Combined, the three construct an image of
U.S. women after feminism: wealthy (all attend college), openly
acting on their own sexual desires, treating men as objects for
fantasy, manipulative of men, and attacking men for their own
sexuality. With this skewed characterization, women (feminists)
are shown to be the chief representatives and actors of social efforts
to objectify and manipulate veterans.

The ideological motivation and essential bankruptcy of a gender
equation between women and men is revealed in this opposition,
as the very group whose treatment the veterans' is to parallel
through the metaphorization of rape—women—is *also* the group
against whom they are structurally posed—women. The only way
out of this paradox within the frame of the narrative is yet more
revealing for the strategies of masculinity: that the parallel between veterans and women works only in comparison with the
Vietnamese girl, whose suffering is presumed on numerous levels
to be like that of the veteran ("victims" of a government, nationalism, war, military strategies, etc.). Such a shift in the logic of the
equation requires a separation between women so that the oppres-
sions women suffer at the hands of men—literalized in the novel
as rape—are substantially different for Vietnamese and U.S.
women.[15] Consequently, women in their relations to men cannot
be viewed as a "class" sharing conditions of social relations, but
only as fragmented groups whose interests, behaviors, and experi-

ences are not aligned. Paradoxically, feminism is shown to be that which separates rather than binds women. In addition to breaking down the very basis upon which gender categories are enacted— i.e., the hierarchical oppression of women by men—such a separation allows for the possibility of suggesting that U.S. women have not been raped, as have Vietnamese women,[16] and that (again unlike Vietnamese women) they are victimizers rather than victims of men.

In one of the most powerful moments of this novel, Cathy has a dream in which she acts out her initial sexual fantasies about Paco. After making love, Paco

> arches his back and reaches up to his forehead and begins by pinching the skin there, but he's working the skin loose, and then begins to peel the scars off as if they were a mask. . . . I close my eyes and turn my head, and urge him off me with my hips—but I think now that he must have thought I wanted to fuck more.
>
> He's holding me down with that hard belly of his, and lays the scars on my chest. It *burns* . . . [ellipsis in text] and I think I hear *screams*, as if each scar is a scream, . . . Then he's kneeling on my shoulders . . . and he's laying strings of those scars on my face, and I'm beginning to suffocate. . . . And he lays them across my breasts and belly—tingling and burning—lays them in my hair, wrapping them around my head, like a skull cap. And when each scar touches me, I feel the suffocating burn, hear the scream. (pp. 208–9)

Though Cathy is raped in this scene—"I think now he must have thought I wanted to fuck more"—the focus is not on her pain or her screams but on Paco's and the screams of the men whose scars he bears, those screams that have been "rattling all over God's ever-loving Creation like a BB in a boxcar" since the novel began and now come to rest, briefly, on Cathy's resisting body. It seems, in fact, that because the encounter only occurs as rape to Cathy retrospectively, it was not rape at all but misunderstanding— "he must have thought"—or projection on her part. This dream reinforces at the close of the novel the implied distances between U.S. and Vietnamese women, as Cathy's rape, unlike that of the Vietnamese girl, is ambivalent and more a product of her own fantasy.

But like the Vietnamese girl, Cathy is made to bear the marks of countless anonymous men, marks impressed upon her through explicitly sexual actions. In this, the last scene of the novel, it is as if she is having to suffer the pain of these men, to pay for their scars, as if she were their cause. Because clearly, in the terms of this narrative, she "deserves" this pain, as punishment for her manipulation, her teasing, and her inability to see Paco's suffering as anything more than grotesque. Here, in a repetition of the paradoxical characterizations of women in *Paco's Story*, she rejoins her Vietnamese counterpart in both bearing responsibility for Paco's/veterans' suffering: the Vietnamese girl as literal and Cathy as metaphorical ambusher. (That this was Paco's job in the platoon, to lay illegal booby-traps for the enemy, shows that it is not the act itself but the point of view from which it is committed that is important, underscoring a basic difference between the ways that men and women "see.")

But isn't this Cathy's dream and not Paco's? Isn't this her own guilty psyche speaking out and not some kind of masculine retribution? The ghosts explained earlier that they are the impulse behind Paco's own nightmares—dreams of execution, escape, panhandling, waiting to leave Vietnam uninjured but never hearing his own name called for departure: "when Paco is all but asleep, *that* is the moment we whisper in his ear, and give him something to think about—a dream or a reverie" (138). I cannot help but see them producing Cathy's dream as well, especially since it is a dream that shifts the pain of the war—the scars—from Paco to Cathy, so that when she awakens, her dream "made her skin crawl" with living reminders of Paco's suffering. Cathy's dream enables Paco to live out what the ghosts' earlier explain is a desire Paco shares with "the rest of us ... to fuck away all that pain and redeem his body. By fucking he wants to ameliorate the stinging ache of those dozens and dozens of swirled-up and curled-round, purple scars" (p. 174). Transferring their scars and their screams to Cathy's body, Paco and the ghosts can "redeem" their own.

But because this can happen only while "fucking," (or, more clearly, while raping a woman), it is a transitory relief that must seek other outlets and be reenacted on other bodies, from Vietnam to the United States. This reading of Cathy's dream and the ghosts' desires makes the novel's final paragraphs far more ominous than they would initially appear. Paco leaves immediately after reading Cathy's dream:

> Suddenly, Paco ... doesn't want to read anymore, flips the diary shut and sits up, puts the chair back where it was, and replaces

the diary precisely where he found it. . . . He tiptoes to the door, jimmies it open from the inside, and leaves, thinking, Whatever it is I want, it ain't in this town. (p. 209)

He then packs his bag, goes out to get the same bus that brought him to town, and "is soon gone" (p. 210). It appears as if Paco and the ghosts that follow him are so horrified by this subterranean perception of their desires that they must run from the person who has "seen" them for what they are. And yet, if, as I read it, the ghosts are in some way responsible for Cathy's dream, principally because that dream acts out Paco's and the ghosts' (all men's) stated desires to "redeem" their bodies through women, and if, as with the Vietnamese girl and Cathy, women do not really "see" at all, then Paco's departure is not so much one of fear and self-repulsion as of completion. Paco leaves Cathy, not with his scars literally placed upon her, but with his signature inscribed upon her through her diary. The diary is the form of sexualized inscription deferred by the metaphorization of rape. In such terms, Cathy's diary is less the source of Paco's departure than of his "rape" of her, this time by placing his scars upon her body. In contrast to the Vietnamese girl, Cathy survives her rape. The even more important contrast is that her "scars" are not visible but inscribed in the diary, apparently deferred, but none the less visible to Cathy. Paco's "story" has been told, heard, and recorded, now by a U.S. rather than a Vietnamese woman's body, solidifying its participation in U.S. dominant culture. Through Cathy, the war and the masculinity it inscribes have truly come "home."

And now Paco leaves this small U.S. town and travels to another, where there will be another female body and another nightmare, but the same "story" of necessarily uncompleted "redemption" of the masculine body. There, Paco will unravel his scars onto yet another female body, inscribing her with the "tattoo" of masculinity. But unlike Paco's scars, or Gallagher's infamous dragon tattoo, and unlike the markings on the back of the Woman Warrior, or even those on the body of the Vietnamese girl, these lines are not visible—are present only in diaries and sensation—and not subject to the explanation, "I was wounded in the war." They are instead the unseen sexualized inscriptions of masculinity, erasing the scars of its own desexualized image.

## N O T E S

1. Larry Heinemann, *Paco's Story* (New York: Penguin, 1986), p. 103.

2. Maxine Hong Kingston, *The Woman Warrior* (New York: Knopf, 1977), p. 34.

3. "Purse strings and apron strings" suggests a link made frequently in Vietnam representation between the feminine and those who control the economy of the government, particularly in narratives like *Rambo: First Blood, Part II*, or *Missing in Action, I* and *II*, or *Uncommon Valor*, in which the feminine characteristics of the government—weakness, a willingness to negotiate, inaction, and duplicity—are pitted against a strong, active, and decisive male—Rambo—as explanation for why the war was lost. For a fuller discussion of this point, see my "The New Vietnam Films: Is the Movie Over?," *Journal of Popular Film and Television* (Winter 1986), 13(4):186–95.

4. Though length does not permit full discussion of this point, it is important to note that the direction of deferral of violence is clearly racially motivated, as the violence between men that erupts in a scene of sex with white women is displaced as rape of the Asian girl. In such terms, race becomes the outlet for the repression of sexual violence necessary to the social enactment of gender.

5. Because women were (and still are) not allowed in combat in the United States, this criterion of having fought in the war indexes an exclusively male population.

6. *The Remasculinization of America: Gender and the Vietnam War.* (Bloomington: Indiana University Press, 1989).

7. I would want to argue here for a distinction between a "neutral" voice that cannot be identified as gendered and an appropriative voice that speaks as both men and women and is thus reiterating "neutrality" as gendered.

8. An example of a different narrative that insists on rather than eludes sexual difference in rape is Emily Prager's fascinating Vietnam short story, "The Lincoln-Pruitt Anti-Rape Device," in which a device originally designed to kill the enemy through a sexual seduction finds its fullest use as an anti-rape device used by all women and not simply U.S. vs. Vietnamese, in *A Visit to the Footbinder* (New York: Vintage, 1982).

9. Foucault's arguments appear in *La folie encerclée* published by the Change collective in 1977.

10. Teresa de Lauretis, *Technologies of Gender: Essays on Theory, Film, and Fiction* (Bloomington: Indiana University Press, 1987), p. 37.

11. "De-briding Vietnam: The Resurrection of the White American Male," *Feminist Studies* 14.3 (Fall 1988), 14(3):525–45.

12. *Man and Woman, War and Peace: The Strategist's Companion* (New York: Routledge and Kegan Paul, 1987), p. 24.

13. Though Wilden's method of identifying symmetrized oppositions has a shadow relation to Derridean deconstruction, I find Wilden's analysis more useful here because he begins, not with a critique of the represented oppositions (man/woman), but with an assumption of *real* situations of oppression that result from hierarchical relations. In this way, Wilden's analysis is grounded in and consistently returns to critiques of actual oppression, something that many forms of deconstruction have been remarkably adept at avoiding, both as theory and as practice.

14. This metaphorization and neutralization in reinforced in many current U.S. dominant cultural representations through the elaboration of child abuse. Because the category "children" is culturally projected as gender neutral, and

because the abuse of children is not gender specific, the concept of rape as non-gendered supports a cultural rhetoric of rape as not predominantly a mechanism for enforcing the dominance of men over women. While I by no means want to suggest that child abuse is not a real or a serious crime, its popularization as an issue for television, magazines, etc. in recent years fits *both* an increased social awareness of child abuse *and* the kinds of reinscriptions of masculinity I am discussing here.

15. A corollary to the separation among women is a similar distancing of men who fought in the war from those who did not, so that Ernest Monroe, veteran of World War I, is unable to understand Paco's experiences, and it is only to Jesse, the wandering Vietnam veteran, that Paco can talk about Fire Base Harriette. Echoing a divide typical of Vietnam representation between those who fought and those who did not, *Paco's Story* appears to break down gender categories here as well. What prevents such distinctions from being real challenges to the operation of gender in Vietnam representation is the continued stability of the masculine point of view that is not divided but is instead a unified voice of war—and masculine—experience. What such distractions indicate is the historical specificity of masculinity and its relations to the gender system.

16. I do not mean to suggest that there are not distinctions between the experiences of white women and women of color especially in their subjection to rape as a form of nationalism and imperialism. What I am arguing is that narratives like *Paco's Story* simplify those distinctions so that identifications between women's experiences cannot exist at all.

# The Vietnam War and American Music

## DAVID E. JAMES

*Noise is a weapon and music, primordially, is the formation, domestication, and ritualization of that weapon as a simulacrum of ritual murder.*
  Jacques Attali, Noise

*Even the sound of despair pays its tribute to a hideous affirmation.*
  Theodor Adorno, "Commitment"

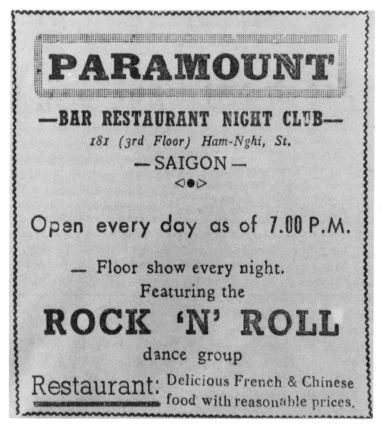

From the *Saigon Post*, December 31, 1968.

**July 1954.** On Sunday July 4, French forces abandoned the town of Phuly to advancing Vietminh insurgents. Though the town had previously been considered a key point in the communications between Hanoi and the lower Red River delta, Premier Pierre Mendès-France declared that the pullback had strengthened the French military situation. On July 5, at Sam Phillips' studio in Memphis a young white man recorded "That's All Right (Mama)," a song written and recorded in the forties by a black bluesman, Arthur "Big Boy" Crudup. On July 10, after the record was first broadcast on WHBQ, the radio station's switchboard was jammed with callers. That evening the record was played over and over; rock and roll as we know it was on the air, and Elvis Presley on his way to stardom. The same day, having been informed that the French had recognized an independent sovereign "State of Vietnam" in a secret treaty signed with Emperor Bao Dai, Ngo Dinh Diem, an anticommunist Vietnamese nationalist, agreed to form a government. On July 18, in Geneva, Tran Van Do, Foreign Minister of the French-created state, rejected drafts of a final declaration that allowed the country to be partitioned into two separate zones. On July 19, "That's All Right (Mama)" was officially released; eventually it became a regional hit, reaching number one in the Memphis Country and Western charts. On July 20, French delegates signed a cease-fire agreement with delegates representing Ho Chi Minh's Democratic Republic of Vietnam. The agreement required all troops to withdraw to opposite sides of a provisional military demarcation line; troop levels were to be frozen, and elections were to be held in the summer of 1956.

**May 1956.** 350 U.S. military personnel were sent to Vietnam. The number one record at the time was "Heartbreak Hotel," Elvis' first for RCA, where Phillips had sold him for $35,000. During the Vietnam War, RCA's Department of Defense contracts averaged $300 million a year.[1] Thom Gunn had already noted that, whether or not it was real and though it turned "revolt into style," Elvis' pose might also be a "posture for combat."[2]

Conceived as far apart as Jamestown, where the first African slaves were landed in 1619, and Tourane, which the French first shelled in 1858, rock and roll and the Vietnam War were born at the same time. The synchonicity marks and initiates a register of interdependencies which in retrospect seem so intricate that we can hardly imagine one without the other. If we understand the

invasion as the most ambitious adventure of American imperialism, itself the "highest stage" of capitalism, and at the same time
its most catastrophic reversal to date, and if we understand rock
and roll as the summary late-capitalist art form, which during the
period of the war replaced Hollywood as the primary vehicle of
cultural imperialism but also became the arena of many kinds of
dissent—if we understand rock and the war in such extended ways,
then the integration of an international cultural economy in a
similarly globalized economy of the political was clearly inevitable.

While the agencies of this mutual determination exist primarily
in the United States itself, the impact of the political and the
musical crises upon one another has incoming and outgoing international ramifications for the world historical fate of capitalism
itself. The musical rupture, that in less than two decades would see
what was thought to be a temporary delinquency reorient all other
musical and then all other cultural practice of any kind to its tow,
was symptomatic of a libidinal crisis for the West that could be
resolved only by negotiations with precapitalist cultures. For as an
appropriation of Afro-American blues (itself previously a synthesis
of European and African modes), rock and roll was—whatever else
—a response to the psychic atrophy of hyperrationalized capitalist
culture. This "retreat from the West"[3] met an advance from the
East; while not the first successful war of decolonization, Vietnam
was the first clear victory for an "underdeveloped" country over
the strongest imperialist power. (This pivotal function for the third
world in both political and cultural developments informs the particular plangency of Afro-Americans' musical response to a war
whose costs they so disproportionately bore.)

Given the hegemony rock and roll eventually achieved, the political function of post-World War II music generally is crucially
(though not entirely) figured in rock's own contradictory position
in capitalism and in the relationship of other music to it, as mediated by that position. While the aesthetic and social rituals of
liberation and resistance that organize rock's massive sonic pleasures cannot be understood apart from its multiple forms of insertion in capitalist production, still it is not clear how far the commodity function of rock (summarized by the dominance of the
mass-market record) circumscribes any challenge it might otherwise propose to late capitalism. In respect to issues such as the

228

determination of the music by the dominant mode of its production and the latter's position in monopoly capitalism—the relation between the musical text and its operationality—three general positions have been proposed: that the music is not determined by its production; that it is totally determined; and that its position generates limits or internal contradictions that may or may not be articulated in the music.[4]

Late 60s euphoria provided a fertile ground for celebrations of rock that either ignored its corporate insertion or saw the music as triumphant over it. These, the ideologies of rock itself, found a millenarian expression in John Sinclair's proposal that rock supplied the form of and the means to social transformation. His notions of a "guitar army" of rock and roll guerrillas, and of the rock generation as a class affiliated with other revolutionary groups throughout the world reflect the most incandescent social desire, emblematized in the figure of the crossed rifle and guitar and summarized in the proposal that "Rock and roll is not only a weapon of cultural revolution, it is the model of the revolutionary future. At its best the music works to free people on all levels, and a rock and roll band is a working model of the post-revolutionary productive unit."[5]

But even at the height of the counterculture, critiques of rock as an internalized control system or as a spurious and administered revolt, promoted by and compatible with the corporations, were available if not nearly so fashionable: "In fact rock, rather than being an example of how freedom can be achieved within the capitalist structure, is an example of how capitalism can, almost without a conscious effort, deceive those whom it oppresses."[6] Or, as Marcuse had written five years before, "the music of the soul is also the music of salesmanship."[7] With the corporate adoption of counterculture rhetoric, (epitomized in CBS' late 60s' advertisements in *Rolling Stone* that claimed that "The Revolutionaries are on Columbia") and the evaporation after the early 70s of movements for progressive social change, only naively collusive journalism and advertising itself have been able to ignore what has become an increased, and increasingly overt, accomodation of rock to corporate priorities.

More recent attempts to retain some aspects of 60s' utopianism have resorted to theories of mediation. These have taken several forms. It has become commonplace to distinguish cycles of populist, expressive authenticity that decay into sanitized commercial shallowness: Elvis Presley in the mid-50s (and more recently, the Elvis of the Sun Sessions only); the "British Invasion" and Bob Dylan in the mid-60s; and punk in the mid-70s. Such diachronic distinctions may be ordered synchronically to separate at any given time authentic from nonauthentic practices, either within rock, or within contemporary music as a whole to distinguish rock from other musics. Accepting that rock is intrinsically—not incidentally or partially—a mass-market commodity product,[8] these distinctions recognize integral contradictions even in "good" rock, and attempt to account for the music's pleasure within the functions of leisure and youth in late capitalism. The best of such theories attack the assumption that corporate culture is a closed totality and emphasize that the disjunctions and antagonisms within the complex of apparatuses that constitute rock and roll create "sites of affective empowerment which can provide strategies of resistance, evasion, and even counter-control."[9] The spheres of affectivity thus "excorporated" from the hegemony sustain "a form of cultural rebellion, but never of political revolution."[10] More penetrating and nuanced than previous accounts of music consumption, Grossberg's model of the subjectivities that different points in the apparatus allow nevertheless fails to situate rock in either history or in the other musical practices it displaced and those that continue to surround it.

Jacques Attali's much larger historical perspectives allow the disjunctions between empowerment and impoverishment to be elaborated diachronically. On the one hand, the overall organization of twentieth-century music around the commodity record signals the supersession of the era of "representation" that constitutes so-called classical music (the enactment of standard music texts by individual performers) by the era of unalloyed, uninflected "repetition." On the other, while Attali recognizes contemporary music's role in the production of demand and consumption needed by the material surplus of late capital,[11] he also suggests that alongside and indeed abetted by records is "a new practice of musical production, a day-to-day and subversive practice" (p. 141) in a variety of forms of popular performance, a return to the conditions of precapitalist *jongleurs:* "no study is required to play this kind of music, which is orally transmitted and largely improvisational. It is thus accessible to everyone, breaking the barrier raised by an apprenticeship in the code and the instrument. It has developed among all social classes, but in particular among those most oppressed. . . . the number of small orchestras of amateurs who play for free has mushroomed" (p. 140).

Attali's thesis that "change is inscribed in noise faster than it transforms society" (p. 5) allows him to project the decentered, performative, amateur musics that flourish in the gaps in industrial production into some similarly participatory social formation. This mutual facilitation of the utopian and the dystopian represents the ambivalence of postmodernism itself; but it also returns us to the 60s' models of rock as a revolutionary popular practice, a form of folk music.

Like "the folk," the concept of folk music is a politically charged Romantic fabrication; we inherit the tradition of putatively authentic songs either from the eighteenth century via bourgeois antiquarians like Cecil Sharp and Francis Child, whose aesthetics bore little relation to the cultural program of the modern working class [12] or from Communist attempts deliberately to construct a proletarian music in the 30s. Nevertheless, the concept of folk music, retained as a heuristic, can illuminate the limits of commodity music. The idea of a popularly created and constantly rewritten collective musical practice outside the commodity function, one without individual authorship and without a distinction of producers from consumers, is valuable not just because it invokes a preindustrial ideal which some future society may rehabilitate, but because it designates present practices that constantly inflect and intersect with the operationality of industrial music.

Whereas film, to take the most prominent counterexample, allows the public *only* the position of consumers (though it is significant that the period of the Vietnam War also coincided with the most extensive popular practice of film ever), the material conditions of music are such that everyone may practice it. Though highly monopolized, the postwar music industry has been less rigidly rationalized and hierarchicized than either film or television; it is geared more directly to the youth market and, especially after the mid-60s' rock stars broke the hold of the Tin Pan Alley production line and secured the right to write and produce their own material, it never entirely assimilated its artists to corporate priorities. Indeed the industry's flexibility and the cheapness of starting

231

a band encouraged a plethora of popular practice such that, however it is privileged, commodity production remains only one moment in the totality of musical practices, emerging from and returning to popular production.[13]

Analysis of the political significance of contemporary music is incomplete, then, if it is limited to the recordings of the major companies or to clarifying the ideological limits of commodity production; rather it demands that industrial production be understood in its relations to the total field of musical practice—which is by definition generally undocumented. Thus a complete account of the music of the Vietnam War would include at least the following: the different effects of the war on various styles of music and modes of musical production; the ways each of these represented or otherwise addressed the war; the psychological positioning generated in different musics and the articulation of these libidinal economies with the war's other economies; the uses made of music by the various parties involved in the war (including the U.S. soldiers,[14] the domestic resistance, the Vietnamese patriots,[15] and the South Vietnamese entertainment industry—and the transformation of motifs as they pass amongst all these); the effect of American music upon Vietnamese music, notably the growth of South Vietnamese rock and roll bands;[16] the place of music among other cultural practices in the period of the war, especially the use of music in films and other forms of representing the war; and the relation of the American music industry to the other industries by which the war was prosecuted.[17] Together, these produce a field bounded on one side by the place of the Vietnam War in the history of music and on the other by the place of music in the history of the Vietnam War.

As a propaedeutic to this total study, here I propose what is primarily a content analysis of the lyrics of the music of middle- and working-class urban white youth between approximately 1965 and 1985, paying particular attention to the representation of the American soldier in different modes of musical production.[18] The analysis demonstrates that the ideological positions made available by hegemonic industrial culture barometrically reflected the changes in the general public consensus, and conversely that dissident or minority attitudes were mobilized only in marginal musical practices.

## Folk Music

Any approach to music through lyrics has the obvious limitations of excluding purely instrumental music and nonverbal musical meaning which may overdetermine words when they are present. Despite the spate of late 60s' apologists for rock-as-poetry,[19] the social power of rock and roll has often been understood as a function of the polysemy of its lyrics,[20] their availability for investment with individual or group significance. To take a presently important instance, in Vietnam American GIs endowed such songs as The Rolling Stones' "2000 Light Years From Home," The Animals' "We Gotta Get Out Of This Place," Porter Wagoner's "Green, Green Grass of Home," The Box Tops' "The Letter," and Peter, Paul, and Mary's "Leaving on a Jet Plane" with meanings they could not have had elsewhere. Often entailing a willful ideological transgression of the original, appropriation of this kind allows industrially produced music to imitate the "folk" function of populist production, and sometimes even to initiate it. The instability and indeterminacy of the lyrics of popular music mark the limitations of the present approach through them, and ensure that certain kinds of musical meanings will not be accessible here. These limitations may not be discounted, but rather must be included in the procedures of analysis, which consequently must begin by differentiating between music which marginalizes its words or uses them as essentially arbitrary vehicles for sonic effects and music which aims to articulate specific ideological positions by precise and comprehensible statement. In general, the importance and availability of the lyrics decreased as folk music became rock and roll, which allows us to understand increasing indeterminacy—increasing verbal inarticulateness—as a historical function, coincident with the escalation of the war.

Nowhere is it clearer that rock and roll involved the migration of a primarily performative folk practice to one of recording than in the case of Elvis Presley. Indeed the miscegenation of that first single, with the blues "That's All Right (Mama)" on one side and the country song "Blue Moon of Kentucky" on the other, figured all the subsequent formal and political (racial) contradictions of rock and roll; and it also figured the migration of two sets of lyrics from a folk to an industrial mode of production. But the energy and the major artists of this first fusion quickly dissipated, leaving the end

233

of the decade open to softer reworkings of traditional songs. The industrially assimilated folk music of the Kingston Trio ("Tom Dooley," 1958) promoted a revival of the popular music of the proletarian and antiracist struggles of the 30s, music which had been anathema during the cold war. The songs of Communist organizers, the Wobblies, Woody Guthrie, and also black religious song were popular on records; but they also supported a revival of the spectrum of amateur and semi-amateur popular performance which became increasingly self-conscious in respect to international politics and the politics of musical styles and modes of production in the first half of the 60s.

Growing from civil rights and nuclear disarmament protest, this movement eventually passed into war resistance. The folk music of this period involved all kinds of popular participation, all kinds of ways of using previously authored texts and all kinds of musical production, so its political significance cannot be assessed simply in reflectionist terms. It must be supplemented by consideration of the various subject positions the lyrics imply. The re-voicing of the lyrics, subvocalized or aloud in singing, is an almost diagramatrically explicit instance of the way in which pronomial shifters create ideological positioning. In singing first-person lyrics, one identifies with the discursive or narrative voice, and so the characterization of the narrator is the stage for the construction of political positions.

Buffy Sainte-Marie's "Universal Soldier," which though released as late as 1964 made no mention of Vietnam, epitomizes the least radical of this folk music. Reflecting the antimilitarism directed equally at East and West of the anti-nuclear period, the song attacked all soldiers, whatever their race, religion, or politics. Rather than a hero or the victim of political forces—the two roles that would subsequently compete in the theory of the GI—the soldier was blamed for all tyrants from Caesar to Hitler. And though finally Sainte-Marie suggests that his orders come from "you and me," nevertheless the common soldier "really is to blame" for war.

Whatever the value of blaming war on soldiers—and ironically it was echoed in late-60s' attempts to end the war by organizing GI resistance—as a transhistorical generalization it allowed no analysis of the agencies and functions of the specific military undertakings, no recognition that the historical effect of the common soldier was any different in Vietnam from what it had been in World War II. A movement, associated especially with Phil Ochs, to replace this unspecific and therefore sentimental and/or collusive protest music with more precise topical reference made consideration of Vietnam possible.

Ochs' intervention was focused by the chart-topping success in 1965 of Barry McGuire's "Eve of Destruction," a song sufficiently vague in its ideological orientation that it could align fear of nuclear disaster with both anti-Communist and civil rights issues in suggesting an equivalence betweeen all the "hate in Red China" and that in Selma, Alabama. While extremely controversial and often accused of communist subversion,[21] the song could project only a melodramatic foreboding without analysis of its political causes. Referring to it, Ochs insisted on a difference between "songs that make a point like [Bob Dylan's] 'Hattie Carroll' and songs that make vague philosophical points that can be taken anyway by anybody"[22]—which is exactly the difference between a folk and a rock function. His own more specific writing reflected his belief that the folk singer had to become a "walking newspaper" to compensate for the mendacity and irresponsibility of television and the mass media.[23] Ochs himself wrote songs about the Kennedy assassination, the Bay of Pigs, and (beginning as early as 1962) several songs about Vietnam, including "Talking Vietnam Blues" (1964), "Draft Dodger Rag" and "I Ain't Marching Anymore" (1965), "The War Is Over" (1967), and "White Boots Marching in A Yellow Land" (1968).

Unlike Sainte-Marie, who marks her emotional distance from the soldier by using the third-person narrative mode, in "Talking Vietnam Blues," Ochs assumes the persona of an American adviser in Vietnam. But rather than identifying ideologically with him or sentimentalizing him, he exploits his naivete so as to satirize the U.S. training program and its support of Diem. The narrator details the activities of the soldiers as they advise the ARVN troops; "commie snipers" who "never fight fair" shoot at them although they're only trainers, and in retaliation they burn villages that hide "red apes" and move the people to relocation camps. In the jungle he meets the ghost of Diem, who admits that the Americans are fighting for "diem-ocracy," for the rule of his family and the Christian domination of a "backward Buddhist land." The use of the personae of the GI and Diem and his shifting ironic positions allows Ochs to expose the American military intervention and its domestic implication; his recognition of Vietnam as a "South East Asian Birmingham" attests to the song's ancestry in the civil rights movement as well as looking forward to the ideologies of third world solidarity of the second half of the decade, while the fact that the song was written when the American involvement stood at only 15,000 underlines his prescience and acumen.

The humor that allows Ochs to solve the double bind of needing to attack the war without attacking the soldiers is common in protest songs of this period. Tom Paxton's "Lyndon Johnson Told the Nation" (1965) and his later "Talking Vietnam Pot Luck Blues" (1968), where the Americans ensure the VC get "smashed" by sharing marijuana with them, use the same strategy. In a social movement that aspired to general popularity, the GI could be directly addressed only when his resistance to the war obviated the need for such a shield of humor. Pete Seeger's "Ballad of the Fort Hood Three" (1966), for example, celebrates three soldiers who were court-martialed for refusing to go to Vietnam. The song gives thumbnail sketches of their backgrounds, but also interpolates their specific reasons for refusing to kill Vietnamese. For example, Private Dennis Mora from Spanish Harlem claims that in Vietnam he would be "supporting a dictator who holds Hitler his hero" and so chooses rather to fight "the war on poverty." Seeger gives these men a public voice, a traditional broadside function that is underlined by his adaptation of a traditional modal-scale melody.

As group singing during marches, demonstrations, and eventually in GI coffee houses became one of the antiwar movement's important rituals of social bonding, the folk song movement mounted an opposition simultaneously to the war and to Tin Pan Alley. Eventually it developed its own star system that privileged the commodity record, albeit on small companies like Elektra and Vanguard, but still the early 60s did produce a participatory musical practice of substantial cultural weight and range that radically revised the social relations and ideological possibilities of capitalist music. In this practice, records were by definition marginal, and where they did exist they did not instance themselves and were not made to valorize invested capital. Rather they preserved other activities and made them publicly available.[24] The scope and possibilities of these musical practices not organized around commodity records may be limned by the reference to the accomplishments of Barbara Dane, a jazz singer in the 50s who in the 60s sang and worked in many other ways for the civil rights and the war resistance movements. Her musical practice involved at least four areas: organizing protest concerts, publishing songs, organizing GI resistance, and publishing records by both the domestic resistance and Vietnamese patriots.

1. The Sing-In For Peace, a concert at Carnegie Hall, September 24, 1965. Coordinated by Dane for a committee of a hundred folk singers. Featuring sixty performers and attended by 5,000 people, the concert lasted in two shifts until 3 a.m., after which over 360 people marched to Washington Square, where they continued to sing until dawn.[25]

2. *The Vietnam Songbook*, co-edited by Dane and Irwin Silber in 1969. In the lineage of IWW's *Little Red Song Book* and the CPUSA's *Red Song Book*, this collected more than a hundred antiwar songs from all over the world including the songs of the Vietnamese themselves. The introduction recognized that the collection covered a wide range of different types of song: "simple pacifist" songs and those "designed to expose the hypocrisies of Amerian jingoism"; "organizing tools for demonstrations and mass actions" and "expressions of support for the struggles of the Vietnamese people" (p. 7). Some came from famous singers like Seeger and Ochs while others were anonymous; some were from Vietnamese soldiers and others from the domestic resistance. Because it is totally outside the corporate publishing system (and in fact it was closely associated with the independent newspaper, *The Guardian*), it could be unequivocal in its support for the Vietnamese people. The songs cannot all be summarized, but the refrain from the last one may represent the compilations' project: "For our people we march to the front / We'll wipe out the very last Yankee, / And proudly fly our Liberation flag."

3. In the late 60s, to support and encourage resistance by the GIs themselves, the movement established a network of coffee shops near Fort Hood, Fort Bragg, Fort Dix, and most other army bases across the country. Opening an album of songs Dane recorded there (*FTA! Song of the G.I. Resistance*, 1971), is "Join the GI Movement," in which a chorus of soldiers sing the refrain to Dane's stanzas. In this song she speaks as a GI, but instead of Ochs' ingenuous one, hers is a fully self-conscious resister, aware of the army's systematic denial of human rights ("if you won't be a killer" the army will put you in jail) and its class bias:

> The gen'rals ride fine horses,
> While we walk in the mud.
> Their banner is the dollar sign

> While ours is striped in blood!
> (Chorus)
> Join the GI Movement,
> Come and join the GI Movement.

This song completes that identification of the singer with the soldier refused by Sainte-Marie, assumed but ironized by Ochs, and quoted by Seeger. Conversely, singing along in the chorus positions the soldiers inside an ideology of resistance—confirming, encouraging, and producing their outlaw recalcitrance. This music is essentially performative; though the record was offered for sale and so enabled the social rituals it documents to be reproduced, essentially it is just a *record*, the trace of a musical event that was its own end. Its life as a commodity was extremely limited, and quite outside the apparatus of the mass media. Dane in fact had to form her own company, Paredon Records, to distribute it.[26]

Paredon Records was founded by Dane and Irwin Silber in 1970, initially to distribute a collection of *nueva canción* recorded in Cuba, and eventually to distribute political music from all over the world. As well as *FTA!*, the first ten releases included music from Angola, Belfast, China, and the domestic black movement; also included were two records of Vietnamese music, *Vietnam: Songs of Liberation* and *Vietnam Will Win*. These last are especially important in light of the government's persistent misrepresentations of the Vietnamese, which made the circulation of Vietnamese self-representation to counter U.S. propaganda an important cultural task. New York Newsreel, for example, made distribution of Vietnamese films a major priority; Paredon's records of Vietnamese folk songs and of liberation songs written by both the NLF and the North Vietnamese is part of the same project, though it is unlikely that the Vietnamese music was as immediately functional as the Vietnamese films.

These independent practices and apparatuses—and though it was unusually vigorous, Dane's work was part of a tideswell of similar endeavors—had economic functions different from those of commercial music, and indeed these economic and social differences supported the political contestation; nevertheless the dissident and the industrial practices are dialectically interrelated. So while the political continuity between the antiwar movement and the communist organizing of the 30s supplies the grounds for the musical continuity (and in fact the Dane song discussed above is based on one of the most famous of 30s' labor songs, Aunt Molly Jackson's "I Am a Union Woman" [1931], with her chorus of "Join the CIO" replaced by "Join the GI Movement"), protest music often consisted of rewritings of pop songs. The various addresses to President Johnson at Dane's Carnegie Hall concert, for example, included Joan Baez's brilliantly audacious recontextualization of the Supremes' "Stop, in the Name of Love." Similarly, the *Vietnam Songbook* contains obvious rewritings and self-conscious parodies: "Let the Good Times Roll" ("Let the Gook Heads Roll") and "Mac the Knife" ("McNamara").[27]

But even while politicized folk-music sustained these forms of anti-industrial operationality and independent distribution, it was also itself becoming a part of the dominant record industry and—in its less politicized forms—of mass culture. As public opinion turned against the war, antiwar songs in a folk style became increasingly visible. By 1967, Joan Baez's "Saigon Bride" (1967), Malvina Reynolds' "Napalm" (1965), Tom Paxton's "Lyndon Johnson Told the Nation" (1965), and Arlo Guthrie's "Alice's Restaurant" (1967) were all noticed by the *New York Times* as specifically antiwar recordings.[28] Similar songs include Tom Paxton's "The Willing Conscript" and "Ain't That the News" (1965), and "Talking Vietnam Pot Luck Blues" (1968); Judy Collins' "Thirsty Boots" (1965) and Eric Andersen's own version the next year; Pete Seeger's "Bring Them Home" (1966); Tim Buckley's "No Man Can Find the War" (1967); Joni Mitchell's "Fiddle and Drum" (1968); and Joan Baez's album of antiwar songs, *Baptism: A Journey Through Our Time.*

But it is with Bob Dylan, whose early songs like "Blowin in the Wind," "Masters of War," and "A Hard Rain's A-Gonna Fall" were used by the movement through the decade, that the costs of the migration of folk music into industrial culture may most clearly be seen. Dylan never mentions Vietnam specifically in any of his lyrics,[29] and by the time the war was the major issue, he had rejected topical reference and folk music generally. His attacks on Ochs as being a journalist rather than a folksinger instance the former,[30] while the 1965 Newport Folk Festival crystallized the latter. The 1963 Festival had been the highpoint of the folk movement, ending triumphantly with the Freedom Singers, Peter Paul and Mary, Joan Baez, and Pete Seeger all joining Dylan to sing "Blowin' in the Wind." But in 1965, with his first rock album *Bringing It All Back Home* and a single from it selling very well, when Dylan sang "Like a Rolling Stone" in black leather with an electric guitar, he was booed from the stage. He returned only to retract his earlier moral outspokeness with an acoustic, "It's All Over Now, Baby Blue."

In the subsequent controversy, arguments that Dylan had betrayed the folk tradition were matched by arguments that he had simply adapted it to an electronic age. While both blues and country singers had used electric guitars since the early 40s,[31] electronification was a polemical issue, not because the materialist argument that it figured corporate insertion was raised, but because it symbolized the ambitions of the music industry, of rock and roll. Abandoning acoustic instruments summarized rejecting a music in which communalism and populist contestation were still possible for one which consolidated a categorical, industrial division between performer and audience. On the other hand, while the revitalization of rock and roll by folk had by 1968 killed the folk movement itself, it still allowed the claim that rock was the folk music of the present to recur in the more millenarian vocabulary of the late 60s counterculture. Folk-rock and eventually "rock" were at once central to countercultural utopianism and also so profitable for the corporations that musical content and function pass into new patterns of determination.

*Rock*

In late 60s rock, commonly reckoned as the golden age of rock and roll when it attained a maturity unimaginable for the delinquent rebellion of the 50s, there are numerous references to the war; but the first—and virtually the only widely popular—song specifically about Vietnam was "I-Feel-Like-I'm-Fixin-To-Die-Rag" (1967) by Country Joe and the Fish, a song that was transitional between the folk and the rock modes of production. Stylistically, the song's folk origins are clear, and in fact Macdonald had begun his career singing folk and eventually returned to it.

Admitting that Uncle Sam is "in a terrible jam / Way down yonder in Vietnam," the song invites American men to help him; it also reminds Wall Street of the "good money to be made / By supplyin' the Army," and promises American mothers and fathers the honor of being "the first in your block / To have your boy come home in a box." In the refrain the narrator makes his strongest identification with the GI:

240

And it's one, two, three, what are we fighting for,
Don't ask me I don't give a damn, next stop is Vietnam.
And it's five, six, seven, open up the pearly gates.
Well there ain't no time to wonder why, Whoopee, we're gonna
die.

The equation of historical incomprehension and ecstatic death
is a key trope in accounts of the GI's battle experience; it is endemic in rock songs about the war, and also informs the use of rock
and roll in other representations of the war. Otherwise, the fair-
ground populism invoked by the jaunty rhythms, the calliope and
the kazoo, subtly modernised by the all-but-subliminal "psychedelic" chant, and the alternating verse and chorus structure—all
these are folk idioms that sustain the verbal detail, but also insu-
late its macabre irony. And though the humor and the sing-along
jocularity are finally undercut by a coda of machine-gun fire, they
recall the ideological tensions that produce Och's irony and suggest
a function for the song somewhat different from that of protest
music. Though the lyrics position the listener as a GI about to leave
for Vietnam, and though the song was popular with GI's in Vietnam, it is directed primarily to the domestic refusal, to those who
are *not* going to Vietnam.

Reflecting this orientation, criticism of the war in rock is sub-
merged in or displaced by the politics of sexuality, lifestyle, and
drugs. Even though in the period 1968–70 popular music in general
evidenced an unprecedented "complexity of lyrical themes,"[32] finally what is remarkable about late 60s' rock, not least in the San
Francisco Renaissance, is that its central instrumentality in countercultural formation coincided with a virtual absence of any cogent analysis of the war or even critical attention to it. Even in the
most "political" of the records of the time, the Jefferson Airplane's
*Volunteers* written at the height of the domestic resistance, the
status of the injunctions to revolution is ambiguous. The opening
cut, "We Can Be Together," and the final one, "Volunteers," celebrate what is apparently a unified militant generation: "We are
outlaws in the eyes of America" and "Look what's happening in the
street / Got a revolution, got to revolution." But in fact epigramatic
invocations like "Either go away or go all the way" refer to drugs
—not to social contestation—and musically the most elaborate
tracks on the album, "Hey Fredrick" and "Eskimo Blue Dreams,"
are both meandering drug hallucinations in the mode of Dylan.

241

The war is of course objectionable, but it is engaged directly only in respect to the threat it entails to the countercultures' disaffiliation—a threat which only became severe as the late 60s troop buildups made the draft a reality for the middle class. The music celebrates antimaterialism, spiritual reawakening, and social disengagement; but the dominance of idealist thought in the countercultures prevented structural social analysis except for theories of youth as a class in revolt against a generalized establishment, an ideology well-fueled by the passage of the postwar baby-boom into an economic expansion, itself at least partially the result of the war. But however luridly or libidinally the generational conflict was mythologized, in general the music was not able to consider its own position in respect to either the domestic or foreign operations of corporate and state power. Like the social movement it made possible, hippie music was ideologically and economically assimilable.

Some examples of reference to the war in late 60s rock.

*From 1967:* The Buckinghams' "Foreign Policy" included war along with ignorance and bigotry as threats to children, and interpolated a quote from Kennedy arguing that peace was a basic human right; the Box Tops' "The Letter" could be construed as dealing with a letter to a GI; the Association's "Requiem for the Masses" hinted at Vietnam via the metaphor of matadors who fell "before the bull."

*From 1968:* The Animals' "Sky Pilot" was an unusually explicit and mordant indictment of army chaplains, culminating in the soldiers returning from battle and "the stench of death" to confront the sky pilot with his own words, "Thou Shalt Not Kill"; The Doors lamented the death of the "Universal Soldier," while finding consolation in the fact that for him the war was over; The Byrds' "Draft Morning" and "Wasn't Born to Follow"—adjacent tracks on their critically acclaimed *The Notorious Byrd Brothers* album—both celebrated refusal to serve in the army.

*From 1969:* "American Eagle Tragedy," an eleven-minute epic by Earth Opera, described a kingdom falling into ruin as the king laughs and stumbles in his countinghouse, and "sends our lovely boys to die / In a foreign jungle war"; Creedence Clearwater Revival indicted the inequities of the draft in "Fortunate Son"; John Lennon and the Plastic Ono Band pleaded that peace be given a chance; in "Wooden Ships," Crosby, Stills, and Nash described a meeting of two dead soldiers; they share food, then wooden ships take them away, past "silver people on the shore" to a place where they will be free.

*From 1970:* The Guess Who deplored the "American Woman"'s "war machine" and "ghetto scene"; in "Izabella," Jimi Hendrix became a GI calling to his lover with the claim that "All of this blood is for the world an' you," while in "Machine Gun" "evil men," oblige him to kill; Crosby, Stills, and Nash hailed the domestic resistance in "Four Dead (Ohio)."

*From 1971:* Emerson, Lake, and Palmer ironically commemorated a "Lucky Man," one who, though he had "white horses / And ladies by the score" went to fight "for his country and king," only to be found by a fatal bullet; in "War Pigs," Black Sabbath attacked the politicians and the rest of the war machine of "Generals gathered in their masses / just like witches at black masses" before envisaging them crawling on their knees to an apocalyptic judgement; and even David Bowie mentioned the war in "Running Gun Blues."[33]

None of these describes the war in any detail, in terms of either its historical or political meaning, or the experience of the fighting men. Instead, it is typically displaced into a fantasy medieval landscape or displaced by an idyllic dream-vision of childhood regression or psychedelic projection. Incapable of approaching the reality of the war, all these songs can mobilize against it is a vague pacifist lament. John Lennon's "Give Peace a Chance"—of all these songs "perhaps the most popular and frequently heard at antiwar moratoriums"[34]—exemplifies an endemic refusal of ideological or historical specificity. All these—and indeed all rock songs—could be functional within the rituals and other social practices of the antiwar movement, and on many levels rock music supplied the libidinal and imaginative energy of contestation. But by the same terms, the music was equally functional in social quietism and indeed the prosecution of the war itself.[35] The reproduction of the political contradictions of the counterculture in its music was facilitated by two primary and enabling features of rock, an ambiguous relation between martial and musical violence, and the indeterminacy of the lyrics. Together these produce a discursive ambiguity, intrinsic to rock semiology, which clearly distinguish rock from folk. They also allowed the war an indeterminancy of its own; it became a surrogate for violent energy of any kind, especially erotic. Exemplary is the musical simulation of gunfire. While the quotation of gunfire, either real or simulated, in songs midway between folk and rock (like "Fixin-To-Die" and the Fug's "Kill For Peace") and even in soft-rock songs (like "Draft Morning") signifies danger and fear, in rock-proper sonic violence of this kind is the essence of the music and itself the site of aural pleasure.

Jimi Hendrix's "Machine Gun," which in the 1970 New Year's Eve performance recorded on *Band of Gypsies* he dedicated to "all the soldiers fighting in Chicago and Milwaukee" and also (almost as an afterthought) "to all the soldiers fighting in Vietnam," epitomizes the ambiguity of the ecstatic energy of destruction which allows rock and the war to become interchangeable metaphors for each other. In the elliptic narrative, Hendrix is first a soldier being torn apart by a machine gun; then he picks up his axe and "fight[s] like a [Vietnamese?] farmer" and kills someone else. The pun on axe allows his guitar to become the gun and justifies the stacatto arpeggios of distortion and the other aural pyrotechnics of Hendrix's simulation of the gun's devastation.[36] While he ostensibly deplores the violence of his gun/guitar, in fact it registers a phallic mastery celebrated in and by the music. The essence of Hendrix's signature style, it is subsumed in the orgasmic oblivion that transforms an ostensibly political lament into an erotic melodrama, a heavy-metal "Hey Joe." Even though its intensity derives from black music and from the social experience of black Americans, "Machine Gun" is the essential Vietnam rock record;[37] as the summary instance of the fungibility of military, musical, and sexual violence, it proves that you can't have the ecstasy of lightning without the thunder of unreason.

Within the programmatically antipolitical terms of hippie ideology, the absence of attention to Vietnam can be seen as a deliberate refusal, an enactment, for example of Ken Kesey's proposal that the only way to end the war was to "turn your backs and say ... Fuck it."[38] This blind idealism could contain virtually no place for the soldier. Only to the extent that the GI hyperbolically enacted the counterculture's own disengagement by deserting—by saying "Fuck it" in the only way his social position allowed—could he be accommodated in what understood itself as an opposition to *all* versions of the war, left and right alike. Consequently the songs form this milieu that can be specific about the war are those which refer to draft refusal. The Byrds' "Draft Morning," Steppenwolf's "Draft Resister," Bob Seger's "2 + 2" (1968) and the Flying Burrito Brothers' "My Uncle" (1972) are the most explicit. In the last, the singer decides to take a bus to Canada rather than pay a debt to his "uncle" by fighting for glory in a war which he cannot assess. Otherwise, the disappearance of the GI from the music, especially after the turn of the decade when the draft ceased to be an issue, leaves a void which persisted through the era of corporate rock in the first half of the 70s. But in the late 70s, punk's new negotiations with violence produced very different contradictions, and in the 80s, concurrent with revisionist right-wing rewritings of the war, a new phase of Vietnam War songs entered the cultural mainstream. These songs about returned veterans synthesized and cosmeticized two previous marginal traditions: pro-war Country and Western songs and punk's politically unaffiliated flirtation with violence.

## The Veteran

During the war, a continuous tradition of prowar (and so pro-GI songs) was maintained, primarily in the idioms or social milieux of country music.[39] It began with the most famous and financially most successful of all Vietnam songs, Staff Sergeant Barry Sadler's "The Ballad of the Green Berets" (1966), a number one hit and a golden record. To a military march, it sketched the career of a Green Beret, one of "America's best," who "meets his fate" and dies "for those oppressed." With his last words, he requests that his widow ensure that his son also become a Green Beret—a genealogy that precisely illustrates the thesis of Sainte-Marie's "Universal Soldier."

Subsequent releases along similar lines had two main themes: first, that the United States was fighting a defensive war which, if it did not take place in Vietnam, would have to take place on the U.S. mainland; and second, that the American soldiers who had already died legitimated the war and demanded its successful resolution. Often the songs organized a comparison between the patriotic soldier and the cowardly and dishonorable war protestors. Examples include Merle Haggard's antihippie songs and his "A Soldier's Last Letter"; Pat Boone's "Wish You Were Here, Buddy" (1966); Dave Dudley's "Hello Vietnam" (1966); Stonewall Jackson's "The Minutemen (Are Turning in Their Grave)" (1966); Autry Inman's "Ballad of Two Brothers" (1968) and a "Ballad of Lt. Calley." To the tune of "John Brown's Body," the last of these contrasted the soldiers "dying in the rice fields" with an unnamed "they" who "help our defeat" by "marching in the street"; for this narrator, the tragedy of My Lai is that a hundred soldiers were killed. But the 80s revivals differed from these in that, unlike the one-dimensional conviction of Sadler's Green Beret (who may be killed but is never emotionally or ideologically confused—he is one of the "men who mean just what they say"), the veteran is now severely traumatized. The contradictions and tensions of the war are internalized in the mind of the veteran, who consequently becomes "a maladjusted psychopath."[40]

This had been foreshadowed in the first phase of punk which, though in general as antipolitical as the hippie subcultures, included more or less aestheticized instances of both extreme left and right ideology. Both of the two seminal (pre-) punk bands, the New York Dolls and the Ramones, included a song about an unstable veteran on their first albums: respectively, "Vietnamese Baby" (1973) and "53rd and Third" (1976). The latter depicted a deranged Green Beret, who since his return to the United States had become a homicidal, maniacal killer, very similar to the hero of Scorsese's *Taxi Driver* of the same year. A homosexual prostitute, he is pursued by the police for knifing someone to prove he is "no sissy." This vet is quite at home with the punks, gluesniffers, and Nazi storm troopers who populate the Ramones' postapocalyptic urban landscape, a milieu in which the war provided a vocabulary of violence that could be raided for sheer affect.[41]

The synthesis of sympathy for the soldier with recognition of his trauma was first made in music situated between folk and rock in the early seventies, notably John Prine's "Sam Stone" (1971) and then Harry Chapin's "Bummer" (1975). The latter describes the career of a black criminal; already pimping and pushing in high school, in Vietnam he wins six purple hearts and a Medal of Honor, but when he returns he drifts back into crime and is eventually killed by the police. Two, more easily consumable, versions of the same motif appeared in 1982: Charlie Daniels' "Still in Saigon" and Billy Joel's "Goodnight Saigon." Daniels' narrator, who could have gone to Canada or school, but decided not to "break the rules" comes back to find that the legitimacy of the "rules" has quite collapsed. While his father calls him a vet, his younger brother calls him a killer and everybody says he's "someone else." From this loss of identity, Saigon appears a haven of stability, a place where he did know who he was. The tour of the narrator of Billy Joel's "Goodnight Saigon" similarly takes him from Parris Island to an asylum, and in between passing the hash pipe and playing the Doors' tapes, the soldiers all go down together.

> We came in spastic
> Like tameless horses
> We left in plastic
> As numbered corpses

These images are derived as much from a decade of cultural exploitation of deranged vets, especially from the films of the late 70s, as from any actual experience. The Joel song, for instance, is a verbal pastiche of Michael Herr's *Dispatches* set to a musical pastiche of early 70s David Bowie. And they clearly do the ideological work of the emerging right-wing hegemony. For while, irrespective of the degree to which the protest songs of the folk era sympathized with the GI, they were able to maintain a clear analysis of the war, and all the rock songs at least implied a moral indictment of U.S. imperialism. Now any real critique or resistance has evaporated. In the chaotic phantasmagoria of psychedelic firefights, all moral distinctions have become impossible. And so Joel's narrator can say: "And who was wrong? / And who was right? / It didn't matter in the thickest night." This new model of the GI as victim made him a pawn in 80s' political exploitations of the war, much as he had been a victim in the war itself.

The right was able to theorize the veteran without contradiction; he was the victim of the Vietnamese Communists, of the domestic protesters, of the liberal press, and of the administration which only halfheartedly pursued a necessary and laudable war. But the liberal left had to distinguish between the GI as victim of the war and the GI as agent of the violence inflicted on the Vietnamese people, had to recognize the GI's trauma without using it to legitimate the invasion.

This is the ideological context in which, in 1985, Bruce Springsteen released a single, each side a song about a veteran. On "Shut Out the Light" (the B-side), the returning soldier is welcomed by his family and girlfriend, and his father is confident that his son's factory job will await him (though of course, since this is a Springsteen song, the factory has closed). Unable to adjust back to his old life, the vet goes to a dark river in the middle of rainy woods and thinks about where he has been. Held in check by a violin dirge, the sympathy is understated, and Springsteen doesn't capitulate to the sentimental, collusive melodrama of Daniels or Joel. But there is no question that the veteran is anything but a victim, and no attempt to relate his condition to the political function of the war or its effects on the Vietnamese.

The other side attempts a more complex reading, but it is also more ambivalent. In "Born in the U.S.A.," Springsteen describes a working-class hero who has been taking kicks all his life, his first when he "hit the ground," since then in a scrape with the law that sent him to "a foreign land," and now, on his return, in the form of unemployment and an uninterested and powerless Veterans Administration. This appeal for sympathy for the veteran is more intelligent than Joel's or Daniels' in locating his problems, not psychically in an overwrought imagination, but socially and politically in a depressed economy and lack of government assistance. But there are still unresolved tensions in the song, an undigested racism in the mention of "the yellow man" the hero was taught to kill, but a much more substantial problem in the disparity between the stanzas of social satire and the sing-along chorus. The repeated "Born in the USA," which should have registered a bitter irony by focusing the misery of the forgotten man or attacking the government, instead made the song available for a chauvinist celebration of mindless patriotism. The failure of the song as a whole to create the ideological position the stanzas imply is recorded in the plausibility of the appropriation of Springsteen by conservative columnists like George Will, by his being claimed by both Mondale and Reagan in the 1984 presidential campaign and, most pointedly, in a bumper sticker that was common at the time of the song's popularity: "Bruce: the Rambo of Rock." The song's indeterminancy allowed it to be immediately assimilated to a transformation of 70s' guilt about Vietnam into a cultural program that would authorize a new Vietnam in Central America.

This disparity between the song's ostensible strategies and its actual operationality illuminates ambiguities on several levels. It can be seen as a tension between the discursive content of lyrics in rock and roll and the way musical functions rewrite them; it can be seen as a tension within Springsteen himself, by which his mobilization of a vocabulary of small-town industrial modernity covers for a reactionary nostalgia ill at ease with less realistic rock modes; it can be seen as a tension between the artist's progressivism and its deflection by his white, largely middle-class audience; or it can be seen as a calculated manipulation of the politics of

From *The Nam, No. 2.* Copyright © 1987 Marvel Entertainment Group, Inc.
All Rights Reserved.

guilt—and of the spectacle of authenticity—by an artist for whom, finally, sincerity is even less available than it is for the overt self-fabrications of synthesizer post-modernism against which his image defines him. Together these contradictions make the song a summary of the contradictions of late capitalist culture generally. But there is yet a further edge to them.

Springsteen's identification with the soldier is, as we have seen, in a tradition of similar positioning that always marks an ideological stance. Here, sympathy for the veteran turns into a celebration of the United States and the glory of all who are "Born in the USA." In this apotheosis, the veteran becomes the *type* of all contemporary heroes. As Springsteen appropriates this heroism to his own self-spectacularization, as he (and via him, the audience) *becomes* the veteran by singing as the veteran, so the veteran becomes Springsteen. By incremental repetition, the choruses accumulate more and more weight—and more and more ambiguity; the soldier is "ten years burning down the road"; then he is a "a long gone Daddy in the USA"; and at last he is "a cool rocking Daddy in the USA." Finally, the imperialist soldier has become a rock star.

## NOTES

It is impossible for me to mention all the many people who in so many ways helped me in this essay; in place of my thanks, let me summarize what I understand to be at stake in our collective project by dedicating it to the memory of Benjamin Linder.

1. Steve Chapple and Reebee Garafalo, *Rock 'N' Role Is Here to Pay* (Chicago: Nelson-Hall, 1977), p. 220.

2. Thom Gunn, "Elvis Presley," *The Sense of Movement* (London: Faber and Faber, 1957).

3. Richard Middleton, *Pop Music and the Blues* (London: Victor Gollancz, 1972), p. 141.

4. In another approach to these issues, Lawrence Grossberg has isolated four frameworks in critical writing on rock and roll: discourses that attack rock as a profit-making commodity that distracts youth from real social problems and produces gendered, racist subjects of capitalism; discourses that attack it for failing to meet the criteria of great art; discourses that understand it as determined by the economies of youth and leisure; discourses that see it as a form of folk practice, however it is mediated by capitalized institutions. Lawrence Grossberg, "I'd Rather Feel Bad Rather Than Not Feel Anything at All," *Enclitic* (Fall 1984), 8(1–2):95–97.

5. John Sinclair, *Guitar Army: Street Armies / Prison Writings* (New York: Douglas, 1972), p. 117.

Other important defenses of rock along these lines include the belief that, despite the record companies' exploitation, rock still communicates revolt to otherwise isolated people—R. Serge Denisoff, *Great Day Coming: Folk Music and the American Left* (Urbana: University of Illinois Press, 1971), p. 138: and the belief that rock provides an image of community to audiences fragmented by capitalism—Greil Marcus, *Mystery Train: Images of America in Rock 'N' Roll Music* (New York, Dutton, 1976), p. 44. Belief in rock's revolutionary potential was shared by the fundamentalist right; David A. Noebel in particular assembled what is one of the most detailed histories of left incursions into popular music. His jeremiads quote in complete agreement the prognostications of the most fervent rock apologists, and his listing of antiwar folk songs has not been bettered. David A. Noebel, *The Marxist Minstrels: A Handbook on Communist Subversion of Music* (Tulsa: American Christian College Press, 1974), pp. 241–42.

   6. Michael Lydon, "Rock For Sale," *Ramparts* (June 1969), 7(13):22.

   7. Herbert Marcuse, *One-Dimensional Man* (Boston: Beacon Press, 1964), p. 57. This, essentially the Frankfurt School position, may be traced back through 50s' sociologists like David Reisman to Adorno's 1940s' articles on jazz and radio, where he argued that even "good" (i.e., European art) music is radically altered by both the processes of mechanical reproduction and the social relations of commodity art. See, for example, Theodor Adorno, "A Social Critique of Radio Music," *Kenyon* Review (Spring 1945), 7(2):208–17.

   8. Simon Frith, *Sound Effects: Youth, Leisure, and the Politics of Rock 'N' Roll* (New York: Pantheon, 1981), p. 6.

   9. Grossberg, "I'd Rather Feel Bad," p. 101.

   10. Lawrence Grossberg, "The Politics of Youth Culture: Some Observations on Rock and Roll in American Culture," *Social Texts* (Winter 1983), 8:104–26.

   11. Jacques Attali, *Noise: The Political Economy of Music* (Minneapolis: University of Minnesota Press, 1985), p. 103.

   12. Dave Harker, *Fakesong: The Manufacture of British Folksong" 1700 to the Present Day* (Philadelphia: Open University Press, 1985).

   13. The paradigm of industrial renewal from popular practice remains that of northern cities of England in the early '60s; in 1963, there were 20,000 amateur groups in England, including 400 in Liverpool and 600 in Newcastle. Dave Harker, *One for the Money: Politics and Popular Song* (London: Hutchinson, 1980).

   14. Accounts of folksinging among GIs date from a sidebar in *Time*, March 4, 1966, "The Purple Heart Boogie." The two Lansdale collections in the Library of Congress contain several hours of songs by American and South Vietnamese soldiers, mostly recorded in Vietnam between 1964 and 1971. Three main broadcasting systems competed with each other in Vietnam: The Armed Forces Radio in Vietnam (AFRVN) which censored both news (e.g., about the antiwar movement) and the music it played, especially songs supposed to be about drugs (it sometimes played songs only once so as to refute the charge of censorship); clandestine stations operated by GIs, sometimes even broadcasting from aircraft; and Radio Hanoi where "Hanoi Hannah" mixed hard rock with propaganda. Some of this material has been recovered and assembled into a series of radio documentaries, "Vietnam: Radio First Termer," by Alexis Muellner of Interlock Media Associations (P.O. Box 619, Harvard Square Station, Cambridge, Mass. 02138). For accounts of the music listened to by American soldiers, see especially Charles Perry, "Is this Any Way to Run the Army?—Stoned?" *Rolling Stone*, November 9, 1968, pp. 1–8; and Michael Herr, *Dispatches* (New York: Avon Books, 1978). Michael McCabe details the American antiwar movement's rebroadcasting of Radio Hanoi programs. McCabe, "Radio Hanoi Goes Progressive Rock," *Rolling Stone*, March 18, 1971, p. 8.

   15. Among documentation of such music, see especially the two anthologies of songs by the armies and guerrilla detachments of the NLF and the artistic

ensembles of North Vietnam and the Provisional Revolutionary Government assembled by Paredon Records in the late 60s: *Vietnam: Songs of Liberation* and *Vietnam Will Win.* Thi Quyen Phan records the use of folk music for morale building among the jailed South Vietnamese resistance; though they were regularly beaten for doing so, inmates taught each other songs on the grounds that "teaching songs in prison is revolutionary work, and so is learning them for this gives you optimism and faith." Phan, *Nguyen Van Troi: As He Was* (Hanoi: Foreign Languages Publishing House, 1965), p. 77.

16. For which see Tom Marlow, "Yea, We're the CBC Band and We'd Like to Turn You On," *Rolling Stone,* November 26, 1979, pp. 28–29; "The Saigon Rock Festival Rolls," *Rolling Stone,* July 8, 1971, p. 16; David Butler, "Saigon: The Vietnamization of Rock & Roll," *Rolling Stone,* April 10, 1975, p. 20.

17. Corporate ownership of rock and roll, the integration of music companies' other industrial conglomerates, and the Defense Department business of these last are all sketched in Chapple and Garofalo, passim. The collusion of rock musicians themselves—not to mention their hardly credible disingenuousness—is perhaps summarized in a remark by Keith Richards which they quote: "We found out, and it wasn't years later till we did, that all the bread we made for Decca was going into making little black boxes that go into American Air Force bombers to bomb fucking North Vietnam" (p. 86).

18. Here I only very briefly consider the presence of the War in Country and Western music and various Black musics. Nor do I consider the implications of the virtually complete absence of reference to the War in art music; in respect to this last quietism, the abstractness of music is less a determinant than are, on the one hand, the incorporation of the apparatuses of so-called classical music within the other apparatuses of state power and, on the other, the idealism of the aesthetic avant-garde. The July 1969 issue of *Source: Music of the Avant Garde* (no. 6) contains some documentation of occasional efforts to politicize avant-garde music. Notable instances include the conclusion to Luigi Nono's opera, *Gran Sole Carico d'Amore,* which refers to the mourning of Vietnamese mothers, and Daniel Lentz's *Hydro-Geneva, Emergency Piece No. 3,* in which the performer asked the audience to pour hydrogen peroxide solution into their ears and to " 'think/hear' others' skin melting in far-off lands."

19. Richard Goldstein, *The Poetry of Rock* (New York; Bantam, 1969), see also David Pichaske, *The Poetry of Rock: The Golden Years* (Peoria, Ill.: Ellis Press, 1981).

20. Thus, while virtually all rock has lyrics, usually either only a chorus is intelligible, or the meanings are indeterminate. Apologists for rock (e.g., Marcus, "A Singer and a Rock and Roll Band," p. 93 and Grossberg, "I'd Rather Feel Bad," p. 101) often argue that the meaning must be vague enough that all can rewrite it for themselves, while Frith asserts that inarticulateness is the conventional sign of sincerity (p. 35).

21. In fact, a contemporary study of college students revealed that only one-third of its hearers understood the lyrics. See R. Serge Denisoff, *Sing a Song of Social Significance* (Bowling Green, Ky.: Bowling Green State University Press, 1983), p. 153.

22. Pichaske, p. xx.

23. Phil Ochs, "The Need for Topical Music," *Broadside* (March 1963).

24. Alongside and often counter to revisionist attempts to reclaim the war for the right, the 1980s saw a revival of similar decentered musical production by veterans and their sympathisers. This often did occur as live performance (eventually of a substantial scale like the July 4, 1987 "Welcome Home" concert at Landover, Maryland, presented by HBO) but, possibly influenced by the independent record production of the post-punk period, it also resulted in

scattered independent records and cassette tape projects that cover the entire political spectrum. Some examples: a tape, *Incoming,* and a songbook, *Songs For America,* by Jim Walktendonk (P.O. Box 3472, Madison, Wis. 53704); a tape with photographs, *Bong Son Blues: Surrealism From Vietnam, 1969,* by William Scaff (Little Sun, P.O. Box 1850, Monrovia, Calif. 91016); a tape anthology of songs by and about veterans, *Tape Talk,* vol. 3, and an album by Country Joe Macdonald, *The Vietnam Experience* from Rag Baby Records, Box 3316, San Francisco, Calif. 94114. *Broadside 172* in April 1986 was devoted to "GI Songs of the Vietnam War" and included information about several independent tape projects. Creating an underground network of information and support, these must be considered authentic subcultural production in opposition to the culture industries. For further information, see Lydia Fish, "Sources for Folk Music of the Vietnam War and Vietnam Veterans' Music." Checklist available from Department of Anthropology, Buffalo State College, Buffalo, N.Y. 14222.

25. John Dillin, " 'Sing-In Assails Vietnam War," *Christian Science Monitor,* September 27, 1965.

26. A similar album was made by the antiwar movement within the U.S. Airforce: The Covered Wagon Musicians, *We Say No To Your War,* also distributed by Paredon.

27. It also includes a song not recognized as a parody, "Every Day, The Movement's Getting Stronger," that was transcribed from the singing of an American POW broadcast over Hanoi Radio. Though it escaped the attention of the transcribers, the fact that the song simply substituted for half the words of Buddy Holly's "Everyday," would have added a powerful resonance.

28. Tom Phillips, "Vietnam Blues," *New York Times Magazine,* October 8, 1967, pp. 12–22. Baez's remarkable "Where Are You Now, My Son" is an instance of how a strong position in the record business could secure exposure for quite articulate oppositional music. One side of the album consisted of ambient sound she recorded in Hanoi in Christmas 1972, with the sounds of bombing interspersed with a ballad that took for its point of departure the cry of a Vietnamese woman searching among the rubble for her dead son.

29. And not until 1984 did he write a song specifically about Vietnam; "Clean Cut Kid" described how an American youth became a trained killer and then a traumatized veteran who eventually kills himself.

30. Anthony Scaduto, *Dylan: An Intimate Biography* (New York: New American Library, 1971), p. 264.

31. Harker, *One for the Money,* p. 131.

32. Richard A. Peterson and David G. Berger, "Three Eras in the Manufacture of Popular Music Lyrics," in R. Serge Denisoff, ed., *The Sounds of Social Change* (Chicago: Rand McNally, 1972), p. 290.

33. About half of these were released as singles and half only as album cuts. Of those released as singles, only "Sky Pilot," "Fortunate Son," "Who'll Stop the Rain," "American Woman," and "Give Peace a Chance" reached the Top Twenty; only "American Woman" (significantly, by a Canadian group) reached number one, holding that position for three weeks.

34. R. Serge Denisoff, *Songs of Protest, War, and Peace* (Santa Barbara, Calif.: Clio Press, 1973), p. xiv.

35. See the remarks of Lee Ballinger, a veteran: "Despite what some may choose to think, rock and roll was never fundamentally *anti*war; it was a soundtrack for the entire process, of which opposition was only a part. Rock also served to let civilians forget about the war, just as it allowed those who were in Vietnam or had somebody there to make it through just one more day without doing anything about the situation," Lee Ballinger, "Deja Vu," in Dave Marsh, ed., *Rock & Roll Confidential* (New York: Pantheon, 1985), p. 210.

36. In his "Izabella," a similar pun identifies the guitar Hendrix is playing, the machine gun he supposedly holds in Vietnam, and Izabella, the woman he dreams of holding on his return.

37. A similar appropriation of the war as a marker of violent sexuality is Iggy's celebration of his performance in "love in the middle of a firefight" in "Search and Destroy" (1973). In the late 70s this confusion modulates into the social exploitation of the deranged veteran. Note also the cold irony of the name of Bob Dylan's 1975 Rolling Thunder Review. The obverse appropriation also informs the soldiers' understanding of their experience of the war through the vocabulary of rock and roll epitomized in the report that in Vietnam "putting the weapon on 'automatic fire' was called putting it on rock and roll." Herman Rapaport, "Vietnam: The Thousand Plateaus," in Sohnya Sayres et al., eds., *The Sixties Without Apology* (Minneapolis: University of Minnesota Press, 1984), p. 141.

38. Tom Wolfe, *The Electric Kool-Acid Test* (New York: Bantam, 1968), p. 199. The directness with which all kinds of black musics spoke out against the war, especially after 1970, provides an illuminating counterexample. Several songs were very explicit: Edwin Starr's "War" and "Stop the War Now" (1970) reached the top of the charts; The Temptations' "Ball of Confusion" (1970) reached number 3; Marvin Gaye's "What's Goin on" (1971) reached number 2; and Freda Payne's "Bring the Boys Home" (1971) ("What they doin' over there now / Bring them back alive / When we need 'em over here now / Bring them back alive") reached number 12. Later Stevie Wonder's "The Front Line" spoke directly to the racism by which blacks, 14 percent of the population, constituted 20 percent of combat troops. Other black musics were equally direct. Blues songs including John Lee Hooker's "I Don't Want to Go To Vietnam" (1969), J. B. Lenoire's "Vietnam Blues," Junior Wells' "Vietcong Blues" and, in the mid-80s, Robert Cray's "Sonny"; reggae like Jimmy Cliff's "Vietnam" (1970) all attacked the war with a forthrightness employed by no white music after folk. Jazz musicians in the 60s, most notably Archie Shepp, were often very articulate critics of the war; records such as Freddie Hubbard's *Sing Me a Song of SongMy* (1971) and The Revolutionary Ensemble's *Vietnam* (1973) are instances of music constructed specifically in opposition to the war.

39. For an overview of pro-war Country and Western music, see Jens Lund, "Fundamentalism, Racism, and Political Reaction in Country Music," in R. Serge Denisoff, ed., *The Sounds of Social Change* (Chicago: Rand McNally, 1972).

40. Rick Berg, "Losing Vietnam: Covering the War in an Age of Technology," in this collection.

41. Use of the war in punk and post-punk culture includes band names like Agent Orange, the MIA's, the B-52's, and Fugazi, and songs about the war— including The Clash, "Charlie Don't Surf" (1980) and "Straight to Hell" (1982); the Stranglers' "Vietnamerica" (1981); GBH, "Vietnamese Blues"; Paul Hardcastle, "19" (1985); Minutemen, "Vietnam" and "Price of Paradise" (1985); Stan Ridgeway, "Camoflage" (1985).

# Poetry

## W. D. EHRHART

*The Congress shall have power to lay and collect taxes ... to ...
provide for the common defense and general welfare of the United
States.*
  *Art. I, Sec. 8, Para. 1*
  *U.S. Constitution*

## Responsibility

The sun taps on the kitchen table;
coffee boils. As birds awaken
trees beyond the window, I think of you
upstairs: your naked body curled
around a pillow, your gentle face
an easy dream of last night's love.
It's Friday; summer.

Somewhere
in another country to the south,
government troops are stalking
through a nightmare; a naked body
in the dusty street behind them
sprawls in rubbish, and a woman
in a house with the door kicked in
pounds fists on empty walls. There,
the news is always bad, the soldiers
always armed, the people
always waiting for the sound
of boots splintering wood.

What if you and I were wrenched from sleep
by soldiers, and they dragged me out
and shot me? Just like that; just
the way it happens every day;
the life we share,
all the years ahead we savor
like the rich taste of good imported coffee,
vanished
in a single bloody hole between the eyes.

Would you fix the door and go on living?
Or would the soldiers rape and shoot you, too?
Idle thoughts. Things like that don't happen
in America. The sun climbs;
the coffee's gone; time to leave for work.
Friday, payday, security:
money in my pocket for the weekend;
money for the government;
money for the soldiers of El Salvador,
two hundred bullets to the box.

# Parade Rest

Today, they held a tickertape parade
in New York City: Welcome Home,
Vietnam Veterans,
America's Heroes—

ten years after the last rooftop
chopper out of Saigon;

ten, fifteen, twenty years
too late for kids not twenty
years old and dead in ricefields;
brain-dead, soul-dead, half-dead
in wheelchairs; afraid to share,

afraid to sleep, afraid of trees,
and alien; invisible; forgotten;
even the unmarked forever AWOL.

You'd think that any self-respecting
vet would give the middle finger
to the folks who thought of it
ten years and more too late—

yet there they were: the sad
survivors, balding, overweight
and full of beer, weeping, grateful
for their hour come round at last.

I saw one man in camouflaged utilities;
a boy, his son, dressed like dad;
both proudly marching.

How many wounded generations,
touched with fire, have offered up
their children to the gods of fire?
Even now, new flames are burning,
and the gods of fire call for more,
and the new recruits keep coming.

What fire will burn that small
boy marching with his father?
What parade will heal
his father's wounds?

(May 7th, 1985)

## The Invasion of Grenada

I didn't want a monument,
not even one as sober as that
vast black wall of broken lives.
I didn't want a postage stamp.
I didn't want a road beside the Delaware
River with a sign proclaiming:
"Vietnam Veterans Memorial Highway."

257

What I wanted was a simple recognition
of the limits of our power as a nation
to inflict our will on others.
What I wanted was an understanding
that the world is neither black-and-white
nor ours.

What I wanted
was an end to monuments.

From *To Those Who Have Gone Home Tired: New & Selected Poems*, copyright © 1984 by W. D. Ehrhart, Thunder's Mouth Press, by permission of the author.

# A Relative Thing

We are the ones you sent to fight a war
you didn't know a thing about.

It didn't take us long to realize
the only land that we controlled
was covered by the bottoms of our boots.

When the newsmen said that naval ships
had shelled a VC staging point,
we saw a breastless woman
and her stillborn child.

We laughed at old men stumbling
in the dust in frenzied terror
to avoid our three-ton trucks.

We fought outnumbered in Hue City
while the ARVN soldiers looted bodied
in the safety of the rear.
The cookies from the wives of Local 104
did not soften our awareness.

We have seen the pacified supporters
of the Saigon government
sitting in their jampacked cardboard towns,
their wasted hands placed limply in their laps,

their empty bellies waiting for the rice
some district chief has sold
for profit to the Vietcong.

We have been Democracy on Zippo raids,
burning houses to the ground,
driving eager amtracs through new-sown fields.

We are the ones who have to live
with the memory that we were the instruments
of your pigeon-breasted fantasies.
We are inextricable accomplices
in this travesty of dreams:
but we are not alone.

We are the ones you sent to fight a war
you did not know a thing about—
those of us that lived
have tried to tell you what went wrong.
Now you think you do not have to listen.

Just because we will not fit
into the uniforms of photographs
of you at twenty-one
does not mean you can disown us.

We are your sons, America,
and you cannot change that.
When you awake,
we will still be here.

# A Confirmation

*for Gerry Gaffney*

Solemn Douglas firs stride slowly
down steep hills to drink
the waters of the wild Upper Umqua.
In a small clearing in the small
carved ravine of a feeder stream

we camp, pitching our tent
in the perfect stillness of the shadows
of the Klamath Indians. Far off,
almost in a dream, the logging trucks
growl west down through the mountains
toward the mills in Roseburg.

I hold the stakes, you hammer:
"Watch fingers!"—both laughing.
Both recall, in easy conversation,
one man poncho-tents rigged
side by side in total darkness;
always you and I, in iron heat,
in the iron monsoon rains—
not like this at all; and yet,
though years have passed
and we are older by a lifetime,
a simple slip of thought, a pause,
and here: nothing's changed.

For we were never young, it seems;
not then, not ever. I couldn't even cry
the day you went down screaming, angry
jagged steel imbedded in your knee—
I knew you would live,
and I knew you wouldn't be back,
and I was glad, and a little jealous.
Two months later, I went down.

We all went down eventually,
the villages aflame, the long
grim lines of soldiers, flotsam
in the vortex of a sinking illusion:
goodbye, Ginny; goodbye, John Kennedy;
goodbye, Tom Paine and high school history—
though here we are still, you and I.
We live our lives now
in a kind of awkward silence
in the perfect stillness of the shadows
of the Klamath Indians.

# Notes on Contributors

**Rick Berg** currently teaches English, film, and critical theory at Scripps College. He has written on film, television, literary theory, and renaissance drama. He was drafted into the Marine Corps and he served as an enlisted man in Vietnam from February 1968 to March 1969.

**Noam Chomsky** is professor of linguistics at the Massachusetts Institute of Technology. He is a longtime political activist and critic of U.S. imperial policies throughout the world. He is the author of many books and articles on U.S. foreign policy, international affairs, and human rights, including *Toward a New Cold War, The Political Economy of Human Rights* (with Edward S. Herman), *The Fateful Triangle*, and *On Power and Ideology: The Managua Lectures*.

**Michael Clark** teaches American culture and critical theory at the University of California, Irvine, where he is the Chair of the Department of English and Comparative Literature. He has published essays on literary theory, early American literature, and Vietnam in popular culture. He is currently completing a book on language in early colonial America. In addition, he has compiled annotated bibiliographies on the works of Michel Foucault and Jacques Lacan for Garland Publishing.

**W. D. Ehrhart** enlisted in the Marine Corps in 1966 at the age of seventeen, serving in Vietnam from February 1967 to February 1968 and earning two Presidential Unit Citations, the Navy Combat Action Ribbon, and the Purple Heart Medal for wounds received in action in Hue City during the Tet Offensive of 1968. His volumes of poetry include *To Those Who Have Gone Home Tired* and *The Outer Banks*. He is also the author of three works of nonfiction prose, *Vietnam-Perkasie, Marking Time*, and *Going Back*, and the editor of *Carrying the Darkness*.

**David James** teaches in the School of Cinema and Television at the University of Southern California. His most recent book is *Allegories of Cinema: Film in the Sixties*.

**Susan Jeffords** teaches feminist theory at the University of Washington. Author of *The Remasculinization of America: Gender and the Vietnam War*, she is at work now on a book on representations of women and combat in the United States.

**Carol Lynn Mithers** is a freelance journalist working out of both Los Angeles and New York. Her work has appeared in the *Village Voice*, the *Nation*, the *Los Angeles Times*, and the *New York Times* as well as in *California, California Business, Glamour, Mirabella, Ladies Home Journal, Redbook* and *Mademoiselle*. She is currently completing a book on a 1970s psychotherapy cult for Addison-Wesley.

**John Carlos Rowe** teaches American literature and critical theory at the University of California, Irvine. He is the author of *Henry Adams and Henry James: The Emergence of a Modern Consciousness, Through the Custom-House: Nineteenth-Century American Fiction and Modern Theory, The Theoretical Dimensions of Henry James*, and *At Emerson's Tomb: The Politics of American Modernism*, as well as essays on critical theory, American culture, and the Vietnam War. He is at present completing *The Americanization of Vietnam: Representations of an Undeclared War*.

**Claudia Springer** teaches in the English Department and Film Studies Program at Rhode Island College. Her articles on representations of war and on American films with Third World settings have been published in *Wide Angle, Genre, Literature and Psychology, Phoebe*, and in the forthcoming anthology, *Unspeakable Images: Ethnicity and the American Cinema*. She is currently working on a book about computer discourses and sexuality.

**Stephen Vlastos** is a professor in the History Department of the University of Iowa. His teaching and research interests include Japan; peasant studies; and Vietnam War history and historiography. Publications include *Peasant Protests and Uprisings in Tokugawa Japan, 1600–1868;* "Opposition Movements in the Early Meiji Period," *Cambridge History of Japan*, vol. 5; and "Television War," *Radical History Review*.

# Index